Where There's a Will

EMILY CHAPPELL worked as a cycle courier in London for many years, telling her story in *What Goes Around*. Since then she has explored the world on her bike, and committed to enabling others to do the same. Her writing has featured in *Vogue*, *Cyclist*, *National Geographic* and the *Guardian*.

@emilychappell

Where There's a Will

Hope, Grief and Endurance in a Cycle Race Across a Continent

Emily Chappell

This paperback edition first published in 2020

First published in Great Britain in 2019 by
PROFILE BOOKS LTD
29 Cloth Fair
London EC1A 7JQ
www.profilebooks.com

3 5 7 9 10 8 6 4 2

Typeset in Sabon by MacGuru Ltd
Printed and bound in Great Britain by
CPI Group (UK) Ltd, Croydon, CR0 4YY

A CIP catalogue record for this book is available from the British Library.

ISBN 978 1 78816 152 7
eISBN 978 1 78283 491 5

For my grandmothers, Elizabeth and Fay

You are neither here nor there,
A hurry through which known and strange things pass
As big soft buffetings come at the car sideways
And catch the heart off guard and blow it open.

(from 'Postscript', by Seamus Heaney)

Prologue

I woke up on my back. All around me the long grass quietly tossed and turned in the wind, and above me the moonless sky was fading from indigo to grey. For a moment or two I was blank, not knowing where I was – perhaps not quite remembering *who* I was – and lacked the energy to wonder how it was that I might have ended up here, in the corner of this field.

I turned my head to the left and saw the outline of my bike, lying in the shelter of the hedge. And there beside it were my orange helmet and my cycling shoes, neatly lined up as I always left them when I stopped for these brief snoozes. Now I remembered. I was in a race.

I had crossed the border into Slovenia a few hours before, and suddenly the world had darkened and quietened. Italy's ubiquitous mopeds and bustling late-night gelaterias gave way to a smooth road that led me calmly through lightless villages, only discernible because my headlamp caught the yellow road signs that announced their presence, and past grassy fields, which I regarded with indecent longing until I finally, inevitably, gave in to my exhaustion, stepped through an open gateway, took my shoes and helmet off, and lay down on the ground.

The previous evening I had noticed myself becoming obsessed with sleep, the way an anorexic obsesses about food, unable to think of anything but what I denied myself, constantly making plans I wouldn't allow myself to carry out, appraising every garden and grass verge I passed for its sleeping potential, but forcing myself to push onwards until I found the next one. I despised myself for my weakness whenever I caved in and lay down. The race leaders were only sleeping twenty minutes a day. I had had over an hour in a park in Treviso that afternoon. That ought to be enough.

I had been following a long, straight road that ran west to east, just north of Venice, and although it only passed through a few settlements large enough to be mapped as towns, it seemed constantly populated along its length with hamlets, and houses, and restaurants, and supermarkets, and where there weren't any of these things there were farms and orchards and vineyards, mostly fenced off or separated from the road by a ten-foot ditch with water at the bottom, all apparently designed to prevent an exhausted cyclist from getting a moment of the sleep she persistently denied herself.

As the night drew on I stopped ever more frequently, for an espresso to keep me going, or a gelato that I only ate so that I could more legitimately ask the heavily made-up waitresses if I could use the bathroom, and if they might fill my bottle. Since the bottle was an aerodynamic, space-ship-shaped affair, designed to fit onto the aerobars of my bike, I usually had to explain, using pidgin Italian and sign language, what it was and how it was filled, and as closing time drew near I clearly failed at this, because a few miles down the road I discovered that the last waitress had in fact handed the bottle back empty.

I slept for ten-minute stretches on the grass outside a deserted garden centre, and in the woods between a shopping mall and a playing field, disturbed by a curious hedgehog who came snuffling through the scorched grass and very nearly walked into my leg, before turning tail and scuttling off into the darkness. Sometime after midnight I was woken up by two sets of headlights shining straight onto me, and when I opened my eyes, blinking into the unexpected blaze of light, I saw a couple of silhouetted figures staggering towards me as if in a nightmare, while muttered conversations from the two cars, and a piercing female voice asking '*esta male?*' told me that I had been wrong in my assumption that no one at this out-of-town restaurant would notice an exhausted cyclist and a well-laden bike, briefly resting in its gardens. I leapt apologetically to my feet, grabbed my bike, and was on my way again before they were even back in their cars, wondering what they must be saying to each other about what they had just seen, and whether it would be with curiosity, disgust or downright pity that they remembered me.

Now I had left the clamour of Italy behind me, and Slovenia was silent. Few cars passed me – they were all on the motorway, which curved along the higher edges of this valley, often crossing a gulf or gully on enormous concrete stilts, while my smaller road edged gradually upwards along its floor. Alongside me, nothing but empty fields and darkened villages. Above me, the fading sky. All around me, the bullying wind.

When I checked the time on my phone, I was only slightly surprised to see that, despite my sense of waking from long slumber, it was only eleven minutes and twenty-nine seconds since I'd set the alarm, for a generous twenty minutes, before resting my head on the grass, and falling into deep sleep so violently that it felt like dark claws were reaching up from the depths to snatch me under. Sometimes I would hear myself groan aloud as I sank into this whirl-pool – but I would always awaken, cleanly and suddenly, between ten and twelve minutes later, staring up at the sky, wondering where I was and how many hours I had lost, then turning, standing, putting on my shoes and helmet, and getting back on the bike, because really, there was nothing else to do.

Once, in a field outside Verona, I had awoken to find that dawn was breaking above me, and an ant was doing laps of my neck, round and round and round, on and on, wonder-ing if she would ever reach the end.

I had lost sight of the end myself. Istanbul was still over a week's ride away, so impossibly distant that there was no point fixating on it. I thought about the next town, the next bend in the road, the next sleep, the next meal. I reminded myself, as I had many times before, that if I just kept going, eventually my destination would appear.

I got back on the bike, and I kept going.

Chapter One

'What are you *doing* here?' exclaimed my father, tucking his nightshirt into his hastily fastened trousers, and beaming as he forgave me for dragging him out of bed to answer the door at 8 a.m. 'You're soaked to the *skin*! You should have phoned me – I'd've picked you up from the station.'

'I haven't ridden from the station,' I replied, and watched his face change again as the penny slowly dropped.

He bustled me inside, grimacing as he hugged me and the water audibly oozed from my clothes, lit the wood burner, made me a cup of tea, and settled down for a blow-by-blow account. I had left London shortly after lunch the previous day, stopped off for a cup of tea at my brother's workshop in Oxford, and then carried on through the rainy November night towards Mid Wales, fretting about my front light, which was already on the blink, with twelve hours of darkness to go.

I had turned to Twitter.

On overnight ride and front light failing. Can anyone in Chipping Norton, Evesham, Worcester lend me a spare? (Will post back.)

I didn't hold out much hope that this would work, but I entertained a fantasy that someone like me, familiar with the trials of long-distance cycling, would answer my plea, and offer me not only a light, but also a couple of minutes of meaningful encounter with someone who *understood* why I might be cycling 200 miles through the rain, unlike the oblivious staff of the petrol stations I occasionally stopped in.

As it turns out, this was exactly what happened. A few cycling acquaintances retweeted my plea, and within an hour a user called @SirWobbly had replied, offering to lend me a light if I was still anywhere near Worcester. And a few miles out I became aware of a car parked up ahead of me, and a shadowy figure standing in the middle of the road, flagging me down.

'Are you looking for a light, by any chance?' asked the figure.

'Funny you should ask,' I grinned, pulling into the layby.

I couldn't quite believe that a person would drive out in the middle of the night to lend a bike light to a stranger, but things became a little clearer when he explained that he was a long-time audax rider and, as such, perfectly accustomed to hanging around in lay-bys at odd hours, in the company of sleep-deprived people in Lycra.

Although it originates in France, I can't help but think of audax as a peculiarly British phenomenon. It's an amateur sport in which participants ride extremely long distances, completing a prescribed route within a prede-fined time limit. The minimum any audaxer will consider worthwhile is 200km, and the most popular distances are 300km, 400km and 600km, along with hallmark events such as Paris-Brest-Paris, which takes place every four years, attracts riders from all over the world, and covers 1,200km in just ninety hours. There are no winners in audax. Success is measured simply by whether you complete the ride before the cut-off – and despite the incredible achievements of its riders, it has successfully dodged the limelight for years, partly thanks to the self-acknowledged stereotype of the audaxer as a socially awkward middle-aged man, powering sternly through the rain on his Dawes Galaxy, and carefully avoiding eye contact as a volunteer serves him his cup of tea and plate of baked beans in one of the draughty village halls that typically host audax controls.

I had fallen in with a crowd of audaxers soon after I took up cycling, and although I had only been on one or two of the shorter rides, I had developed a strong admiration for these riders, who covered the sort of distances each weekend that most people would consider a lifetime's achievement, worthy of sponsorship and media coverage and universal admiration. Often, when I read of a new round-the-world record, or when a roadie friend would boast about the 200km sportive he was training for that summer, I would think of the audaxers, many of whom will quite happily cover 400 miles in a weekend, before heading back to work on Monday morning, simply because they claim to enjoy it.

Although he was more gregarious than the stereotype, my new friend seemed in many ways a typical audaxer. He was in his fifties, bald and slightly stout, with no physical indication whatsoever that he might be capable of cycling hundreds of miles a day. And yet, he informed me as I sorted through the collection of lights laid out in the boot of his car, he would be riding Paris-Brest-Paris for the fifth time that

August. I should have a go at it myself, he suggested, telling me of the festive atmosphere that follows riders from Paris all the way to the coast and back, villagers cheering them on and shops and bars opening through the night to fuel them.

'It's like nothing else,' he said. 'Can you imagine that happening in this country? It's something you should experience at least once.'

'Ah, I'd love to,' I replied, 'but I'm planning on doing the Transcontinental.'

I hadn't fully known that this was the case until I let the words out of my mouth. The Transcontinental was a race across Europe – covering the unfathomable distance from Belgium to Istanbul. It had only existed a couple of years, and was strikingly different from any other bike race I had heard of. Riders were forbidden outside support (unless it was unplanned and spontaneously offered by people they met), so would have to carry everything they needed (or buy it as they went), and there wasn't even a set route – just four checkpoints, spaced out across the continent. Unlike the bloated monsters of the Tour de France and the Giro, the Transcontinental had no publicity caravan, and almost no spectators, save for a few family and friends who would turn up at the start to set the racers off, then watch online as their satellite trackers crept across the map.

Thirty riders had competed in the first year, setting off with minimal fanfare, and mostly camping in fields as they flitted across Europe, riding up to 400km a day. The following year many returned, more joined them, and it was rumoured that 2015 might see over 100 competitors.

I had never entered a race before, let alone one 4,000km long, and I was puzzled by my growing conviction that this was something I wanted to do – that I *could* do. I wasn't a stranger to long-distance cycling. I had worked as a bike messenger for several years, riding around 300 miles a week, and when that initially impossible challenge mellowed into a daily routine, I'd spent eighteen months cycling across Asia. But I had never thought of myself as an athlete. Couriering was a job – albeit a fairly active one – and bike touring had felt more like an indulgent backpacker lifestyle than a physical challenge. Until now I had looked on my strength and fitness as enjoyable side effects of my chosen lifestyle, rather than assets in themselves.

Admitting my ambition to race the Transcontinental felt dangerously presumptuous, yet I recognised the vertiginous feeling of saying it out loud. I had felt the same when I got a job as a cycle courier, worried I wouldn't last the first week – and when I tremulously set out to cycle round the world, hoping that in doing so I might turn myself into the kind of person who was capable of such a thing.

I knew Sir Wobbly would have heard of the Transcontinental, though in classic audax fashion he offered no admiration, acknowledging my intention with a nod and a grunt and continuing to extoll the delights of PBP. This stranger was now under the impression that I was someone who would casually announce 'I'm planning on doing the Transcon', as if I spent every summer cycling 300km a day across Europe. It was starting to become official, and I now had less than a year to live up to myself.

I accepted a bright front light, thinking as he handed it over of all the miles of tarmac it must have illuminated, and Wobbly convinced me to take a spare back one as well, tutting maternally over what might happen if my only other red light fell off and I didn't notice.

'Would you like a chocolate-covered coffee bean?' I asked, anxious to offer him something in return for all this generosity. 'Or I've got some squashed bananas?'

'Oh no,' he replied. 'I've got piles of food for *you*!' And then, concerned he had been slightly dismissive of my offerings: 'although that's the best offer I've had in the last ... fifteen seconds.'

He gave a cheeky grin, and handed me a pack of Snickers bars, and a bag of dried fruit, and some energy bars, gleefully piling up the food until I could carry no more. Then he checked the lights were securely fastened to my bike, gave an approving nod when he saw I was riding fixed, told me to get in touch if I needed rescuing within the next two hours, and sent me on my way, passing me with a cheery toot of his horn a moment later.

The following day, as I basked in paternal pride and the glow of the wood burner, relishing the comfort of dry clothes and remembering how horribly my sodden shorts had chafed over the last fifty miles, the entries for the Transcontinental opened.

The race was the brainchild of Mike Hall, a Yorkshireman in his early thirties who had set a new record for circumnavigating the world by bicycle, covering the requisite 18,000 miles in ninety-one days of cycling. The day he rode triumphantly back into Greenwich I was battling into a hot headwind in the Taklamakan Desert in China, and a couple of months later I still had over a thousand miles to go to Tianjin, where I planned to take a ferry to South Korea and, thanks to China's reluctance to grant me any useful length of visa, only eleven days before I had to leave the country.

I had ridden 100-mile days before, but never eleven in a row, and never with 50kg of luggage on my bike. I was buffeted by wind and rain, diverted by roadworks, slowed down by an unexpected mountain range, and as I struggled through China's industrial heartlands, found my eyes itching, my lungs rasping, and my skin powdered dark grey by the chemicals hanging in the air. After a few days of non-stop riding I set out each morning as exhausted as I had felt the previous evening, panicking over the miles still to come. It felt impossible that I could ride another century (and then another, and another), but I had no choice. Outstaying my visa would provoke a bureaucratic nightmare I didn't have it in me to handle. And tempting though it was to shorten the day, and tell myself I'd make up the miles later, I knew I'd only end up falling behind, and making matters worse.

I often thought of Mike Hall during that ride, imagining him (from the reports I'd read of his achievement) as one of the gruff elderly gentlemen I'd followed on audaxes or chased unsuccessfully through the Peak District, knotted legs pumping metronomically astride their hand-built steel frames, faces inscrutable beneath their beards. The knowledge that someone had done something so much harder than I was attempting helped to bring my woes into perspective. If he had covered 200 miles a day, for three months, with legs and lungs and bicycle, then I could surely get through this. I would picture him riding as I rode – occasionally alongside me, but more often in that curious way our minds have of simultaneously witnessing and inhabiting that which we imagine. I wasn't yet convinced of my own strength, but I was of his, so I relied on him to prop me up through my periods of misgiving and self-doubt. But most of all, I looked to him as a new pinnacle of achievement, towards which I could aspire without any particular hope of competing with what he had done, but with some promise of getting farther than I might have otherwise. As far as I was concerned he was a pioneer, breaking a path into unknown territory – 200 miles a day! – that I would never have had the courage to forge myself, but knew I might one day want to follow.

When I met him, shortly after flying home from Japan in 2013, he wasn't quite as I'd expected. I'd hung back nervously at the start of the evening, a high-profile charity event organised by adventurer Alastair Humphreys, as the other speakers mingled, introduced themselves and swapped stories. I was one of only two women (and had in fact been asked to talk specifically about my gender, as though that were my specialist subject), and everyone else seemed to be a tall, muscular young man with a chiselled jawline. I wondered which of them would turn out to be Mike Hall. The hero I'd thus far known as an abstract collection of strength, endurance and achievement was about to manifest himself in flesh, as if he were a normal person like the rest of us.

Eventually I asked Al to point him out, and was agreeably surprised when my gaze was directed to a man, shorter and stouter and scruffier than I'd imagined, sitting alone at the other end of the row – as if he were as shy as I was. His fuzzy brown hair was in need of a cut, and his gut bulged an inch or so over his belted jeans. I was captivated.

I think, had Mike Hall really been the Greek god I'd imagined, I could only have been less impressed once the flickering image I'd held in my head solidified into flesh. I'd quickly have realised that, like the avenue of young men stretching between us, he was insurmountably different from me, and therefore no longer a valid figure of aspiration. No matter how hard I trained, or how far I cycled, I would never be one of these men, with their expedition beards, their rangy limbs and their broad shoulders. Even at my strongest, six months previously, as I pedalled frantically through China, my days of lean muscularity had been regrettably brief. Now, after two months of couch-surfing in a wintery London, I had settled into the despair that had hovered like a dark cloud over the final month of my trip, and reverted to pale podginess. My hair was lank and dull, and I had nothing to wear but a laddered base layer and the stained hiking trousers I'd bought in Esfahan a year previously.

'I thought she'd be wiry and waif-like,' remarked a friend, in an online interview he published around that time, 'but she looks sturdy, stocky and strong' – which my unhappy mind translated as 'much fatter than I expected'. I couldn't help but think I was failing to live up to my own reputation. And now here was Mike Hall, apparently failing to live up to his, but I liked him all the more for it.

I was too shy to talk to him for most of the evening, then mustered my courage at the last possible minute, and pursued him up the stairs of the auditorium as he and his friend reached the door of the cinema, shrugging on their jackets. I caught up with him in the foyer and introduced myself, even though presumably he now knew who I was from my talk. I didn't like to assume he'd have paid much attention to someone whose achievements were so pedestrian compared to his.

'And I think I just wanted to say ...' I said, mainly because I had to say *something* to him, now that I had his attention, 'that I really am amazed by what you've done – because I know from what *I've* just done how hard it must have been, and I know I couldn't do it.'

He thanked me with an air of polite surprise, seeming as embarrassed as I was. Through his moustache, I spied the ghost of a harelip.

'How have you been?' I asked. 'I mean, how are you coping, since you got back?'

'It's not been the easiest,' he mused. 'I wasn't on the bike much for a bit. I've picked up a few days' courier-ing in Cardiff now, in fact,' he said, with a nod to indicate that we had this in common, 'and … well, I'm taking the antidepressants.'

His candour surprised me, and for a moment the differ-ent versions of Mike Hall jostled against each other in my head – the record-breaking hero, versus this softly spoken, melancholic man who'd had trouble leaving the house. I was still a few weeks away from admitting I was in a similar state myself, but then, he was a little way up the road from me, having finished his ride six months earlier.

'But it'll pick up,' he told me. 'You know, when you're going through a really bad patch on the bike, and you tell yourself "this won't last".' He paused, and smiled for the first time. 'And you know, when you're going through a really good patch, you know that won't last either.'

We both laughed, and he turned to the man beside him, as if to apologise for the hold-up, then back towards me.

'We're going for a pint, if you fancy it?'

I fancied nothing more than sitting in the corner of some booming central London pub, quietly exchanging stories with one of the few people who wouldn't expect me to behave like the prodigal cyclist, but I reluctantly excused myself and rejoined my friends, who had pub plans of their own. I failed to keep up with most of their conversation though. The talk I'd given, even though it had only been six minutes long, had wrung all my language and energy out of me, leaving me no verve with which to respond to people's questions, or follow their tangents. I excused myself after one drink, and gladly got back on my bike to pedal through the cold night, to the spare room in south-west London where my four panniers and their contents were currently piled.

Mike and I crossed paths fairly regularly in the years that followed, at bike shows and other such events where we were invited to talk about our respective adventures. One bright spark at the Leeds Festival of Cycling had the idea of making us race against each other on the rollers, and I was embarrassed when Mike completed his 500m when I was barely halfway through mine, leaving me spinning and hyperventilating alone. I didn't know if he would consider me worth remembering, but when I emailed him a query about the time race entries opened for the Transcontinental, his response said, 'It'll be great to have you on the race. Just get your entry in when you can.'

I felt I had overcome the first hurdle a month later, when he offered me a place. Now, I told people, with an optimism I didn't feel, I had six months to transform myself into a road cyclist. I had never owned the sort of bike I would need for the Transcontinental, and – aside from the eighteen months I'd spent pedalling a touring bike across Asia – almost all of my cycling had been on my fixed-gear courier bike.

I tried to ignore the other racers, many of whom were already broadcasting their training plans and route research over social media. My friend Leo had pinned a map of Europe to his living room wall, the location of each checkpoint marked with a pin. He showed me the kit he was amassing, described his training rituals, and told me he planned to ride the first 1,000km of the race in just over two days, and reach the first checkpoint – Mont Ventoux – in the early hours of the morning, to avoid climbing in the heat. I envied his confidence as much as I did his broad shoulders and lean muscles. I was scared even to imagine how long it would take me to reach Ventoux.

I didn't have a clue how one was supposed to train for an

event like this, so I decided simply to do as much cycling as I possibly could, with a conviction that the more I suffered before the race, the less I would suffer once it started. Which is how I found myself lining up for the Bryan Chapman, a popular and infamous 600km audax that takes riders from Chepstow to Anglesey and back again, routing them over every hill. Wales is one of the smallest countries in Europe, but there was still a fearful symbolism in riding its length twice in a single weekend, made worse by the fact that the Bryan Chapman had hovered in my consciousness for years as a comfortably unattainable target, that other riders had managed to achieve, but that was unquestionably beyond me.

The night before the ride I ensconced myself miserably in the corner of Wetherspoons in Chepstow. I quite often stopped in Wetherspoons for breakfast if I'd been riding all night, enjoying the cheap coffee and bacon rolls, the luxurious toilets, and the company of gentle, red-nosed men on their first pint of the day. But now I sat alone, ignored by the tipsy teenagers who made up Wetherspoons' evening clientele, scanning the menu to find the most calories for the least money, and texting every friend I could think of to seek some comfort for my building sense of dread.

I had stumbled into riding the Bryan Chapman in much the same way as I had the Transcon – I had spoken my intentions out loud, people had taken me seriously, and now I had to do it. The ride was sold out, but Sir Wobbly came to my aid once again, like a fairy godfather, revealing that he had been on the board of Audax UK, and that he could almost certainly get me a place. ('Only you might have to pretend you're me.') I knew, somewhere in the furthest recesses of my mind, that I was entirely capable of finishing this ride, but this knowledge was so expertly hidden by my habitual fear and self-doubt that I rarely met it face to face, and as I sat there in Wetherspoons, gloomily chewing on a microwaved burrito, the fear and self-doubt flew about my head like bats, feeding off each other, growing bigger and bigger.

I felt hopelessly unprepared for this ride. I had never ridden 600km in one go, and here I was, hubristically taking on the most difficult 600 on the audax calendar. I fretted over whether I'd packed the right kit – whether I even owned the right kit. I should have got round to replacing my shoes before now, but had succumbed to my usual strategy of using clothes and components until they literally fell apart, reasoning that this minor inconvenience was worth the money I'd save by getting an extra few weeks' wear out of them. But now I was worried that the soles of my shoes had become so thin that I might actually wrench them loose as I rode.

Placated by the reassurances of friends and the calories of Wetherspoons, I struggled back up the hill to camp beside the community centre where the ride started, feeling weak and uncommonly tired; nothing like the ball of energy you'd want to be, setting out on a forty-hour ride. The following morning I packed my tent away at 5 a.m. and hovered at the edge of a gathering crowd of tall men in Lycra, standing around with their cups of tea, discussing important matters of audax. I had no one to talk to, so busied myself with multiple teas, repeated toilet trips and unnecessary last-minute adjustments to my bike and kit. It was a relief when we finally set off, in a chorus of beeping Garmins and cleats clipping into pedals, chasing each other along the chilly lanes of Monmouthshire in the grey morning light.

And by the time we reached the first control at Talgarth,

I realised I had left my doubts behind in Chepstow, like a skin I'd sloughed off or a chrysalis I'd emerged from. A man I befriended over breakfast assured me that there was no obligation to follow the set route, as long as you visited all the controls, and we successfully dodged the Bank Holiday traffic by crossing the River Wye and following a leafy lane up through Boughrood and Erwood, chattering along two abreast as the other riders struggled through the fumes on the A470.

'The ride used to go this way anyway,' he told me, as we pedalled out of Rhayader towards the chain of Victorian dams that submerged farms and hamlets in order to send Welsh water to Birmingham. Two other men had joined our peloton, but charily decided there was no need to add one of Wales' most famous climbs to what was already a painfully hilly route. I was familiar with the Elan Valley, having grown up a few miles east, near the head of the Severn, and although I knew it wouldn't be an easy detour, this was trumped by the comfort of a road that held no surprises. Besides, it was a beautiful day to be out, just at the point where spring tipped over into summer, the sunshine throwing itself about the heavens, the clouds rolling busily along above us, and an orchestra of birds and insects heralding our progress through the country.

I eventually lost my breakfast friend on the climb up towards the watershed between Rhayader and Cwmystwyth (he waved me on apologetically, telling me that his legs weren't having a good day) and set about chasing the white-haired man in the green-and-yellow jersey I could see up ahead of me, occasionally disappearing round a corner or over the brow of a hill, never quite within my reach. I was intoxicated by the strength of my legs, which seemed to be infused with all of the brightness and beauty of the day, and the unexpected plot twist that, here I was, riding the Bryan Chapman and, rather than grimly struggling and just about hanging on, I was *enjoying* it.

Chapter Two

The Transcontinental began in Belgium, a week after the Tour de France finished in Paris, and I arrived by bike, distracted by a burgeoning love affair that felt far more important than the pedestrian logistics of trains and flights. I sailed peacefully through the night, arriving in Geraardsbergen just as the cafés opened, and didn't question the wisdom of riding so far just before the race. An all-night ride was no longer a challenge, and I was relieved to blow away the cobwebs of the last few weeks, to pass from one element into another.

I settled down in a riverside café and ordered the first of many espressos, my plan being to keep myself awake till nightfall, ensuring that my last sleep before the race would be as long and deep as I could make it. After a couple of hours, I looked up to see a tall, tanned figure in white Lycra, bending to examine the bike I'd parked outside.

Juliana was one of the few other women in the race, and therefore ostensibly my competition, though neither of us had quite succeeded in seeing it that way. She was acknowledged to be one of the world's strongest endurance riders, having established a women's round-the-world record the same year Mike Hall set the men's, ridden in the first Transcontinental, and come fourth overall in the inaugural TransAm Bike Race, which had crossed the US the previous summer. Before reinventing herself as a cyclist she had had a rather different life, growing up in a cult, which she left after the suicide of her sister, and eventually denounced in a best-selling memoir. Her decision to cycle round the world had been prompted by the death of the man she loved, who was killed by a crocodile in the Congo. To most people she was an improbable, larger-than-life character, but she and I had somehow ended up becoming friends, each relieved to find another woman who took such evident delight in cycling hundreds of miles without sleep. Six weeks previously we had ridden from London to Edinburgh together, my fears that she'd outpace me quickly dissipating as we chased each other up the country, gossiping over pub lunches, giggling in the aisles of Hexham's twenty-four-hour Tesco as we bought gardening gloves for our freezing hands, and exchanging details of our saddlesore at top volume as we sped through the traffic jams on our way into Edinburgh.

The arrival of a friend made me feel a little more like I belonged here, and the two of us spent the next twenty-four hours drifting from café to café, eating chips and pasta, and watching the town fill up with racers. Many of them already knew Juliana, from previous races or by reputation, and I was most amused when an Italian man, on meeting her in person for the first time, staggered back and (apparently even to his own surprise) began to cry. I teased Juliana about their mutual embarrassment, once she'd posed for a photo and got rid of him.

As midnight approached we pedalled slowly up to the top of the Kapelmuur, where the bars heaved with anxious Lycra-clad men, and dozens of bikes lined the narrow cobbled road. The crowds of spectators lit their flaming torches, and wives and girlfriends kissed the racers goodbye, promising to see them in Turkey. Then the clock struck, a bell rang, and we rode a slow procession around the town, before climbing back through the market square and finally wrestling our bikes up the cobbled climb to the start line, trying to keep our momentum, improvising lines between our fellow riders, sightreading the camber and gradient of the torchlit stones as we ascended through the roaring crowds. Occasionally I heard my own name ringing out from the melee.

At the top of the Muur we tipped over into silence, as suddenly as when a diver slips from air into water, and within minutes I rediscovered the familiar world of focus and motion, the night air rushing past my face, my tyres murmuring against the tarmac, and the gentle darkness enveloping me like a blanket. The building angst with which I'd awaited this race blew away behind me like a lost glove, instantly forgotten as I remembered that this was a place that held no fear for me, and a moment I could happily have held on to forever.

I had spent that summer living in the past and the future – condensing my memories of the last five years into the book I was writing, casting my mind ahead to the challenges that this race might hold, and delightedly anticipating my happily ever after with the woman I'd just met. Now I was finally on the road, there was comfort in the knowledge that what was done was done, what I'd not done would be left undone, and all I could do now was keep moving forward.

A country lane gave way to a cobbled farm track, nettles and brambles crowding in from either side, and I momentarily despaired – only a couple of hours into the race, and I was already getting myself lost, tangled in briars while the competition glided over tarmac. But my dismay was only momentary. In England or Wales, such a road would invariably lead to a remote farmhouse with an angry dog, or simply disappear into a ploughed field. But I knew this must be one of Belgium's legendary cobbled roads, and that it must lead *somewhere*, and that even if it didn't, I had all the time in the world to extricate myself, because, really, I didn't stand a chance of winning this race, or even doing particularly well, so I might as well do some exploring along the way. My front beam lit up the uneven *pavé* ahead of me, and the undergrowth clawed at my bare legs as I steered myself around potholes. Lightning shimmered on the horizon, heralding the storms we'd been warned about back in Geraardsbergen. I wanted to stop for a moment, to savour the silence that would crowd in as my wheels stilled and my breathing slowed, to enjoy the sense of being cradled by the hedgerows, here on this tiny lane, somewhere on the earth's surface with the flickering sky above me. But I was here to ride, so I rode on.

Minutes later I turned onto a main road and found myself back in the race. The riders were disembodied, visible only as bundles of flickering lights and glowing reflective stripes until I caught them. I accelerated past a pair of stocky men, carrying on until I'd left them a good way behind and felt I could maintain my position, then a couple of faster riders shot by, one with his head down and his teeth bared, the other with a shout and a wave.

'Hello love,' called Juliana's voice, and Juliana herself sailed past, ghostlike in her white Lycra. I chased her for a while, but she was riding harder than I'd ever seen her go before, and far too fast for me to keep up with.

We'd agreed that whoever made it to Istanbul first would get the beers in, and I recalled the dual fantasies I'd entertained before the start – one in which I ground to a triumphant halt beside the Bosphorus, looked all around for Juliana and realised I'd beaten her; the other, far more likely, in which I staggered into the final checkpoint to find her waiting for me with two cold bottles of Efes.

A few hours previously we'd chinked our espresso cups and hugged each other as the riders started to empty out of the bar towards the start line, and I noticed my body beginning to fizz with excitement, as if someone were opening bottles of champagne behind my rib cage. She had smiled affectionately at me, but seemed distant and preoccupied. I wondered if she was thinking about her knees, which were still damaged from the TransAm, and had bothered her on our Edinburgh ride. Maybe it was just that a start line held less excitement for her. She had seen a few more than I had.

It was strange that we liked each other so much, I thought, and that our mutual regard seemed to have supplanted any sense of competition, to the extent that we relished racing together no matter what the result. 'You're chasing my tail, I'm happy. I'm chasing your tail, I'm happy,' she had said in a text the previous week. Perhaps it wasn't that we'd lost our sense of competition. Perhaps it was that we both knew we'd be competitive *anyway*, no matter who we were chasing, and it was comforting to share the road with someone who felt the same way, who knew that, no matter how sincerely either of us might strain to overtake the other, the real race would always be against ourselves. I hoped our paths would cross during the ride – that I'd see her bike parked outside a café, and tiptoe in to surprise her, or that I'd spot her ahead of me on one of the long climbs, and slowly reel her in before losing her again on the descent.

I watched as she drew ahead, overtaking the other riders one by one as the road rose into France, and the discreetly spaced pools of light cast by people's dynamos staggered up towards the restless sky as if mounting a ladder into the darkness.

⠿

'It's Emily, isn't it?'

I started and looked round to see where the voice was coming from, momentarily taking my eyes off the road that rolled out ahead of me like a corridor, lined with columns of plane trees, through which the Saône Valley scrolled past like a frieze.

'Sorry for making you jump,' said the wiry Englishman who'd spoken. 'I remember you from the Bryan Chapman – I think you took the Elan Valley detour like I did?'

'Oh yes,' I replied. 'That was me.'

'I'm Shell,' he said. 'Name's Sheldrake, but everyone calls me Shell.' I noticed he was wearing the same jersey that he had in Wales – the broad green and yellow stripes of Leicester Forest Cycling Club – which was all I remembered of him, having followed it like a hare up the climb out of Rhayader towards Cwmystwyth, and never quite managed to catch it. Now, in the steamy air of central France, just before the sun set on the second day of the Transcontinental, he had caught me.

'How's this one going so far?' he asked.

'Oh, surprisingly good! I got majorly lost yesterday – or

at least, I planned my route a bit stupidly – and ended up doing lots of gravel, and I assumed that everyone else must be long gone, but people keep catching me up now, so I'm obviously not the slowest.'

'No, I'd say you're going well,' he replied. 'Where did you sleep? *Did* you sleep?'

'Yep – I had to,' I told him. 'I had a rough patch late afternoon – just could *not* keep my eyes open, and I was crawling along, riding through all this gorgeous parkland, seeing good places to sleep and not letting myself. Then I stopped in a little village, and had a drink.'

I paused, remembering the wretchedness I'd felt as I hunted for a café, the contempt exuding from its proprietor as she charged me €2 for a 200ml bottle of orange juice, and my despair as I sat in the corner, propped my head up on my hands, and allowed myself to sink into unconsciousness. I was less than twenty-four hours into the race, which had begun on the stroke of midnight, and already felt unable to go any further. It was far too early to sleep – I'd planned to ride a full day before stopping – but there seemed little point in continuing while I felt like this. Practically, I couldn't keep my eyes open. Physically I was weak and slow, my inner calves were rubbed raw by my frame pack, and my face was sore and itchy with lack of sleep. I was furious with myself for stopping, for my slowness, for the shoddy route-planning that meant my day had mostly been spent on unpaved farm tracks. I hadn't seen another rider for hours. But then ...

'And then,' I continued to Shell, glad of a listener, 'it all turned around. I ended up on a farm track again, except this was a really beautiful one. It took me up across these gorgeous golden fields, past massive haystacks, just as the sun was sinking. And then I dropped down into this ancient woodland, and I was rolling along through oak trees and beech trees, with actual deer bounding out of my path.'

The magic of the place still clung to me. My unsatisfying half hour of snoozes, and the expensive orange juice I'd eked out sip by sip, had done their work, and a gravelly uphill road I would have deplored two hours ago now beckoned me onward with the promise of adventure and discovery, eventually dropping me down into a tiny French village, stacked on a steep hillside in the smoky twilight, the sun's final rays glowing on its uppermost rooftops. The road, probably ancient itself, was rutted, covered in loose stones, and in places almost unrideable, meaning that I had to focus closely on keeping the bike moving forward. For most of that evening, the race – and everything I knew – seemed a long way away, as I pedalled along dark empty roads that led me over low hilltops, down through dingles and along valley floors, through the occasional shuttered village and onward into the night.

'I ended up sleeping between some woodpiles at the edge of a village,' I told Shell. 'It was lovely. I think I had about four hours.'

I wanted to tell him that 'lovely' was nowhere near the right word – that as I lay down in my bivvy bag and felt my tired body relax, sinking into the ground as if it wanted to put down roots and claw its way into the soil, I had looked up at the dark sky and the brilliant spray of stars shining down over this lightless French village, and felt a happiness so powerful that I strained to stay awake for a few more seconds, knowing it would be gone when I woke up. There was nowhere I wanted to be more than here, on the damp ground among the snails and woodlice. I had unwittingly been striving towards this moment for the twenty-three hours I'd been racing – and the nine months I'd spent preparing – and just briefly, everything was right: myself, the world, the race, and my place in each of them.

I suspected Shell would understand, but we were riding at such a pace I couldn't muster the words to explain it to him. We rolled along together for a while, chatting about rides we had done, agreeing that the Bryan Chapman was the finest of them all. He had finished the Transcon before, he told me (I remembered seeing a green-and-yellow jersey in the finishers' photo), but wasn't sure if he'd manage it this year – his knees weren't all they should be.

They seemed pretty good to me, I thought, noticing that we had both subtly increased our speed in response to each other's, and were now conversing at a near sprint, enjoying the cooler air rippling over us as the evening drew in. I thought again about the rule against slipstreaming – which we most certainly were not doing – and wondered how much of an advantage was conferred simply by having someone ride alongside you, whether companionably or competitively. I had done almost all of my cycling solo so far, and only once or twice gone out with a local club during my haphazard preparation for this race. I had worried that I'd be left behind, then hadn't known what to do when it transpired that I was faster than most of the men, feeling simultaneously gleeful in my unexpected talent, and worried that I was breaking some sort of etiquette when I overtook them. I suspected that having people to chase and pace myself against was making me ride faster than I would on my own, and wondered if having a faster rider (especially a woman) in their midst was increasing the pace of the whole group. I remembered, one long-ago evening, admitting to a fellow courier that I could no longer match the pace he was setting up Lloyd Baker Street after a couple of pints off Theobald's Road, and his laughter as he abruptly fell back and gasped 'no, *I've* been trying to keep up with *you*!'

'Anyway,' said Shell, 'I'll let you get on for now – I'm going to take it steady for a bit.' And, just like Will on Lloyd Baker Street, he appeared to slide backwards, and left me sprinting into the light glow of the sunset. I waved goodbye and carried on, enjoying the speed that I half-knew would be temporary. A few hours later I rolled down the hill into Lyon, gazing delightedly at the illuminated bridges that stapled the river into place, and wondering to myself why I'd never bothered to come here before – in fact, why I hadn't spent every spare moment of my life riding from European city to European city, since each one evidently held wonders it had never occurred to me to imagine.

It was after midnight, and I shared the streets with late-night taxis, a couple of refuse trucks and a shouting drunkard. I got all the way down to the river before I found anywhere I could buy food, and I ordered a kebab and a can of Orangina from a friendly Turkish Kurd whose homeland I'd cycled through three years previously, then sat on a plastic chair outside his shop, beaming my contentment at all who passed, and looking up Bédoin on my phone, to see how far I had to go to Mont Ventoux.

Two hundred kilometres? But I could ride that in a night, I thought. And if I covered the distance to Bédoin before sunrise, I might inadvertently follow Leo's plan, and climb Ventoux in the early hours of the morning, before it began to bake in the unrelenting Provençale heat – and I might even run into Leo himself, who, if his ride was going well, perhaps wasn't that far away from me after all.

I got back on the bike, waved goodbye to my friends in the kebab shop and muddled my way through Lyon's back streets. But the breezy energy with which I'd swept into town had deserted me, and I stumbled into *culs-de-sac* and one-way systems, at one point backtracking past a block of flats just a second before someone threw an egg from one of its balconies. The road south, when I finally found it, climbed steadily, and I'd barely been riding for an hour before my body felt too heavy and reluctant to continue, and I began looking for somewhere to sleep.

The joy I had felt lying between the woodpiles the previous night eluded me as I dropped my bike inside an open gateway and unfurled my bivvy bag a few metres away, hoping that the flies hovering in the dying beam of my dynamo light wouldn't gravitate to my sleeping body. Although I had felt too tired to go on, I lay, tense and twitching, for at least ten minutes before I dozed off, then woke less than two hours later to struggle out of my sleeping bag, and sweat miserably into my bivvy. Eventually I realised I might as well carry on.

Chapter Three

The shining peak of Mont Ventoux felt a very long way from the swampy darkness of my field outside Lyon, and it turns out it was. It had seemed such a straightforward plan: just to ride without stopping for seven or eight hours, to cover the 200km to the mountain, and to catch up with Leo – and whomever else might be there by now.

I knew from Twitter that the first rider to Checkpoint One had been a young man called James Hayden (whom no one had heard of before), that the favourite, Josh Ibbett, had raced Ultan Coyle up the mountain in pursuit, and that all three had now turned north-east, towards Checkpoint Two in Sestriere. There they'd follow the Strada dell'Assietta, an unpaved military road through the Western Alps, before dropping down to Italy's Po Valley. The social media commentators were hailing a new star cyclist, who looked like he might fill the vacuum left by Kristof Allegaert, the stern

Belgian who'd appeared from nowhere in similar fashion to win the first two races and this summer was racing across Siberia instead. Hayden himself had tweeted: 'Thanks everyone, I'm having the time of my life. This is what I've dreamed of since I was a kid.' I remembered my own fantasies of winning races when I was sprinting around London as a courier, marvelling at the speed and grace I hadn't known I possessed.

I had no idea where Juliana was, but the chances were that, if I'd made it this close to Ventoux, she must be past it, and gaining on Hayden, Coyle and Ibbett. I dropped her a couple of encouraging texts that morning, glad of any excuse to spend a few moments not cycling. The day was hot and hilly, and all I wanted to do was stop, so I did, again and again. I stopped in a car park just after sunrise, and spent twenty minutes asleep under a tree. I stopped two hours later at a coffee shop, washed the previous day's shorts in their hand basin and ordered a second coffee as my excuse to stay longer. The waitress, to my surprise, had heard of the Transcontinental, and wished me well as I left. I briefly saw myself through her eyes – a noble athlete rather than a malodorous tramp – but within an hour the heat and exhaustion were crowding in on me again.

As I turned off the main road into the hills, the landscape corrugated and my feet throbbed painfully in my tight shoes, until I was conscious of every pedal stroke. I stopped in a tiny village at the bottom of a hill, ripped off my shoes and socks and plunged my feet into the ice-cold tank of water underneath a fountain, gasping as agony abruptly turned to relief. The scents of basil and lavender hovered in the air, and a ringing choir of insects pulsed in my ears. I stopped a few villages later, having spied an open café-bar, bought myself another coffee and two ice lollies, and stared grumpily out at the leafy square. I was ashamed not to have pushed on through the ever-present urge to stop, as I'd promised myself I would. But mostly I felt tired, uncomfortable and fed up. Ventoux seemed as distant as it had the previous night, and I failed to muster much interest in getting there. The possibility of finishing this race still felt so remote that it wasn't even part of my reckoning, and the immediate urge to keep moving had evaporated in the stifling heat of the afternoon.

Juliana had responded to my texts. She was within kilometres of Ventoux, but both her knees had given out the previous night, and now she could barely walk, let alone cycle.

'I can't believe it! My own body's letting me down!'

I remembered her trying to hide that she was crying with pain on the road to Edinburgh two months earlier.

'Have you tried resting them? Elevating? Icing?' I asked, knowing it was too late for any of that, and that even if she could buy herself another day, these knees weren't going to let her ride 3,000km.

'Yep, all of that,' she replied. 'I can't even bend them. Looks like you might win this race after all.'

'What are you going to do?' I asked.

'My sister's coming to pick me up from Nice.'

'Where are you?'

'Aubignan. Just north of Carpentras.'

'Right. I'll try and get there before you go.'

'Yes please. I'd love to see you right now.'

'OK. On my way. Where'll I find you?'

'I'm in a café on the main street. You'll see me.'

'I'm coming as fast as I can. See you soon.'

I rushed inside to pay the bill, suddenly impatient with every wasted second, and hastily recalculated my route.

Aubignan wasn't directly between me and Ventoux, so I abandoned the .gpx track I'd carefully planned the week before, and struck out across the sun-baked hills, pausing now and again to memorise the next few turnings. The need to see Juliana eclipsed my constant urge to stop, and was a purpose far easier to resolve than my vague intention of making it to the finish line. Breathing heavily, I tried to work out how far off Nice was, and how long her sister might take to drive to Aubignan, but the calculations eluded me, my mind enslaved to forward motion as much as my legs.

I raced over col after col, tucking each one behind me, soaring down into whatever new landscape lay beyond. Hungry, but not wanting to stop or divert, I reached hopefully into my jersey pocket and found my hand closing round the tiny malted biscuits that Juliana and I had been served with our coffee in Geraardsbergen. Briefly marvelling that I'd be seeing her again just a few days later, as if in normal life, I ripped the cellophane with my teeth and wolfed down each small mouthful of crumbs. I was 20km from Aubignan now. I'd be there within the hour.

I had drunk all my water, eaten all my food and burnt off almost all my energy, and as I sprinted along the flat road that led into Aubignan I could feel exhaustion lying in wait, hovering over my head like a kettle of vultures. A car slowed down to drive alongside me and I listened with as much attention as I could spare to what the driver was trying to say, wondering what it was he wanted, since he didn't seem as scornful or hostile as drivers usually do in England.

It took a few seconds for him to realise I was foreign, and for me to work out that I simply didn't have enough oxygen in my brain to hold a conversation, but before he pulled away I caught the word '*agile*', noticed that he and his passenger were both smiling at me, and realised that they had slowed down to compliment me on my cycling. My spirits lifted slightly as I ground my way up the final rise, over the roundabout and onto Aubignan's main street, where I slowed down to peer under awnings and into windows, looking for Juliana. I freewheeled down the hill, fought my way through the busy evening traffic, and cycled back up to the top, looking everywhere for her bike, her white Lycra, her distinctive silhouette. But she was gone. And I was exhausted.

'I'll rest and eat,' I told myself, 'then I'll think about Ventoux.' Put like that it sounded like a plan.

There weren't many restaurants in Aubignan, and even the supermarket was closed. I settled for a bar where the waitress had told me they started serving pizza at 6 p.m. – still half an hour off, but there was nothing else I could do with that time. I'd have to ride Ventoux in the dark, but since the climb currently looked impossible anyway, one more element of difficulty wouldn't make much difference. I sat myself down at the edge of the terrace, trying to calculate how long it had been since I last had a shower.

One pizza wasn't anywhere near enough. I ordered a plate of tiramisu, and polished off the basket of bread, but I didn't feel any better for eating. The heat was beginning to drain out of the day as the shadows lengthened and the sun sank towards the luminous Provençale landscape. I got back on my bike, telling myself that I could stop any time I wanted to, that a couple of hours' snooze in a field might sort me out. But I knew that sleep would have as little effect as the pizza I'd eaten. I stopped at a fountain in Caromb and threw water over my face and arms. It didn't help. I stopped in Bédoin and drank an espresso. It didn't help. The mountain loomed over me, its peak still glowing with the light of day while shadows fell everywhere around.

I tried to explain to myself what I was feeling as I pedalled slowly towards the start of the climb. I wasn't afraid – I hadn't the energy for such grand, decisive emotions. Instead I had a sense of what lay ahead of me being impossible, but also inevitable. I knew that I hadn't the strength to see it through. But nor did I have the imagination to find any better solution than just carrying on. So I carried on, through the outskirts of Bédoin, past its stone walls and olive groves, under an apricot sky that smelt of lavender.

As I turned onto the road that led to the summit I felt something break inside me. But it was nothing like I had imagined when speculating on what terrible things would happen to me during this race. Nothing snapped, or cracked, or shattered. Instead it felt more like melting; a gentle, delicate collapse, like a body falling exhaustedly into sleep after a long day's work. I felt myself start to cry, but in a way that was more a merciful release of tension than an expression of pain.

I had been here before, just once in my life, and always wondered when I might go back. The day after I finished my scramble through Eastern China I stepped off the ferry in Korea and started to ride the 50km to my friends' house. It should have taken less than three hours, but it took twelve. As the sky darkened around me and the rain came down, I pedalled through the business parks of Seoul and Incheon, following signposts that led me persistently round in circles, backtracking again and again, despairing that I would *ever* find a way out of this nightmare. Having slept through most of the ferry crossing, I had apparently forgotten that I was exhausted by my exertions in China, but this must have had something to do with the fact that, eventually, I broke down.

I had always been anxious to keep myself from crying in

situations like this, imagining that if I gave in to the tears it would all be over, and my final remnants of strength and resolve would be swept away in the ensuing tide of salt water. But that afternoon I ran out of the strength I was using to hold them back. Sheltering under a bridge beside the Han River, I sobbed out loud for a few minutes, not caring who saw. Then I made a discovery that surprised me: this wasn't the end after all. Still crying, I got back on the bike. My sobs rippled in and out of me like breath. For half an hour I cycled along weeping quietly to myself, then my mood shifted, the rain stopped, and I finally found my way.

I'd heard of audaxers hallucinating after riding for days without sleep, but I'd never heard of breakdowns like this. 'It'll be easier next time,' I told myself. 'I thought I was about to lose it. Next time I'll know it's just the crying stage.'

Three years later, here I was again, at the crying stage. A couple of tears ran down my cheeks, and a few sobs escaped my lips, quickly dying into whimpers. Somehow I was still here, still cycling.

'It doesn't matter!' I thought to myself. For an instant, I knew what I should have known all along: that riding the Transcontinental was simply something I wanted to do, rather than underpinning my entire character and worth. It meant so much less than I'd thought.

Perversely, rather than removing any incentive to carry on, this realisation boosted me forward. I didn't have it in me to race up Ventoux like a hero, so there was no sense in trying. I could choose to stop, or I could choose to keep going, and if I kept going then I wouldn't be breaking the promises I'd made to myself when I entered this race back in November.

A day ago, my friend Hannah had completed her first

Ironman triathlon. We had met up the previous weekend, to discuss our impending challenges, and as we sat in a sunny pub garden, with plates of carbohydrate and glasses of tap water between us, she told me about her race strategy. She had divided the whole thing into twenty-eight half-hour periods, and for the run she had even planned in advance what she was going to think about during each segment. Half an hour for song lyrics. Half an hour for mathematics. Half an hour for daydreaming.

I was impressed. If anyone asked me about my own strategies for when things got difficult, all I could offer was vague mumbling about having found myself before at the point where I thought I couldn't go on, and always having muddled through somehow. I had a certain amount of faith in my own resilience, without ever having bothered to think through how this resilience *worked*, and what its limits might be. I doubted I would ever plan out my race experience as meticulously as Hannah had hers. It just wasn't my style.

Now I changed my mind. It was 21km to the summit of Ventoux, and I knew that was impossible in my current state. But if I divided the climb into segments of two kilometres, it wouldn't feel quite so bad. I had already ridden half a kilometre without noticing. So if I could find something to focus on for each segment, to distract myself from the magnitude of what I was trying to do, to mask my weakness and cushion my fear, then all I would have to do was ride two kilometres, stop, rest, and then ride two more.

I decided, the idea rising into my awareness fully formed, that for each 2km stretch I would think about a woman I found inspiring, and dedicate that part of the ride to her. Because she had given me the idea, I started with Hannah. I tried to remember everything she'd told me about her

Ironman preparation, hoping I might be able to wring out a few more drops of wisdom. I filled my head with pride for what she had accomplished the previous day, wondered how she was feeling in the aftermath, and looked forward to when, sometime in the hazy future, when all of this was over, we'd drink wine instead of tap water, and compare notes on what we'd been through. I replayed a comment she'd made once, in response to someone else's remark about 'keeping on through the pain' of endurance sports. It's not about physical pain, she said, not unless you're pushing through an injury – it's more of a *striving tension*. She was right: I knew it then and I knew it even more now, on the slopes of Ventoux. No part of me actually hurt, despite the ever-present urge to stop. And why, indeed, did I *want* to stop when the only way I could conceive of getting myself out of this was to keep going? *Striving tension*. I couldn't have put it better.

I must have missed a kilometre marker, because the next one I passed told me I was 3km in. Only 18km to go from here. It was now a work in progress.

The sun had sunk behind the hills to the west, and the colour was draining from the sky. A couple of cyclists sped down the mountain, heading back to their home or hotel, for a shower, dinner, a glass of wine, bed. I wondered what they thought of me, heading foolishly up towards the summit as night fell. They disappeared off towards Bédoin, and the road was quiet once again.

My next segment was dedicated to Sarah Outen – a former hero of mine who had ended up becoming a friend, and who was at that point rowing the Atlantic, the final stretch of a four-year journey, by bike and boat, that had taken her most of the way round the planet.

She might be rowing at that very moment, I thought,

out there in the great blue wilderness between Cape Cod and Cornwall. The gradient had picked up and I was now out of the saddle, breathing heavily, settling into the beat of my pedalling. I tried to match my exertions to what I imagined might be the rhythm of her oars, wanting to help her home across the ocean as much as I wanted her to lend me strength to get me up the mountain. I thought back to the short time I'd spent rowing at university, trying to remember what I knew about technique, to feel the blades locking into the water. For a minute or two I forgot I was cycling, forgot that I wanted to stop, forgot that I couldn't let myself stop.

When that faltered I thought back to Sarah: thought about the oceans she'd rowed, and told myself that if she could manage all of that then I could manage to cycle two kilometres up a nine per cent gradient. I reminded myself that she'd been rowing when I started this race, she'd be rowing all the way through it, and she'd still be rowing for well over a month after I finished. Like Russian dolls, her row enclosed my ride, and my ride contained Hannah's triathlon.

And then I remembered a trick Sarah had told me she discovered the night she had to cycle 270km through freezing rain in Russia. She had imagined an invisible peloton of everyone she knew riding alongside her, pushing and pulling her along, helping her to keep going. That was effectively what I was doing now, I thought, as I pulled up at my sixth kilometre marker, for a sip of water and a quick stretch. I was in amongst the trees now, and between their branches the sky was fading to grey. I switched my lights on.

The next person I invoked was Juliana. I could imagine teasing her that *she* wasn't using her energy, so I might as well take advantage of it. First I thought about what she must have been through over the last three days – the relent-less, sleepless push down to Aubignan, and then the agony of watching her body fail while mind and spirit strained to continue. I remembered sitting beside her in a darkened theatre in Edinburgh, watching the film about the TransAm Bike Race, which Mike had won and she had finished in fourth place, despite cracked ribs, trapped nerves and the beginning of the knee problems that had finally defeated her today. I had marvelled at her refusal to stop, her ability to push on through injuries – knowing that this was what would ultimately differentiate us when we lined up for the Transcontinental.

By now it was almost completely dark, and all around me were the shadows of the trees, black branches against a grey sky; trunks lining the steep road like a crowd of spectators who'd been waiting for me so long that they'd lost interest and turned to stone. Whenever I stopped to catch my breath, my bright dynamo light faded to a glow and I felt the darkness close in around me, nobody there to see how slowly I was riding, how often I was stopping. I remembered a stretch of road Juliana and I had covered in Northumberland, in the early hours of the morning, which had risen and fallen unendingly, each descent shooting us straight into the next climb. It was hard, and we were tired. But it was the height of summer, and we were far enough north that the sky never quite got dark: dead ahead of us, on the horizon, was a smudge of light that slowly faded from silver-grey to blood-red as sunset joined hands with dawn, and as I crested the top of every hill, I had the sense that I was soaring onwards to meet the new day. A couple of miles along that road I found I was doing well – nothing hurt, my legs felt powerful and my lungs were opening up as if they wanted to suck in the whole sky. Part of me still wanted to stop, but carrying on felt wonderful. I didn't feel like that now, but it was comforting to remember that I had once, that I probably would again. That I still had that strength in me, even if I couldn't feel it.

When I got to the eighth marker I decided to give Juliana another two kilometres, since there was still plenty to think about her, and she had distracted me admirably so far. 'You're going to have to ride hard for both of us,' she'd said, when she dropped out, and I reminded myself of this – I *had* to keep going, for her as well as for me.

At this moment, something quite unexpected happened. Up ahead of me I made out a figure standing by the side of the road. A second later the beam of my front light picked out the reflective bands on his tyres and I could tell that he had a bicycle with him. I wondered whether he might be another racer – and then I realised that the wheels were far smaller than mine, and that he was riding a *Brompton*. No doubt he was some holidaying eccentric, who had attempted to ride up Ventoux on a folding bike and ended up taking longer than he planned and having to come down in the dark.

'Ça va?' I called as I approached him.

'Hallo!' he called back, as if he'd been waiting for me, which it turns out he had. 'I am a journalist from German radio. Is it OK to ask you some questions?' And as I passed him he parked his Brompton and began to jog alongside me, dictaphone in hand.

'Umm, yes, OK,' was all I could think to say in response.

I carried on cycling up the darkened road, mostly out of the saddle, since this was one of the sections whose gradient approached ten per cent, and he carried on jogging, firing questions at me just as if we were chatting over a coffee in London or Berlin. It was too dark for us to see each other's faces, and it only occurred to me afterwards that I should have pulled over to talk to him.

He asked how I'd found the race so far, and I told him I'd been enjoying it, though of course I'd had a few low points, and I was quite tired now.

He asked if I'd heard that Juliana had pulled out, and I told him I had, that I was desperately sad about it, that I'd sprinted for hours to try and see her before she left Aubignan, and that I was now riding for both of us.

He asked what my strategy was for the next twenty-four hours, and I told him I was only able to think about the next two kilometres, and was going to have to let the rest of the race take care of itself for now.

After a couple of minutes my surprise at this ambush became amazement that I was managing to hold a coherent conversation while simultaneously riding up Mont Ventoux out of the saddle. It was almost as if I were a strong cyclist, who had everything under control, who hadn't spent the last couple of hours on the verge of collapse. He faltered before I did, and fell back, wishing me good luck with the wind as I pushed on up the hill.

I carried on out of the saddle. It was still hard, but now I was puzzled – I clearly had untapped reserves of energy, if I'd been able to climb like this *and* hold a conversation. I must have more in me than I realised, even if I wasn't quite sure how to access it. As I pushed on, climbing didn't get any easier, but I held more hope of being able to continue. Perhaps my body was rationing its energy, holding it back until I needed it, not wanting me to squander it all when I still had so much further to go.

Now and then a pair of headlights would slant through the trees, and each time I wondered whether this would be the race car, on its way down the mountain towards

Checkpoint Two, cursing myself for not finding out when this checkpoint actually closed. None of the cars stopped though, or even slowed down. I wondered what their occupants were doing up Ventoux at this time of night, and what they thought of me, a lonely light, with a lone cyclist behind.

The trees thinned out as I approached the junction with the road that led down to Sault. When I was ready to descend the mountain I would retrace my steps to this point, and then turn back north, descending on easier gradients and gentler curves towards Embrun, Briançon and eventually the Italian border and Checkpoint Two. Next to the junction, sheltered in a fold of the mountain, was Chalet Reynard, during the day a busy tourist trap, with a restaurant and souvenir kiosks; now locked up for the night and completely deserted.

I pulled over, glad of an excuse to stop, and at that moment a single light appeared on the hillside, and another racer soared down towards me, shouting 'hello!' as he sped past and onwards up the ramp that led towards the Sault descent. Behind him came a couple more, and we called out 'chapeau!' and 'allez!' to each other as they passed, their speed and jaunty good humour a contrast to my feeble exhaustion – but also a foretaste of how things might change if I ever reached the top of this mountain.

I would reach the top, of course, I thought to myself. There simply was no conceivable alternative, unless somehow my life ended during the next 6km. And yet, my imagination still failed me when I tried to think about how I would get myself through what remained. There was no comfort in knowing I'd make it, because I still had to endure so much more of this, and my body still felt empty, my limbs soft, my mind limp.

There was no escape from the wind now, and as I pressed on upwards it roared and surged around me like a wild animal, one moment rushing into my face, so that my weak arms wavered as I tried to keep the bike straight; one moment bounding down the scree slope that towered above me, threatening to push me right off the road and down the mountainside. Twice I had to put a foot down, then wait for a break in the wind in order to push off again, zig-zagging across the road to find the easiest gradient. And at one point I actually got off and pushed, using all of my fading strength to move the bike forward, cowering as it and I were battered by the wind, straining towards the next bend in the road, where I'd be momentarily sheltered in a fold of the mountain, and could catch my breath, and then get back on.

This was impossible, I thought. It was too hard; my progress was too slow. I had effectively failed anyway, since I was now reduced to walking.

I thought about Jenny Graham, a woman I'd met in Edinburgh the day after Juliana went home, lining up for a race through the Pentlands to absolve what she saw as her failure to complete the Highland Trail, a notoriously difficult off-road race around the north of Scotland. She'd ridden, pushed and carried her bike over mountains and through rivers, through days of torrential rain, barely stopping, barely sleeping. When I praised her resilience she seemed embarrassed, and I thought about how unheroic she must have felt, pushing and pushing, sometimes covering as little as thirty-four miles in twelve hours, before finally giving up when she could no longer squeeze her swollen feet into her shoes. She had thought herself as pathetic as I thought myself now. But if she had, she was the only one – everyone else, myself included, was in awe of her strength, her resilience, her unswerving determination.

I was still doing it, I reminded myself. As long as I kept moving forward, even if I was walking, even if I had to stop every five minutes, I was still in the race, and I would make it to the top of the mountain, no matter how long it took.

Looking down to my left, over the night-time lightscape of Southern France far below, I told myself that I must already have gained over a kilometre in elevation, and just for a moment, allowed myself to look proudly back on what I had accomplished so far, rather than fearfully forward at what was to come. I no longer felt the urge to stop, I discovered; no longer had any sense of beginning, or end, or of anywhere else I might be. I had become a creature who climbed – there was no room in me for any other impulse, no reason or logic behind it, no sense of destination or reward. My awareness was narrowed to the dark road curling up the mountainside ahead of me, the cold moonlight as it fell on the silvery scree slopes around me, and the fierce racket of the wind above my head.

I knew, distantly, that my arms and legs were trembling with exhaustion, and I was slightly too cold in my thin cycling jersey, but stopping to put on another layer was beyond me. I remembered what Reinhold Messner had written about his solo ascent of Everest, thirty-five years previously: 'I can scarcely go on. No despair, no happiness, no anxiety. I have not lost the mastery of my feelings, there are actually no more feelings. I consist only of will.'

Maybe that was the stage I had reached – no energy left for any thought or feeling apart from the will to go on. I went on. It was all there was to do.

The wind shrieked and bellowed, now dying down for a moment, now pouncing on me as I rounded a spur of the mountain. Sometimes it tossed me from side to side like a dog breaking a rat's neck. Sometimes I was thumped mercilessly, like a boxer losing a fight, backed into the corner of the ring, the second before the whistle blows. Just occasionally a gust would gather behind me, and lift me gently up to the next corner as if a stronger cyclist were riding alongside me, her hand on the small of my back, helping me along.

The lights of a car appeared round the next bend, and I quickly put my hands back on the hoods, and tried to look like I was still a serious cyclist, in case it was the race car. This time it actually was, and I pulled over for a brief chat with Mike as if it were the most ordinary thing in the world, to run into him on the slopes of Mont Ventoux in the dark.

'You're nearly there,' he told me. 'And Kevin and Marion are up there in the red camper, doing the night shift. See you in Sestriere!'

So the checkpoint wasn't closed after all. And what was more, Kevin and Marion were people I actually *knew*. Momentarily, I remembered that there was a world beyond the mountain – a world in which I would find brightness, and comfort, and people. But the thought was whipped away by the wind, and the darkness closed in again.

A flight of steps cut into the mountainside on my right, and I realised I was passing the memorial to Tom Simpson, who had died here in 1967, four years younger than me, having pushed himself so hard that his heart gave out. It's traditional for riders to pay their respects at this point, but I feared that if I stopped now I'd never get going again, so I gave Simpson a nod as I passed, and wondered if I'd ever be back here, perhaps on a sunny September afternoon, to stop for a moment or two, and leave my bottle or my cycling cap as a tribute.

I had just over a kilometre to go, and I knew it would

be hard won. I could see the summit by now, and make out the shape of its red-and-white meteorological tower through the darkness, but to get there I had to fight my way through gusts of wind that were trying to push me off the road as surely as riptides might try to drown me. I edged across the mountain, clinging on like a fly as it grew steeper and steeper, and the drop to my left became ever deeper, a mile of sky between me and the ground. Just after the marker that told me it was 500 metres to the top I got off the bike, and started to push it, bent double with the effort, braced against the battering wind.

And finally I was there, staggering up onto the flat summit, nothing more above me but the tower, standing resolutely there like a lighthouse on a dark night. And there in its lee was a small red camper van, its windows glowing, a telltale Transcontinental banner pinned to its side.

I parked my bike against the side of the building and rummaged in my seat pack for a malt loaf and my jacket and gloves, knowing that I'd get cold when the glow of exertion wore off. And then I strolled over to the door of the camper van, which slid open as I approached, amazed that Kevin and Marion were going to encounter me as the person they'd always known me to be, rather than as an exhausted creature flayed and drained by the climb.

'Emily!' said Marion's delighted voice, and I stepped up into warmth and brightness and closed the door behind me.

Chapter Four

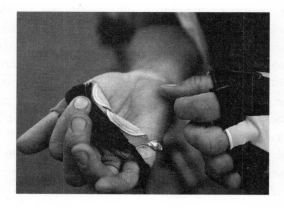

A few hours' ride away the air was warm and full of life, humming with insects and flocks of cyclists who'd sit on my wheel for a few miles before calling out 'bonjour!' and overtaking with a cheery wave. Everyday life carried on, unaffected by and unaware of the other world I'd stumbled into on the slopes of Ventoux. A waitress imperiously served me cappuccino and a *baguette au jambon*, and my senses embraced the warm, crackling crust of the bread and the sweet creamy butter with such opulent pleasure that I knew I must owe myself hundreds, if not thousands of calories. It was still early, I realised – just after breakfast time – but I'd been up so long I'd thought it was the middle of the day.

Just before dawn, I'd awoken on the chilly concrete terrace of Chalet Reynard, and swept down the eastern side of the mountain with the sense I often have after a big pass, of having crossed a border or breached some boundary, of discovering the world all over again. As the light rose around me a vaster, more austere terrain revealed itself. I left the pine trees behind and descended into the golden fold of Provence that harboured Sault, joined a small knot of hungry Transcon racers outside a soon-to-open *boulangerie* and then, fortified by hot pastry, set off into the mountains.

An hour later, stopping to drink from a fountain at the apex of a long sunny climb, I'd glanced back to the summit of Ventoux, now bathed in sunlight, its white scree like snowfall, the tower an unremarkable speck. The red van was probably still up there, and Marion and Kevin might even now be stamping the brevet card of some exhausted racer, congratulating them on making it to Checkpoint One. But their climb would have been very different and they – indeed most other people – would never have any idea of the sight and sound of Ventoux at night. My few hours up there felt like a secret few would ever share.

'It's five to midnight,' Marion had announced, half to me and half to Kevin, as I tore open the wrapper of my malt loaf and he entered my time and race number on a clipboard beneath those of all the racers ahead of me. 'That means you've made it in under three days. Well done!' She stamped and signed my brevet card.

Three days to ride a thousand kilometres. That wasn't so bad, I thought to myself, realising I must have done more cycling than I thought, in amongst all the stops for coffee, McDonald's, ice cream, more coffee, water, twenty-minute snoozes, *patisserie* and more coffee.

I begged the wifi password from the waitress, rediscovered the internet for the first time since the previous evening's dinner in Aubignan, and found, to my great surprise, that the world hadn't forgotten me after all. In an email entitled 'Mont Ventoux', and sent on the stroke of midnight, my parents told me:

> We've been tracking you up that hill off and on for most of the evening. You've made it, wow, well done. You must be thrilled ... and maybe just a little bit tired. ☺

There was an email from Cherry, an old university friend:

> Amazing efforts. I am loving following your dot. Enjoyed armchair following you up Mont Ventoux last night immensely. Jen said 'surely she'll wait until tomorrow morning? But ... it's DARK now'.

There was a text from my sister, with a photo of the meal she was eating while she clicked refresh every three minutes and my dot crawled along the winding red line that was the road up the mountain. A man I didn't even know said he'd used Street View to imagine he was riding the final 5km alongside me, and congratulated me on my success.

Marion had posted a picture of me, sitting in the van with my malt loaf, and I was surprised, as I sometimes am after a difficult period on the bike, to see that I looked very much like the self I'd always been, with little external evidence of the extremes to which I'd dived on the inside. Looking at me, you'd never know I was anything less than human.

All of a sudden, sitting in that café, surrounded by oblivious tourists and elderly cyclists, I was back on the mountain in the dark. Except that now the experience was transformed. I hadn't been alone, unseen, forgotten in my struggles. Instead, all around me in the darkness, floating just out of sight, were dozens of people willing me on, wishing me well – just like Sarah's invisible peloton; just like the imaginary cyclist whose hand (in the form of a tail-wind) had occasionally rested on the small of my back. I had attempted to haul my exhausted self up Ventoux by calling on the strength and support of stronger people and, unaware though I was, it had been there all along.

I had known – of course – that my progress was visible to people on the internet. I was even aware that dot-watching, as it's come to be known, had turned out to be an addictive pastime, with Transcontinental fans all over the world theatrically bemoaning their two-week productivity slump as they watched the race unfold in one browser window while failing to do any work in another. But I hadn't quite understood that I was part of this – that they'd be watching *me*, or that my progress would be of interest to anyone other than my father. It had certainly never crossed my mind that dot-watching, and the dot-watchers themselves, might affect my experience in the race, much less support me through it. I suspect no one did, when long-distance cyclists first strapped GPS beacons to their bikes as a safety precaution, presuming their whereabouts to be of interest only to their immediate family and anyone needing to rescue them if things went wrong – just as no one could have predicted, when Facebook first launched, our fascination with the ongoing minutiae of each other's meals, daily routines, family members, and all the other coordinates that make up an ordinary life.

Dot-watching has effectively become another channel of social media, its attractiveness – and, let's make no bones about this, addictiveness – rooted identically in the promise of continual reward, which keeps users refreshing their screens compulsively. And, perhaps less like social media, whose memes, jokes, rants and disclosures leave us hungry, unsatisfied by what we've been given rather than eager for what's to come, dot-watching offers a connection to something that is actually, physically, unambiguously happening. Each dot, crawling across the map, is a person, crawling across the landscape, and between the three-minute updates, watchers are free to imagine the effort, the tension, the grind and rhythm of the pedals, the laboured breath, the tiny adjustments as a rider balances her bike around corners, the texture of the road, the warmth of the sun or the chill of the night air, the wind as it ripples against the rider's face, the way she wavers with exhaustion, or charges forward, electrified with a few hours' sleep and a strong coffee. And then the map is reloaded, the rider is further along, and the dot-watcher marvels yet again that this has happened in real time. Not that much has changed, and that's the point. Dot-watching doesn't promise surprise or enlightenment – just the gratification of witnessing someone complete a seemingly impossible feat minute by minute.

It could become more or less a full-time job, if you cared to cross-reference the map with the riders' social media feeds, the official race pronouncements, Street View and local weather reports. By the third year of the race, everyone had realised just how intrinsic the internet was, not only to its existence, but to the way it was witnessed by fans, adjudicated by the race crew, experienced by riders and portrayed to the outside world. The Transcontinental was far too long for spectators to get much out of turning up in person – apart from the crowds at the start and a few family and friends at the finish line, we were far more likely to run into fellow racers than the eager roadside fans who line the route of the Tour de France. And, unlike the

Tour, the Transcon wasn't televised to millions. I'd grown up watching grimacing men battling it out on high mountain passes, the camera so close to their faces that you could make out the sweat dripping off their noses. When Ultan and Josh were racing up Ventoux, all viewers had to go on were a couple of dots, a few hairpins apart, and a distant photo taken by a member of the race crew. What they were going through, and the second-by-second progress of their pursuit, was left to dot-watchers' conjecture and admiration.

The Transcon's obliqueness recalls the earliest days of the Tour, which was founded to improve circulation of a newspaper – but how could you honestly report on a race so long, on a peloton so strung out, without any sort of remote surveillance or videography? Little wonder cheating was rife in the early days (racers occasionally even skipped sections by taking trains), and little wonder journalists and fans quickly evolved mythologies around their favourite riders. Unlike a game of football, where spectators can absorb themselves in the minutiae of players' skill and technique for the full ninety minutes, a long-distance bike race like the Tour (and now like the Transcon) mostly took place out of sight, obliging its followers to spin stories to fill the gaps, and to reconstruct the race from what scattered evidence they had available.

Early Tour fans would wait at the side of the road for that prized, fleeting moment when their idols became flesh, but otherwise they relied on second-hand accounts written by journalists, believing (or disputing) whatever the papers told them. Fans might not even know what their favourite racers looked like, and they admired their exploits from afar, judging a rider by his reported distances and speeds, rather than the persistence with which he attacked his rivals, the honest agony of his disappointment as he was dropped, or the grace of his cadence as he mounted a col.

At least with the Transcon, the tracker provided a steady thread of truth – a line of facts, drawn across the map, around which the mythologies could be spun. A few months after I'd got home, someone commented on my blog to say how much she was still enjoying piecing together the race, as one rider after another published long-form reports of their adventures. The media streams that surround the Transcon, I realised, perfectly reflect their times in that they are largely self-curated. A fan chooses how much or how little time to spend following the race. She selects the riders she likes to follow – perhaps the leaders, or perhaps the ones a day or two back, because they tell a better story. She might prefer a more visual account, in which case she'll focus on Instagram rather than Twitter, meaning that a lot of the amateur race commentary passes her by, but that she has a clearer idea of how it looks from the saddle, what the riders are eating, where they spread their bivvies out, and the views from the baking switchbacks where they've momentarily stopped, to soften their despair of ever reaching the top of this climb by sharing it with their friends. Another dot-watcher might take a more analytical approach, monitoring the average speed of his preferred riders, keeping an eye on how much rest they're getting, and speculating over how this might affect their progress over the next few hours, given the prevailing wind and the precise gradient of the long climb they're about to encounter.

Commentating on the Transcon is likewise entirely democratic. Whereas in the old days a race would have been recreated via the authority of just one or two sources (newspapers, and later on radio and TV channels), now anyone can pitch in, and their expertise is judged by their pronouncements rather than their platform. Mike had initially attempted to produce daily blog posts, but it was increasingly evident that he didn't have time to do this justice, and that it was unnecessary anyway, given that anyone who wanted to see what was going on in the race could follow the #TCR2015 hashtag, and read through what everyone, racers and dot-watchers alike, had been saying over the last few hours: who was steaming ahead, who'd been held up with mechanicals, who was at McDonald's, and who, like Juliana, had caused widespread mourning by retiring from the race.

I checked the hashtag myself, sitting there in that sunny garden, and was both alarmed and amused to see a tweet about me:

@emilychappell is riding her very own race/parcours

A screenshot showed my dot where it was right at that moment, taking an apparently unnecessary detour through the mountains while everyone else's streamed north-east along a valley. I hastily paid the bill, retrieved my bike from the tangle of carbon and steel outside the café, and sped off to catch them up, wondering if I'd make it to Sestriere that night. My map showed me it was less than 200km away.

⁚⁚⁚

Fourteen hours later I admitted defeat, knowing, as I rolled into Briançon, that this would be the night I caved in and found a hotel. The vigour with which I'd flown through the mountains that morning was a distant memory – now the urge to stop pedalling was almost constant, and I frequently paused by the side of the road to catch my breath, relax my head onto my bars in an attitude of despair, and give myself some relief from the burning in my shorts. As the heat of the day took hold, I'd longed to stop and rest in every field I passed, and given into my baser impulses whenever I passed a petrol station or anywhere selling ice cream.

My exhaustion no longer felt critical, but had diffused into a rotten mood. The road from Embrun had climbed and climbed – not in the vicious switchbacks I'd endured earlier that afternoon, but in long consecutive ramps, so that I had the curious feeling of riding up stairs. At one point I'd loosened my gloves to check my throbbing hands, and found they were pink and raw, with blisters forming under the skin. My spirits dropped another couple of notches. There was no way, if I continued to ride, that these blisters wouldn't swell and then break, leaving raw flesh to grind against the rough suede of my cheap cycling gloves.

I grumpily circled the centre of Briançon, thinking of all the minutes I'd wasted that day, and wondering how few of them had made the difference between the hotels being open and the hotels being closed. I resigned myself to another hour of cycling, a chilly berth somewhere in the mountains, and a hungry push on towards Sestriere in the early hours of the morning.

All along the street people sat at tables, surrounded by the detritus of long, leisurely meals, and no doubt contemplating an early night and a reasonable amount of sleep. There are times when I'd regard such a scene smugly, wondering if these poor people had ever witnessed the sun rising after a long night on the bike, or felt the midnight winds storming across Mont Ventoux, but right now it seemed depressingly evident that they'd got it right, and I'd got it wrong. There was even the predictable table of

English louts, catcalling me as I rolled past. I ignored them, but they weren't dissuaded.

'Hey! Yes, you!' shouted one of them, waving me over.

I am never less amenable than when summoned by loud men outside bars, and was about to turn tail and ride for the hills when another of them shouted, 'Are you with the race?'

Oh. I swung round and rode cautiously towards them, still half-assuming they were a bunch of drunken idiots for whom I'd be part of the evening's entertainment.

It turned out they were mountain bikers, on holiday in the area, who had been sitting at this table all evening, and quickly noticed the passing stream of tired-looking roadies. After flagging one down and asking what was going on, they had started buying beer and pizza for all the racers they could catch. On a neighbouring table was a stack of empty pizza boxes, and as soon as they'd convinced me to join them, the younger man jumped up to see if the pizzeria was still open. When it wasn't, he disappeared into the bar and came out with an enormous ham-and-cheese baguette and a glass of beer.

I hesitated momentarily. Should I be drinking beer during a race? And accepting it was an admission that I'd sit here for the time I took to drink it, and really I should either be sleeping or pressing on. Then I thought, with a little inward flourish of recognition, of all the unexpected encounters I've had on my travels; the brief but sincere friendships with people I'd never meet again; the characters who arrive improbably in my life, offering me whatever it is I most need at that moment, be it a drink of water or a bed for the night. I hadn't expected any such meetings on my long, lonely race across Europe – and yet, here were these lovely kind men, and here was this cold glass of beer.

'Is there anything else you need?' one of them asked.

'I think a nice comfortable hedge is next on the agenda,' I told them, explaining that I had missed out on Briançon's hotel rooms, and now planned to ride into the mountains, fuelled by beer and sandwich, and find somewhere to camp. My new friends exchanged glances.

'Well … we've got a spare bed in our hotel room. I mean, we've got a bed each, but there's a van one of us can sleep in. Would you be up for that? I promise we're all totally non-weird. He's married, and I'm …'

They continued in this vein long after I had accepted their offer, assuring me of their non-weirdness all the way back to the hotel, while I assured them in turn that they were making a terrible mistake by allowing a feral ultra-racer into their sanctuary.

I showered for the first time since Belgium, washing my hair with the tips of my fingers so as not to disturb the blisters on my palms. There was nothing to use but a bottle of Lynx shower gel, and I tried unsuccessfully to drag my fingers through the tangles it left, wishing I'd brought conditioner. Washing wasn't the gateway to bliss I'd been imagining. I smelt better than I had, but my skin still prickled with sunburn and stung with saddlesore, and my legs and back were so stiff that I could barely climb into the bath. It was better than nothing though, I told myself, pleased that I wouldn't be offending my roommates with the stench of four days' cycling.

My alarm went off at 4.30 a.m. and I blinked crustily into the thick air of the hotel room, inhaling the fug and fume of three heavy sleepers as I fumbled about for my things, whispered goodbye and crept out into the dark streets, past the brief racket of a rubbish lorry and the occasional lit-up window behind which a *boulanger* toiled, to start another day of riding. The road rose steadily out of Briançon, and I struggled upwards, dismayed that four hours' sleep in a bed hadn't made much difference to my energy levels. On the contrary, I felt more sluggish than I had at any other point in the race, as if the walls of the hotel room had shut me off from the energising effects of the landscape.

Dawn broke, and I gasped to see an enormous switchback, built up out of the mountainside with crenellated grey stone, thrusting above me like a galleon. I knew I should have paid more attention to these things when I planned my route, so that I had at least some idea of which way the road pointed, but I preferred to watch the landscape unfolding before me, every turning, mountain pass and sunrise revealing something I hadn't expected. I struggled on.

An hour later I passed a sign saying 'Montgenèvre' and abruptly the road was lined with ski chalets and resort buildings. I regarded them curiously as I passed, having never visited a ski resort before, and then, to my considerable joy, found a café, noticed another cyclist sitting outside, and settled down happily for my breakfast. The sun began to edge its way between the mountains, casting long shadows and bright pools of astonishing light, and I realised my mood and energy were finally lifting.

The road became vertiginous as I crossed the Italian border, but by now I was singing with delight, screeching my way down a plane so smooth and steep that I wondered whether my wheels would leave it; dropping into the gorge like a stone into a well, then rising like a bird on the other side. The road wound its way up the mountainside, twisting so steeply through villages that the very houses looked uncomfortable, and I wrenched my bike upwards, nodding my greetings to the old ladies who crept along the pavements or took the air from their doorways, but unable to take a hand off the bars to wave.

The grand chalets of Sestriere began to tower over me on the hillsides, and then I was into the town, still climbing out of the saddle, speeding past the ranks of hotels until there, on my left, was one unmistakably trimmed with loaded bikes, and a small noticeboard with the Transcontinental logo. A few racers stumbled about in their cleated shoes or stockinged feet, their legs so stiff that what they wore on their feet made little difference to their gait.

I felt lithe and light in comparison, bounding off my bike and into the hotel foyer, where I was met with a smattering of applause. Unlike the red van at the top of Ventoux, this checkpoint was equipped with a more pedestrian table in one corner of the reception, strewn with papers and staffed by volunteers in matching T-shirts. I noticed people were smiling indulgently at me, and realised that I was beaming like an idiot, greeting everyone in my path a couple of decibels louder than they might have expected at this time in the morning, exuding all the joy and energy of this bright new day, the coffee I'd drunk in Montgenèvre and the brilliance of the mountains all around us.

I turned round from the table to see Mike striding towards me, eyes sparkling, open-mouthed grin mirroring my own, his face alight with recognition. He spread his arms and we hugged tightly almost without meaning to. This was not the encounter I had expected with the Race Director. 'He knows,' I thought. 'He knows me better than anyone else in this room.' For a moment or two I understood that I didn't have to cleave to the role of respectful novice that I'd so carefully painted myself into. Mike already knew that I was cut from the same cloth as him, and his recognition didn't depend on the number of races I'd completed or the records I held.

I tore into the hotel breakfast buffet, although the men had already picked it clean of any sort of protein, halting my Nutella binge only when one of the volunteers came in and handed me her phone. Juliana was on the other end. She congratulated me on making it to Checkpoint Two, and asked how I was doing. 'Brilliant! Wonderful!' I told her. She herself was resting at her sister's, barely able to walk, and miserably ignoring the race as it unfolded on social media.

'I'm only following you now,' she told me. 'Oh, except –' And she mentioned, mischievously, that Katie and Jayne, the only remaining women in the race, were just a couple of hours ahead of me. Since they were racing as a pair we were in different classifications, and even if they reached the finish before me I'd still technically have won, but Juliana knew the powerful incentive of a rival as well as I did. I should have waited long enough to have a shower and charge my phone but, not wanting to waste any more of this crackling energy, I dashed out of the hotel, shouted goodbye to the assembled racers and volunteers, flung myself onto my bike and sped out of town, to where the dusty ribbon of the Strada dell'Assietta ascended into the high mountains.

Chapter Five

A few hours later I was rhythmically descending the tightly piled switchbacks of the Colle delle Finestre – which, in my innocence, I hadn't known I'd be crossing, or even that it existed, let alone its proud reputation and history – feeling the air thicken and moisten around me as I helter-skeltered down into the Po Valley.

I was still humming with energy. The Strada dell'Assietta had, like so many things that frighten me in advance, turned out to be a high point. I'd followed a fellow racer off the tarmac outside Sestriere, quickly losing him as the gravel road reared up into the hills, but not before I'd had a chance to follow his lines, and noticed that he deliberately kept to the smoother parts of the road, where there were fewer loose stones. Naively, I'd assumed that the whole *point* was to ride over the gravelly bits.

I topped out on a windy summit marked by an iron cross,

grinning breathlessly at the clouds rolling through the blue sky above me, the green peaks and ridges falling away beneath me, and the white ribbons of gravel rippling across them, one of which would be my way forward. Here and there I began to see parties of hikers – families with teenagers trailing behind or striking firmly ahead; middle-aged couples with their walking poles, backpacks and sunhats; here and there a couple of trail runners – and thought to myself that this was what a trekking holiday must look like. My own family had only ever spent their summers in Breton campsites, most of my schoolfriends had gone to resorts in Greece and Mallorca, and although I'd heard of people hiking in the Alps, it wasn't until I saw them for myself that I understood what such a trip would look like. I envied these people as I passed them, even while I knew I was doing something I loved more. I envied them the past I didn't share, the years of experience and memories I could have had by now. I hadn't even known what these mountains looked like until today.

Nevertheless, I found myself singing inwardly – and sometimes outwardly – as I hurtled past them, throwing myself exuberantly over the loose, rocky paths, skidding round the hairpins on each descent, and feeling the strength flaming in my legs as I pistonned up each climb. I knew, from my time in the Karakoram and on the Qinghai Plateau, that the thinner air at this altitude should make exertion more difficult, but I felt the opposite. Each breath I took seemed to pull in more air than I thought possible, my ribs rising, my lungs unfurling, as though this was what they were made for; as though they had never before had a chance to show me what they were truly capable of. When I sang, the notes reverberated out of me, deep and throaty, resonating from deep in my core and ringing out towards the jagged horizon, as if there were no difference, as if the air that flowed through my lungs, the wind that whipped about the peaks, the currents and eddies where the birds swerved and played, were all one and the same, and the mountains were reaching their airy fists right into me and pulling me upward.

So I sped down into Susa, thinking to myself that I must magically have acclimatised in the short time I was up there; that now, like a runner who's spent a month on the Kenyan plateau, I would surpass myself down at sea level. A flat road took me east, lined with tumbling greenery and plaited with a couple of bigger roads that all followed the same channel, waiting until the landscape opened out and they could go their separate ways. I was out of the mountains now, I realised, and the next ones I'd see would be the grey karst crags overlooking the Adriatic Sea. A few miles on I spied a pair of racers mounting a slip road alongside me, noticed a blonde ponytail and realised it was Katie and Jayne. They didn't see me, I didn't hail them, and I sped onwards, deciding to myself that I would go on all night, that it seemed foolish to dampen the energy I had drawn from the mountains by attempting to sleep.

The traffic thickened as I neared Torino, racing Vespas down a long boulevard, the grandeur of the buildings increasing as we plunged into the heart of the city and the sinking sun tinted the clouds like spring blossoms. I was passed by two more racers, slipstreaming a muscular young man in a black-and-white skinsuit, who rode a glowing red road bike. I had seen him before, a few hours previously, standing out among the hikers on the Assietta with his sharp edges and bright colours, his head rising as I came into sight, as if I might be someone he was looking for. This was probably an instance of cheating, I thought, of accepting – and probably even pre-arranging – outside assistance, but I wasn't about to tell on them. I crossed a river, spanned by a series of ornate bridges, and carried on into the night.

By the early hours of the morning I had already succumbed to two ten-minute naps, on a grass verge at the edge of an empty car park, and on the pavement next to some darkened warehouses. I was annoyed with myself for failing so quickly in my plan to keep riding all night, and for not being like James Hayden and Josh Ibbett, who were hundreds of kilometres ahead now, and who (as the breathless admiration of their Twitter followers informed me) were stopping only for twenty-minute power naps.

I remember sprawling outside a supermarket later that day, after hours of wrestling the bike into a humid headwind that gave the impression I was riding into a wall of air, that the very atmosphere had turned against me. The sky and the scenery were grey and there was no countryside here, just a succession of unremarkable towns, suburbs, car parks, shopping centres, garages and factories, punctuated by traffic lights and roundabouts and populated with roaring traffic. I plodded, feeling uneven and ungainly, as though the blissful harmony with which I'd flown through the mountains had now fallen out of key. The only reason I eventually stood up from the concrete ledge outside Lidl was that I had eaten and drunk all I could manage, and although I felt no inclination to go on, I also lacked any justification to stay where I was.

A second night, and I found myself following straight roads across a vast plain, fields and marshes surrounding me, and lightning flickering on the horizon like a dying fluorescent bulb. Once I passed a short bespectacled man, standing next to a parked car, cheering out into the night as

I rode by. I wondered if he knew about the race, or was just one of the miscellaneous human beings on various arcane missions that you'll run into on an overnight ride.

I discovered that Italian petrol stations stayed open all night, and that many had café-bars attached, where rotund gentlemen watched me from the terrace as I went stiffly to and fro, filling bottle, downing espresso, topping up on biscuits. My guilty ten-minute naps increased in frequency and intensity, and rather than my body settling gratefully into the earth, it now felt as though something in it was being tugged violently downwards, a taut rope of exhaustion yanking me into whatever vortex or void lay beneath.

I took a wrong turn as I approached Verona, and ended up on a newly built motorway, empty apart from myself, its sweeping acres of tarmac, more space than I'd ever need or could ever fill, easing me down regally shallow inclines towards the city. I had ridden for several miles through this outsized stage set before I realised that it was a ring road, and skirted the edge of Verona instead of plunging through the centre, taking me north when I'd wanted to go east. Wearily, I followed a slip road, a leafy lane, a residential street, and eventually got myself back on course, riding down the centre line through the dark, echoing city, a shocking antithesis to the romance and poetry with which I'd always imbued its name. I rested briefly outside a closed petrol station and my eye caught some movement on the road, like a hawk sighting the flickering of a rodent. Across the forecourt, the pavement, two lanes of non-existent traffic and a central reservation, a cyclist skimmed past, another racer, with his laden bike and powerful lights. He was too far off to notice me sitting there, or for me to shout to him, and we might as well have been ghosts to each other – him in his world, me in mine, both of us a long way from whatever worlds we'd normally inhabit.

I felt a synthetic glimmer of hope as the sky lightened once again and a bakery glowed at me through the gloom, first its warm, sweet aroma, then its lights, open door and reassuring human movement within. I waited behind a trio of bin men, then sat on the edge of the pavement alongside their truck as we all tucked into our breakfasts. In Treviso I devoured two McDonald's meals, then tried to lose consciousness in a nearby park, hiding from the sun under an ant-ridden tree, one hand on my bicycle.

The afternoon became hot as I skirted Venice, on straight, busy roads, trying to avoid the traffic, but grateful for the air-conditioned service stations. I drank a litre of iced tea, ate an enormous pizza and wondered when I'd feel better. I'd forgotten what it was like to ride without a headwind. I spotted another racer outside a petrol station and stopped to talk to him, then didn't know what to say. He was the man who had burst into tears on meeting Juliana in Geraardsbergen, that faraway place, where life's complexities and comforts still existed. We downed litres of water, and set off a few minutes apart. I never saw him again.

I longed for the heat to die down, but it didn't, even as the shadows lengthened and the sunlight deepened to a rich, rustic gold, even as darkness fell and young men charged about on their scooters, the engine noise booming unevenly around me as my head throbbed with tiredness and temperature. I carried on into the inferno, feeling both isolated from the people around me and uncomfortably exposed, as though everyone were staring at me, wondering why I was riding so slowly, why my clothes were so dirty, and what I thought I was doing trying to race when I must now have fallen so far behind the main pack that I'd never catch up.

I passed through Gorizia, on the Slovene border, where I had spent a happy morning on my trans-Asia ride four years previously. Now there was not the slightest sign of warmth or recognition on either part, like an indifferent holiday romance when you ill-advisedly return the following year.

A couple of hours later I woke up on my back, in the corner of a wind-tossed field, and found that there was almost nothing left of me.

⁞⁞⁞

'Excuse me. Are you ... Emily?'

I didn't know who this woman was, but I was grateful to see her. It was 11 p.m., and I had just been discharged from the hospital in Ljubljana. My bike was 50km down the road, at a guesthouse in Postojna, and I was sitting in the corner of the waiting room, anxious that my phone battery might die before I could load a map or a bus timetable.

'I'm Marija. From Twitter?'

I did remember her. She had messaged me a few months previously, introducing herself as someone who had also cycled across Asia. We'd established that she lived in Slovenia, and that I'd be passing through on the Transcon that summer, but since my route wouldn't take me anywhere near her home in Škofja Loka, I'd thought little more of it.

'I thought I should come and see if you were OK,' she explained. 'I was watching your dot and I saw your tweets about being in hospital, and my university is right next door, so ...'

And within moments I was in her car, being driven north to Škofja Loka with the promise of food, a shower and a bed. Marija firmly dismissed my apologies for my filth, my helplessness and the exhaustion that gave my conversation a clumsy staccato quality. She had been there herself, she said, telling me an alarming story of a bike crash on the Tibetan Plateau and a lengthy stay in a Chinese hospital. That was why she had come looking for me. She wasn't sure if, being in an unsupported race, I'd want to accept help, but she thought she'd offer it just in case.

I glanced across at her, tall, bespectacled and strong-looking, thinking what a pathetic bundle I must appear in comparison. She was animated in a way I recognised – this must be a rare chance to share her adventures with someone who'd done similar things, and could sympathise with the experience rather than just marvelling at it. And for my part, I knew that there was no need for apology – Marija had herself been passed gently across a continent by a series of guardian angels, and was delighted to return the favour to someone who needed it.

Her family home in Škofja Loka was large and clean and comfortable, and a selection of leftovers was waiting for me on the dining room table. I ate what I could, while Marija explained my predicament and translated my gratitude to her mother. I then stood under the shower for a long time, staring at the neat tiles on the wall and attempting to reconcile this comfort and order with the din and chaos of the Italian night. The two experiences sat too far apart in my consciousness to be connected by mere hours and miles. Yet one was still as present as the other, so much so that it felt not implausible that I might awaken once again to find myself crawling with ants in the corner of a field.

That morning I had arrived in Postojna as the cafés opened, after an interminable crawl up a narrow valley where the startlingly strong headwind ruptured any momentum I might have found, and exhaustion left me wavering this way and that. Whenever I stopped to rest for a moment my head would drop violently towards the bars as the jaws of sleep snatched at me, and it was an effort to refocus my eyes, straighten my stance and push down on the pedals again to keep riding. As the day brightened I began to see local cyclists, in pairs and groups, out for a Sunday spin in their club kit. Eventually I found an open café, where I sat amongst them, too far gone to gauge their apathy or curiosity. I found, to my detached puzzlement, that I was on the verge of tears, and in fact that I seemed to have only the options of letting myself fall asleep or letting myself cry, but not the resources to remain both awake and dry-eyed. I allowed myself to sleep for a few seconds at a time, my head nodding and then jerking awake in a way that must have seemed comical to anyone watching, and eventually forced myself out the door and back onto the bike.

Further into the town I stopped to buy a fresh bürek from a bakery, but that didn't work either. Having failed to prop up my eyelids with coffee, food or micro-naps, I reluctantly admitted that the only way forward was to find somewhere where I could lie down for a few hours, and sleep properly.

As the road ramped up out of Postojna, I passed a sign announcing *Rooms Only €20*. I didn't know if they'd accept guests so early in the morning, but the old man who greeted me was hearty, kind and slightly curious. He stowed my bike under the stairs, assuring me it would be safe there, showed me the bathroom and let me into a room with three single beds under faded bedspreads. I closed the curtains, lay down on the farthest one and immediately passed out.

When my alarm went, four hours later, I twisted round and sat on the side of the bed with my head in my hands. Apart from having lost the constant urge to close my eyes, I didn't feel any better than I had when I lay down. I let myself cry for a few minutes, wondering if that would help. Alongside the physical soreness and overall exhaustion, I now noticed a firm ache in the left side of my chest, and tried not to leap to conclusions. This couldn't possibly be a heart attack. I was young, fit and active, and surely I wouldn't have been able to cycle hundreds of kilometres a day if I was on the verge of cardiac arrest? I examined the pain, trying to figure out its precise location, and whether it might correspond to some other strain or injury. Taking a deep breath intensified it, as though my swelling lungs were pressing against a bruise or inflammation. Wriggling my arm in its socket made no difference, but lying on my right-hand side did. Perhaps elevating my heart put it under less strain, I conjectured, not really trusting this theory. This was almost certainly nothing to do with my heart. But the ache, so powerful I couldn't ignore it, was deep in my chest, directly under my left breast. I didn't know what else it could be.

I was welcomed into the local clinic by a friendly doctor, who greeted me in fluent English, and ushered me through to the examination room. I only have scattered recollections of what went on in there. I know he gave me an ECG, because I remember him explaining that that was what he meant when he said 'AKG', but I don't have any memory of what that entailed. At one point I realised that the nurse, wanting to take a blood sample or insert an IV, had been swabbing my inner arm for what seemed like an eternity. I must have drifted off again, I thought, and lost track of time – then I looked down and saw a handful of soiled cotton balls next to my forearm, as she wiped my still-filthy skin with yet another. She smiled kindly at me, and I tried to stop myself from crying.

In the end, the doctor sat down opposite me and

explained that he didn't think anything was seriously wrong, but there had been some slightly unusual results, so they were going to send me to the hospital in Ljubljana, to be on the safe side. The ambulance was already waiting.

The highway to Ljubljana was crowded with holiday traffic and we oozed along with it for a few minutes. I heard a siren, watched the cars around us veer onto the shoulder, wondered why we weren't doing the same, then realised the siren was for me. I started to cry again, and couldn't tell if it was from panic or exhaustion.

At the hospital they gave me another ECG, and a chest x-ray, and told me I might have to wait a while for the ultrasound. The young doctor who examined me chuckled as he tried to get his head around what I said I'd been doing.

'Really? 300km a day? For *how* long?'

A few minutes later, as he tried to diagnose my chest pain, he asked if it ever woke me up during the night.

'I haven't been sleeping at night,' I reminded him.

'Oh yes!' He slapped his forehead in a pantomime of realisation.

The ultrasound technician was busy elsewhere, so they wheeled my trolley into a holding area, where a trio of old men with loud coughs were alternately snoozing and chatting. It was only then that I realised what a state I was in. They had taken my jersey off to do the ECG, and as I lay there, with a thin sheet tucked up under my armpits to protect my modesty, I felt the greasy edge of my sports bra crawling against my rib cage. Days of sweating had made me sticky, and the dust and traffic fumes clung to my seeping skin, leaving dark grey tidemarks at the joints of my elbows, the hemlines of my clothing and the folds of my knuckles. My hair felt lank and coarse, and my face prickled with the salt of my sweat and the residue of my tiredness.

For several hours I lay there on the trolley, propped up into a semi-reclined position that made it impossible to get comfortable, wanting nothing more than to sleep, but unable to doze off for more than a minute before I'd be awoken by my throbbing back, by the coughing of one of my roommates or by their loud ringtones, which punctured my dreams and carried on long into my consciousness as the owner gradually noticed that it was *his* phone, and not anyone else's, fumbled about in his pockets and bedding to find it, and then tried to remember which button he needed to press in order to pick up the call.

Occasionally I gave up on sleep and got my own phone out. I reassured family and friends that I was safe and alive, reported my latest adventure to the dot-watchers on Twitter, and tried to distract myself from my predicament with what was going on elsewhere in the race. Leo, to my surprise, was actually a long way behind me. He had been the last rider through Checkpoint One before it closed, and was still nursing himself through the tedium of the Po Valley with podcasts and regular pizza stops. Josh Ibbett was leading the race now, and James Hayden had finally faltered, afflicted by Shermer's Neck – a disorder common only to long-distance cyclists, where his neck muscles had collapsed, meaning he could no longer hold his head up. Someone had posted a picture of him at Checkpoint Four in Montenegro, with strips of black duct tape wound round his chest and forehead, and braced together with another strip to stop his head from flopping forward. He made it as far as Podgorica before admitting defeat, and scratching from the race. Closer to where I was, riders were reporting various physical and existential crises, mostly attributed to the cruel heat and headwinds of the Po Valley. We had thought this would be the easy bit, I reflected – two or three days of flat, after battling up Mont Ventoux and through the Alps. It seemed we'd been wrong.

I couldn't concentrate for long. I craved sleep, yet the coughing, the ringtones and the uncomfortable trolley held me in a state of persistent wakefulness. Eventually I was wheeled in for the ultrasound, which was delivered with an air of brief formality. The young doctor came back in to confirm that they had been unable to find anything wrong with my heart, my lungs or anything else important, and their best guess was that I had strained the muscles between my ribs. I would be fine in a few days, he predicted, as long as I rested properly and didn't try anything silly like riding 300km without sleep. They gave me back my jersey and I was free to go.

After Marija and her mother dropped me off, I sat on the terrace of the guesthouse for the next two days, nestled amongst the geraniums with my swollen legs propped up on a chair. One shin was covered in grazes from a fall on the Assietta, and I watched as the scabs dried and began to peel at the edges, revealing pale new skin underneath.

On the third day I got back on my bike and started riding towards Istanbul. I was out of the Transcon, but I had to get home somehow, and I found I envied everyone who was still cycling. Josh Ibbett had won the race by now, and several others had finished. A photographer called James Robertson was waiting to capture the state they were in as they arrived. All were crumpled and filthy, their once-bright jerseys stained with dust and sweat and in one case even blood, and the lines around their tired eyes exaggerated by the dirt that had settled there.

Leo was still battling through the Balkans when I arrived (having taken a more direct route and a flight from Belgrade), and his girlfriend Kate and I spent a few days watching his dot slowly creep towards us. He wasn't enjoying himself, and in frequent texts to Kate complained of exhaustion, boredom and flare-ups of his eczema and allergies. He only continued, she speculated, because if he didn't finish the race this time round, he'd be obliged to come back and put himself through this all over again.

I, on the other hand, couldn't wait. After a week of recovery and Turkish food I could feel my energy returning, and when we touched down at Heathrow I finally got back on my bike and raced home through the dark streets. I felt invincible, as though I had discovered new powers and couldn't wait to put them to use. Wholeheartedly, I launched myself into the nascent love affair I had suspended during the race, bringing into it the courage and competence the high mountains had infused me with. I was a better, brighter version of myself.

Within a couple of weeks I had finally admitted to myself that London was no longer the place for me, and made plans to leave the city I had called home since my early twenties. My sister and I loaded a van with the astounding quantity of possessions I had accumulated since I moved in with just my bike and panniers at the end of 2013, and drove triumphantly back to the house in Mid Wales where we grew up. My parents had offered to rent me a room until I figured out where I would end up next, and I wondered whether Wales might be my final destination.

As soon as my bike was out of the van I raced off up the hill to watch the sunset. After a couple of hours of cycling, I realised that I couldn't remember when I had last seen a vehicle, and began to worry that perhaps the roads had been closed; perhaps I wasn't supposed to be here. Eventually a set of headlights appeared up ahead and a Land Rover growled towards me, slowing exaggeratedly as it passed. I glimpsed a smiling face under a flat cap, then jumped as the sheep dogs in the back hailed me with a chorus of barking. London was already forgotten.

Chapter Six

The night was full of noises. My tyres rumbled over the loose stones and my breath, already rasping and ragged, roared in my ears, isolating me from the vast silent darkness that no doubt lay beyond. Occasionally another rider would appear out of the night – sometimes ahead of me, but usually from behind, as I was so tired by now that most of my fellow racers were overtaking me – and I'd listen to their rattling bike and their tense, concentrated breath, and watch the brief blaze of their front light as it swept past me. At the end of each lap I'd descend into a muddy arena where crowds of people waited, swathed in down jackets and bobble hats, to cheer on passing riders, or to take the timing chip thrust at them by a breathless teammate, as he climbed off his bike and limped off for a cup of tea, and they mounted theirs and sprinted off up the fire road into the darkness.

The Strathpuffer twenty-four-hour mountain bike race was a new world for me. I wasn't a mountain biker, as I'd been at pains to tell Lee Craigie, whom I'd met the weekend I rode up to Edinburgh with Juliana, and who had suggested we enter it as a pair. I wasn't even much of a racer, but since there was no doubt in my mind that I'd be revisiting the Transcontinental that year, it seemed wise to dip a few more toes into the competitive cycling scene. I knew the Strathpuffer by reputation. It was where Mike Hall had cut his teeth, winning the 2011 event as a solo rider before moving on to even greater things. He had written a detailed blog post advising future riders how to tackle the event, in which he warned of the abrasive mica in the course's soil, and its talent for exfoliating not only a bicycle's moving parts, but the rider's skin, as it seeped through wet clothing. He gave detailed instructions on how to prolong the life of brake pads by using a blowtorch or a household oven to pre-set the friction surface, with expertise borrowed from his 'one-time day job "shaking and baking" high-integrity aerospace electronics'. I sent the link to my brother Sam, who had volunteered to be one of the mechanics for the racers who were sharing our pits, and whose enthusiasm for fixing bikes in difficult conditions seemed to match mine for riding them.

'We have to win, of course,' Lee had said, during one of our few training rides, long after it was too late for me to change my mind. She was a former professional, having retired after the previous year's Commonwealth Games, and I wondered if she believed me when I confessed that my mountain biking experience totalled fewer hours than I'd ride in this race. I suspected that most of our gains would be made on her laps – which, a few hours into the race, were already a good ten minutes faster than mine – and that I'd just have to ride as well as I could, and hope to minimise the losses.

The race, which (like many) promoted itself as 'the world's toughest', took place in the Scottish Highlands in late January, which meant that most of our laps would be completed in darkness, and that there was a strong likelihood of snow and ice. As it turned out, the temperature was unseasonably warm, and hovered around six degrees all night – which meant that within hours the whole course was mud, churned up by thousands of tyres until it was unrideable in places. Sam spent the full twenty-four hours cleaning drive trains with a pressure hose, and told me there was a visible ridge on the ground under his workstand by the time he'd finished.

It wasn't until we'd ridden for eleven hours, and I'd reached the point of submission, where I no longer had the strength either to push myself harder or to conceive of any escape from the tiny cocoon of spluttering breath, juddering handlebars and stony trail leading this way and that way into the night, that I fully understood we were in a race. Between laps I'd retreat to our tent and huddle miserably in my down jacket as the saintly support crew bustled to and fro, boiling kettles, heating soup, mixing energy drinks, hanging up discarded clothing, swapping light batteries, fixing bikes and calculating lap times. Usually, just as I caught my breath and one of them handed me a mug of tea or hot Ribena, I'd look up through the clouded plastic window to see a tall girl in tartan-trimmed Lycra, bent low over her bars as she sprinted for all she was worth up the hill. It dawned on me that she must be our competition.

The second-placed female pair were neck and neck with us for the first half of the race, kept at bay only by Lee's thunderingly fast lap times. Although our tenuous lead was reported to me every time I finished a lap, I barely cared – I knew that as a novice mountain biker I'd be lucky just to survive, and fatalistically assumed that there was no chance I'd make the top of the podium in my very first race. So when one of them finally passed me a few hours after nightfall, I felt relieved. Now I could stop worrying about being overtaken, because it had happened.

Just over an hour later I stood outside the tent with Sam, who was waiting to hand me my bike and whip my down jacket from my shoulders as I set off for another lap. We squinted into the darkness, watching the parade of headlamps bobbing up the hill towards us, trying to guess which one might be Lee's.

'Not that lot, definitely,' remarked Sam. 'They're going way too fast – must be fresh out of the pits!'

But he was wrong. Seconds later Lee thudded to a halt beside me, steaming with exertion, and as I fumbled our timing chip down over my helmet a flash of tartan flitted past us. Lee had managed to regain the lead by a few seconds, and as I sprinted up the long fire road climb that made up the first third of the course, I spotted our rivals performing their own frantic handover outside a tent a few yards up from ours.

A few minutes later, heavy breathing and the purr and stutter of tyres over gravel told me that another rider was drawing level with me. Out of the corner of my eye, I made out long legs, a curly ponytail, and the telltale tartan trim.

We carried on alongside each other, and I struggled to conceal my heavy breathing as the pace rose and rose, neither of us quite sure who was pushing it. Indeed, perhaps it was a joint effort, a common project, a mutual pact of self-annihilation, we two opponents metamorphosed into a team by the very fact of our rivalry.

Despite our differences – she was lean, Lycra-clad, pedalling a carbon hardtail; I was riding an ailing fatbike, wearing walking boots and a fleece jacket – I was, at that moment, closer to her than I've been to anyone. I'd known, since meeting Juliana, that I wasn't the only one who pushed herself relentlessly towards breaking point, who relished the struggle, rather than shrinking from it. But I had yet to witness this first-hand – or to be witnessed myself, by someone who knew where I was going.

The girl's face was impassive, but the slight nodding of her head and slackening of her jaw betrayed that her effort was as great as mine. Where could we go from here? We had another mile of climbing ahead of us, over which I knew we'd continue ratchetting up the pace until we had abandoned any pretence that we weren't sincerely attempting to break each other, and breaking ourselves in the process. My roadie quads could keep her pace on the hills, but I'd be no match for her dexterity over the rocky slabs and chutes that made up the middle part of the course, and I feared the moment when she inevitably pulled ahead of me, knowing that by that point I'd have lost all ability to pretend this didn't matter.

'This is a bit of a battle, isn't it?' she remarked, with a casual sideways glance.

And I muttered something in return, but knew in that moment that it was all over. She had breached my veneer of indifference, and acknowledged our uncomfortable intimacy as clearly and intrusively as a stranger catching my eye in a crowded train carriage. We could no longer pretend we were alone in this, or that it didn't matter. And with that I gave in and let her go, watching the steaming plumes of her breath glowing in the light of her head torch as she sprinted off into the darkness.

Lee and I came second in the Strathpuffer. Zara and Jo extended and then maintained their lead, and finished more than a lap ahead of us, while I continued to force myself onward, my bike slowly failing so that eventually I only had one gear left, and my lungs rasping with the gathering phlegm that I'd spend the next few days coughing up. For a week afterwards my chest rattled audibly as I breathed, and even standing up for any length of time felt like an unreasonable effort. I had never caused myself so much damage.

The following evening, once we had put a tired Sam on the sleeper train, washed our muddy kit and decided to neglect our ruined bikes for another day, we had a subdued Burns Night celebration with our hosts, both bike racers themselves. As the whisky flowed, our Strathpuffer post mortem evolved into a more abstract discussion of the nature of competition, and for the first time I started to pick apart the different ways in which a competitive nature can manifest itself. I had always been told I was competitive, and accepted this as an immutable fact of my character, yet couldn't explain to myself why this hadn't led me to enter races sooner – why I, as an evidently competitive rider, wasn't looking for every opportunity to compete.

Lee recalled the strain of life as a professional cyclist, of lining up at the start of a race surrounded by women she knew well enough (since this was a relatively small scene) to know how their training was going, what injuries they were carrying, what fears and doubts they harboured – and for them to be similarly aware of hers. She recounted the pressure of training for the Commonwealth Games, knowing that this had ceased to be a race that mattered only to her, and feeling the weight of expectation of her coaches, Team Scotland, and the family and friends who had invested in getting her to the start line. I recoiled from her descriptions, which made racing her bike sound less like the escapist solo pursuit I loved, and more like being a tiny cog in a huge, complex machine.

Other people weren't as big a factor in his competitiveness as he'd thought, David countered. He'd battle to overtake people if he could see them, but he'd found this had little to do with the riders themselves – he was effectively just using them as targets, or pegs to pull himself forward. I recognised this. I knew I rode harder with other people around, be they competitors, companions or anonymous strangers.

'Is it harder when you know someone?' I asked, thinking of an abortive skills session with Lee a couple of months previously, where my frustration at continually failing in front of someone I wanted to think highly of me meant that we eventually agreed to go our separate ways and meet at the coffee shop.

'The pressure's higher, definitely,' said Lee. 'Look at how hard the 'puffer was, not wanting to let your partner down.'

Everyone had told us that racing the Strathpuffer as a pair was even harder than riding alone, since solo riders could alter their pace depending on their motivation and energy levels, whereas paired riders were constantly whipped forward by the fear of undermining their partner's efforts (I *knew* Lee wanted us to win), and had just enough time between laps to get sleepy and lose their momentum, before being forced out into the cold once again. We had been sharing our pits with two soloists, who enthused about how much less stressful their way was, and a team of four, who had more than three hours off between their laps, and took turns to mother me during my miserable forty-five-minute rest periods.

I had felt wretchedly incapable, slumping in my chair

while all of these people ministered to me with extraordinary gentleness, doing the things I was no longer able to do myself. Whenever I finished a lap, Sam would seize my bike and take it off to his muddy workstand to undo the damage I'd done in the last hour. Penny and Evan would feed me. Ness would sit beside me and cheerfully try to distract me from whichever parts of me were sore.

I didn't dare tell anyone about that shameful moment when I let Zara pull ahead of me. They were all busy with their tasks, but I had failed at mine, and no longer deserved the care and attention they gave me. And now, over our glasses of Ardmore and Glen Moray, I stayed quiet, not wanting to disrupt the atmosphere of gentle triumph and well-deserved exhaustion with my confession, and realising that in signing up for the Transcontinental for a second year – which I had done as soon as entries opened – I had committed myself to a form of competition I hadn't considered, and was ill-prepared for.

It was all very well to race other cyclists in the streets of London, as I had done for years as a courier, mostly winning, but not caring very much when I did, because the encounter was momentary, the opponent often unaware, and there was no way of telling whether he was at the beginning or end of his journey, riding at his top speed or floating along in a daydream. And when I saw another cyclist ahead of me on a country lane, and stepped up the pace in order to put them behind me, usually I'd never see them again, and they'd feel less like a rival than simply a marker – a sign that I needed to put my foot on the gas for a few minutes.

I had assumed I was used to competition. Now I understood that there was a whole echelon of it that I had missed, and I cringed when I remembered throwaway remarks I'd made about returning to the Transcon 'to finish the job'.

People would be watching me this year, I realised, and they would have expectations. Although I'd failed to finish the previous summer, I had established myself both as a strong rider and as an entertaining one. People had been more aware of my progress than I was myself: one follower remarked with awe that I'd gone for thirty-five hours without sleeping in Northern Italy, and when I stopped in Postojna, Katie and Jayne, who had been keeping an eye on me, knew something was wrong when my dot didn't start moving again after four hours. Jayne was planning to race again as a soloist, and this time I wouldn't have the reassuring presence of Juliana, since she had been offered full sponsorship for the Race Across America.

I'd begun to hear of other women who were entering the race – women who might be stronger than me, might have more experience of racing, might have ridden longer distances; women I knew from a distance, whose social media feeds suggested they were more serious, better equipped, covering more miles. When Jayne told me, in a South London beer garden a couple of months after returning from Istanbul, that she would race again, I had spontaneously whooped and punched the air, overjoyed for reasons I couldn't quite explain to her that I'd have female company in the race, that I wasn't the only one who wanted to do this. Yet alongside my jubilation I'd felt a sour clench of anxiety, which over the next few months blossomed into a disturbing sense of hostility towards my opponents, shadowing my very genuine feelings of affection and camaraderie. Whenever I heard of another woman entering the race, my external delight would be inwardly mirrored by writhing doubt. I'd line my own strengths up against those of my new rival, and find it impossible to say who might triumph.

I began to understand why Juliana and I had managed

to become such close friends, and avoided much sense of competition. Even though we joked that we were rivals, neither of us had any doubt that she was ultimately the stronger cyclist. We'd gained a fairly detailed appreciation of our respective strengths and weaknesses on our rides together. To my surprise I was often faster up hills, but the Transcon had shown me that, despite my firmest intentions, I couldn't resist the urge to stop and rest when I was suffering, whereas she was spurred onward by the very discomforts and stresses that slowed me down. She had ridden through pain that most would find unbearable to finish fourth in the TransAm, and in the Transcon it was only actual bodily failure that stopped her. She had something in her that I didn't, and we couldn't see each other as a threat, because we simply weren't. She knew I'd never beat her in a race, and I knew there was no point trying.

With the other women it was less certain, and therein lay my fear. I would be seen to try, and quite probably also seen to fail. There was no use pretending I didn't care if I was beaten – the fact of entering a race was a declaration that I wanted to win, no matter how low the odds, and I'd line up against women who had professed an identical ambition. I was already used to the way that a long ride would lay me bare, but until now this had been an entirely private experience. Next summer I would enter this vulnerable state in an arena that contained many others, who would witness, share and mercilessly exploit it, while countless dot-watchers looked on. I felt hopelessly unprepared.

I had been relying on my experience of long bike tours, without realising that this was only one part of the equation. So much of the Transcon, I told people afterwards, had felt like the last time I'd cycled across Europe, just speeded up, concentrated and intensified. There was the same thrill of traversing mountain ranges and national borders; the administrative tasks of feeding myself, maintaining body and bike, and finding somewhere to sleep; the brief encounters with curious and apathetic strangers; the particular grammar of long hours on the bike, punctuated by petrol stations, small towns and regular breaks to graze and gaze; the immersion in the landscape, where often I felt that the normal boundaries between myself and the world I moved through had been partially effaced, and we flowed in and out of each other like breath into lungs or waves onto a shoreline.

But I had never raced before, and racing, I now understood, came with its own grammar, its own flow and its own set of anxieties, which I was only just beginning to recognise. Bicycle touring was in my bones; with bicycle racing I seemed to have married into a family whose language I didn't yet speak.

Chapter Seven

In person, Mike undermined his heroic image in almost every way. His Yorkshire accent was a lilting alto, and he held himself with an unexpected levity that frequently found its expression in giggles, especially when an over-enthusiastic hand gesture accidentally made contact with his coffee cup, spraying his T-shirt with a good proportion of the expensive flat white it contained.

We were sitting in a smart café in East London. My first book was published that day, and my main emotion when he got in touch and said that he was in town too, and we should meet up, was relief. My week of interviews and photoshoots had been gratifying, but also surreal and unnerving, as I knew that to accept this as my new reality constituted a chemical change I wasn't ready to undergo. I looked forward to returning to the familiar haven of Mid

Wales, and Mike's smiling face, amongst the pinstripes of Spitalfields, seemed to hold the same promise.

He and his partner Anna were in town to meet with potential sponsors – indeed, as I arrived at the café they had been standing around the table, shaking hands with someone from one of the high-end bike clothing brands. Mike was preparing to ride the Tour Divide from Canada to Mexico – the record time he'd set two years previously wasn't official, because the route had been diverted to avoid forest fires, and having by this point completed the race several times, he'd gained a detailed sense of its pitfalls and opportunities.

I asked him about his preparations, concerned that my planning for the Transcontinental had fallen by the wayside, despite my intention of cultivating an obsession with the race akin to James Hayden's, who had managed to convince a private equity firm to sponsor him, and was now training full-time, determined to win the race in 2016. He had recently posted a picture of himself doing special exercises to prevent a repeat of the Shermer's Neck episode that had ended his race in Montenegro at the same time mine had ended in Slovenia. Mike hadn't experienced Shermer's Neck, but he had already factored it into his plans, and showed me some stretches to help prevent it.

'If you bend your neck forward, flex your foot and then imagine a line running down your back, between the two …' He demonstrated, thrusting a leg out from the table and nearly tripping up a passing suit. I copied him, more carefully.

'That's it. It's mostly about circulation – what happens is, the back of your neck gets compacted, and the muscles end up getting starved of oxygen and deteriorating faster than the rest of you.'

I took note.

'So I'll stretch every few hours, just as I'm riding along. But you'll also want to think about your set-up. I actually put my saddle down a few mil towards the end of TransAm – my muscles were getting stiffer and I didn't have as much reach. It seemed to work.'

I preferred his approach to Juliana's, who in the same race had sown the seed of her ongoing knee problems, thanks to a broken seat post bolt that meant her saddle kept sliding down. She had ignored her pain, whereas Mike was more inclined to see discomfort as a factor that might inhibit his race, and therefore a problem to be solved. I mentioned her plan to race RAAM that summer, and asked if I could pass on the stretches to her.

'How's she doing?' asked Mike.

'Oh, pretty good now, I think. She's finally taking the knee thing seriously. Last thing I heard she was having some sort of injections – cartilage or collagen or something – to rebuild them. And she's got this plan to take RAAM by storm, and show them how much tougher self-supported racers are.'

We smirked at each other. I could tell the same idea had crossed his mind.

'Only problem is, they obviously won't let her enter without a support crew – I've already said I'll do it – and she'll be a nightmare to manage. She's used to riding alone, so she won't want people telling her what to do. Or seeing her when she's falling to pieces.'

I remembered the stories of RAAM riders losing their minds, and the paranoia, hallucinations and occasional fits of weeping brought on by chronic sleep deprivation. I was frightened to see Juliana in such a state, and had no idea how I'd convince someone so headstrong to follow her team's instructions. I had asked about her strategy for avoiding Shermer's Neck, or managing it should it occur, and suggested that we think about it in advance, and bring along a neck brace.

'No,' she'd replied. 'If I start thinking about stuff like that, it'll end up happening. I'll be fine.'

She could do with Mike on her team, I thought. He approached races as complex problems to be solved, each setback a challenge to be improvised through and ultimately learned from. And this extended to his mind, as well as body and bike. On a ride we'd done a couple of months previously he had told me all about 'town draw', explaining how, as he approached any of the settlements along the Tour Divide route, he'd start fantasising about what he'd eat there.

'And you're riding into this town, thinking about the pizza you're craving, and then you get to the town and if they don't have it, you'll grind to a halt, or ride around for ages just looking for pizza. And it's when you stop that you lose time. So I make sure the only thing I crave is being on the bike – you know, when you're on the bike, you're moving forward along the route: that's the only place I want to be.'

I could relate to this tactic more than I could Juliana's unconquerable stubbornness, James Hayden's professionalism. But there was no hurry to leave London this afternoon, so we ordered some brownies, and the conversation turned back to the depression that had troubled us both in the aftermath of big rides, a problem neither of us had fully been able to resolve. Mike recalled how he'd gone to ground for three months after his world record, struggling under the dark cloud that often lies in wait at the end of a long and taxing journey.

'My new hobby was giving up on things,' he'd once remarked. 'I'd go out for a thirty-mile ride, and give up after twenty minutes. I'd start applying for jobs, and give up halfway through the application form.'

'But in the end,' he now reflected, 'I think it was work that saved me, and I think a lot of these professional adventurers – you know the ones, who spend all their time telling people to quit the day job and follow their dreams – miss the point that work is really good for most people. You know, it gives you a routine, and a purpose, and human contact – something to hang your life off, while you get better.'

I smiled with recognition.

'That's *exactly* the experience I had when I got back from my big trip – I was probably a few months behind you. I had the same crash – didn't know what to do with myself, couldn't deal with people – and it was working as a courier that sorted me out. Because, you know, at the very least it got me out the house for ten hours a day, and kept me busy, and meant I got enough exercise that I could sleep. Without that it would have been so much worse.'

I decided not to tell him about the boltholes I'd found around London – in loading bays and doorways and shady parks – where I could cry uninterrupted. Or of the times where I swooped down into the Hyde Park tunnel, where the roar of the traffic echoed off the concrete and meant no one would hear me, and let myself sob noisily for a couple of seconds, just to burn off the immediate anguish so that I could smile pleasantly at the next receptionist. But I suspected he'd have similar tales.

He told me how working – first as a courier in Cardiff and eventually as an engineer at Rolls-Royce – had slowly got him back on his feet, and how within a year he was preparing for his assault on the Tour Divide record. He'd also found time to set up the Transcontinental, which in its first iteration was little more than a small group of pioneers meeting on Westminster Bridge early one morning, posing for photos, and then racing their bikes to Istanbul.

He had achieved a surprising amount during what was probably one of the hardest years of his life, I reflected, remembering the short periods I'd spent between storms of weeping, typing up sample chapters in the rented room where I lived with just the contents of my panniers. At the time I felt hopeless, sure that I'd inadvertently destroyed my life, and would never have the ability to put it back together, but unbeknownst to myself I had been creating the future that we now both sat in: Mike as a respected race director and record holder; me as a published author.

He and Anna had a few spare hours that afternoon, so I recommended the Cycle Revolution exhibition at the Design Museum, suspecting that Mike would jump at the chance to spend a few hours inspecting historically significant bicycles, and pleased to have been the one to bring it to his attention. We hugged goodbye, and I got back on my bike.

⁙

The day after Juliana dropped out of RAAM, the nine of us woke up in a hotel in Durango, Colorado, and wondered what to do.

Sam was disappointed that we'd only made it four days into the race, depriving him of the more serious mechanical breakdowns he would have had to deal with further down the road. But rather than being sad that Juliana's ambitions now lay in ruins, I was euphoric, as if I'd finally reached the top of a long mountain pass I'd been climbing and begun to speed down the descent. For the last four days I'd been watching someone I cared about suffer more and more, knowing that my job was to keep her going despite the pain, rather than alleviate it by letting her stop. Now the worst was over – though Juliana was in a terrible state, hobbling into the breakfast buffet with bags under her eyes, and grimacing as she lowered her saddle sores onto a chair we had prepared with cushions.

She looked better than she had the previous day, though. At around lunchtime she had admitted her neck was hurting, and shortly afterwards her head started to droop. When we stopped to talk through our options, she had to prop her hand under her chin to hold it up. Sam swiftly improvised a brace from a couple of inner tubes, I used the opportunity to rub more sun cream onto her filthy limbs, and we carried on.

We had a long wait for her at the top of the next hill, and when she eventually came into sight she was walking, not cycling, her head bent as if she were scanning the ground beneath her. Her legs were cramping too badly to ride, she said, and we forced some electrolyte drink down her, let her sleep for a while and then pushed her onwards.

A few hours after we had handed over to the night shift we received a mournful call from Billy Rice, Juliana's coach. Juliana was coughing up blood, had a suspected pulmonary oedema and was most definitely out of the race. With minimal discussion, we parked the car and headed for the closest bar.

'Morning team!' Billy seemed to have cheered up now. 'We've gotta get back on the road. If we're quick, we should catch Mike Hall as he comes through Breckenridge. Hurry-hurry!'

Billy was by this point equally tolerated and beloved among our small team for his apparent inability ever to switch off. He bounded off to get ready, while the rest of us stayed huddled over our coffees for a few more minutes. We had already spent four days driving at a cyclist's pace through California, Arizona, Utah and Colorado, wedged into overheated vehicles among Juliana's clothes, food and medical supplies. No one was in the mood to get back in the car, even with the incentive of seeing Mike midway through what was looking like a record-breaking attempt on the Tour Divide.

My excitement grew, though, as we made our way through Colorado's highlands and I recognised the euphoria I had felt on the Strada dell'Assietta the previous summer. An hour or two after leaving Durango's sunny riverside we stopped at the top of the 3,309m Wolf Creek Pass and I danced around the car as soon as I was allowed out of it, bizarrely energised by the thin air, and as gleeful as a child when I thought about what lay ahead. RAAM rules forbade support crew from riding bicycles for the duration of the race, but I had been promised that the next day I could ride for as long as I wanted, and I couldn't wait. And, as long as the traffic was in our favour, we'd be seeing Mike in a few hours. The dot that some of us had been monitoring for the past week would magically and momentarily turn back into our friend.

Mike had posted his phone home from Banff, wanting to eliminate all possible distractions, so he would have absolutely no reason to suspect we might be nearby – as far as he was concerned we were busy with a very different race, hundreds of miles south, out of sight and almost certainly out of mind. I wondered how he'd react when he saw us, and whether this interruption would be welcome. I knew all too well the trance that a rider can get into after a few days of solitude and intense exertion. Would it be healthy to rouse him from it? We might be about to trespass on something private and extremely intimate, and perhaps, as with a rare and elusive animal, it would be better for Mike not to know we were there.

I refreshed Trackleaders impatiently as our little convoy edged its way through Breckenridge's tangled traffic, closer and closer to the blue dot that showed us where Mike was. He had started moving again as we approached the town, and we'd briefly despaired, thinking that we'd missed him, and that he'd disappear onto the trails where our clumsy vehicles couldn't follow. I could jump on my bike, I thought, and chase him down. It would be worth it just to say a quick hello, hand him a bottle of chocolate milk, and see whatever surprise, delight or confusion happened to cross his face.

But the dot paused again at the southern edge of Breckenridge, and a few minutes later we drew up at a gas station to see an unmistakable bike propped up outside, covered in dust, with a cursory sprinkling of Apidura luggage. Inside, dithering between aisles of junk food, was Mike himself.

'Oh, hello,' he said casually, as we crowded eagerly round him. Then a small double-take. 'Umm, aren't you supposed to be …?'

Juliana told him of RAAM's unexpected turn of events, while Billy asked if there was anything he needed, knowing already that he would say no, being as he was one of the most passionate and meticulous advocates of the self-supported ethos.

'No, ta, I'm alright,' said Mike, and Juliana and I instantly had the same idea. I drifted to the back of the store and plucked bottles of chocolate milk from the chiller, while she gravitated to the car and came back with handfuls of her own energy products. While Mike paid for his supplies and tried to get his head round the unscheduled appearance of Billy Rice, we covered his bike with as much food and drink as it would hold, then said our goodbyes and headed off to restock our own vehicle, leaving Mike in peace.

A couple of minutes later he came over to us, his helmet full of the food we'd tried to give him. I noticed he'd either kept or discarded a couple of bottles of chocolate milk.

'I'm going to have to give this back to you,' he said, with the calmness of one whose principles stand comfortably unquestioned. 'But thanks very much all the same.'

He seemed a little less stunned, as if he'd now got used to this intrusion from the outside world. We chatted about this and that as he rearranged his luggage, tightened his straps and got ready for the next push into the mountains.

'I'll see you in Belgium!' I said, by way of farewell. He looked at me blankly for a second, then remembered that, in a life half-forgotten, he was the Director of the Transcontinental Race.

'Oh yes!' he grinned. 'This is the prototype jersey for that, by the way.' He indicated the sleek grey pelt he'd been wearing since he left Banff, and pointed out a couple of tweaks he was planning to make before it went on sale. This was the Mike Hall we knew and loved. I remembered a ride we'd done with Anna and Lee back in March, when he'd told me he was testing some dynamo hubs he'd been sent, methodically wearing out one after the other, to ascertain their average lifespan. It was this painstaking attention to detail, I thought, for testing things to destruction and making them work just right, that had ensured all his past successes, and now put him on course for a new Tour Divide record.

We watched him set off up the hill and vanish into the landscape, then got back in the car and carried on, trying to digest how momentous, and yet also how ordinary it felt to run into a friend so far from home. I remembered Mike stopping to talk to me on his way down Ventoux, puncturing the personal nightmare I was battling through, and calling out 'see you in Sestriere!' as he waved goodbye, with the same nonchalance you might tell your colleagues you'll see them in work tomorrow.

A couple of weeks later we arrived back in Britain to grey skies and the shock of Brexit, and I slid back into the depression that had been waiting for me like a jacket in a cloakroom. The six weeks I'd spent in America had felt like both an escape and a salvation. Before meeting Juliana and the rest of the team in Oceanside I'd cycled south down Route 101, riding alone, sleeping amongst sand dunes as Pacific waves thundered in my dreams, watching the sunlight brighten as I slowly sipped my first coffee of the day, and enjoying a journey comfortably within my capabilities: a good few steps down from the Transcon or the Strathpuffer.

I'd often ridden for twelve hours or more, ignoring all but the world that was immediately around me. For days I neglected emails, avoided social media and managed not to think about the crashing heartbreak that had ensued from the previous summer's love affair. I focused instead on the towering avenues of redwoods, the dappled shade of leaves on the tarmac, the glittering ocean and the windy sky, and nurtured a thin hope that this might be enough – that I had rediscovered a part of myself where I could take shelter.

A day after I returned to the UK, a long phone call with the woman whose love I'd lost dispelled my hope and serenity, and everything was just as it had been before. I remembered Mike's remark that 'giving up on things' had become his hobby in the aftermath of his world record. Crying had become mine. I'd sit at my desk for most of each day, trying not to think about her, overcome with sobs that pounded me like the Pacific waves I'd heard the previous month. I learned new ways of concealing my misery from those I lived with – going for a long bike ride, or taking a hot shower. I debated endlessly whether it was better to let myself cry, let the emotion run its course, or whether I should decide I'd done enough of this, draw a line and make an effort to stop.

As when I'd been depressed after my return from Japan, I conspired endlessly to get myself out of it. I should know my way round my own mind by now, I thought. This certainly wasn't the first time I'd suffered like this, and I knew – rationally if not instinctually – that emotions are often an unfaithful reflection of the actual state of things. Right now I felt very sincerely that my life had turned into a disaster, that I had squandered my potential and opportunities, and that I'd never find a way of salvaging myself and getting through the years that remained. But I also knew I'd felt this before. And between these episodes the coordinates of my life had been exactly the same, yet I had felt infused with ambition and curiosity, excited by the very fact of being alive, of having these years to spend in the world and so many plans that my only real fear was failing to fit them all in.

I am normally someone who *loves* life, I berated myself. So why can't I just go back to feeling like that?

In one of my rare attempts to convey what I was feeling to a friend, I recalled a weekend I'd spent, years previously, in the Indian Himalayas with a group of colleagues, during my brief stint as a financial editor in Delhi. The trip wasn't an unqualified success, and consisted mostly of me saying 'hey, let's go up there!' and charging off towards the nearest cliff face, while the others sat and ate crisps and looked worried. On our way home we stopped off to look at the Ganges above Rishikesh, where it's still a small river, less than five metres wide, rushing along rocky canyons through the pine forests. I lost little time in plunging in and swimming towards the opposite bank. I remember how cool and green the water felt around me (I dreaded going back to Delhi's forty-five-degree heat and intermittent air-conditioning), and how irresistibly strong the current was. Try as I might, I couldn't reach the far bank. I got to just over an arm's length away and kicked and kicked with all my might, but the surging water that held me back might as well have been iron bars. I remember fighting there for a few moments, studying the riverbank just beyond my fingertips, stretching my arms towards the smooth grey rocks, and moss, and pine needles, astounded that I was unable to touch them, despite being so close, and there being no visible obstacle.

'And that's how this depression feels,' I told her. 'The world is *right there* – just past your fingertips – but you can't reach it, no matter how close it seems, and how easy it should be just to step forward, or kick harder, or stretch a tiny bit further, and grasp it in your hand.'

I let everything slip. I couldn't do otherwise. What scraps of work I managed to get done were accomplished between panic attacks and bouts of weeping. I got used to the routine of sitting down in the morning, picking up one task or another and trying to fumble my way through it until the misery burst its banks, then I'd cry for hours, wishing I could stop, wondering if there was anything I could do, or anywhere I could go, that might help me divert this torrent. Some days the storm would pass, and I'd get a few more things done, feeling as empty as if I'd just ridden for several days, and exhausted myself beyond the ability to feel.

I wasn't able to muster any concern about the fact that I was supposed to be racing across Europe the following month. It bothered me that I had become so apathetic about the Transcontinental, especially as I watched others' preparations, seeing how dedicated they were, witnessing how James Hayden's life over the past year had revolved around his goal of winning. The only time I realised I had any feelings at all about it was when a friend – quite wisely – asked me if racing was a good idea, and suggested that instead I stay at home and try to look after myself. The thought filled me with unexpected horror.

Staying at home would mean two more weeks of weeping at my desk, of failing to achieve what seemed the most straightforward of ambitions: simply to change my outlook, and re-engage with the world in the way I always had. I didn't particularly *want* to ride the Transcontinental, but I wasn't afraid of it. The minutiae of crossing a continent by bike were familiar, and a great deal easier than another fortnight of coming to terms with the fact that I didn't fit into the world any more, that I had turned out to be unworthy of the love I thought I'd found. I hoped that the exertion and exhaustion of a long bike ride might function like an electric shock treatment, and force my body's chemicals to mingle and bond in different ways, so that when I emerged, things would be better. At the very least, I craved the brief endorphin flush of finishing a day's riding, and the blissful exhaustion that would guarantee me a few hours of unconsciousness. Travelling to Belgium for the race was an opportunity to change things, and even if it didn't work, the race would fill some of the daunting weeks that stretched ahead of me.

Chapter Eight

Geraardsbergen, when I arrived for the start of the race, was heaving with the mass of nervous men I remembered from last year. In the sports hall, where Mike's pre-race briefing took place, dozens of bikes were bedecked with intricate arrangements of bikepacking bags that their owners had clearly spent months tweaking and redesigning and replacing until they were *just* right. They now eyeballed each other's rigs, offering nods of admiration and tuts of doubt or interest. Some were taking almost nothing; others had strapped a bag to every single point on the bike where one might be carried, and were wearing backpacks and musettes to accommodate the overspill.

I recognised a few women from their Twitter accounts, and made a point of going up to say hello, fearing that they might all be far more serious athletes, who would decline to acknowledge me and then publicly humiliate me once the race started, but knowing that most of them would feel as wary of me as I was of them. They were visibly relieved when I turned out to be friendly.

'That girl there says she's aiming to finish in nine days,' whispered one of them, pointing through the crowds to a muscular woman with long black hair. I decided not to risk introducing myself to her, and calculated that that would add up to around 400km per day.

I had set myself an ambivalent target of 300km, and in my final days of route planning had written down a list of towns that appeared at roughly this interval along my route. The first checkpoint, in Clermont-Ferrand, was around 600km from the start, and it had taken me thirty-five hours to cover that distance in the Bryan Chapman (including stops for meals and a two-hour sleep), so I decided I'd try to get there by 10 a.m. on day three – thirty-six hours. I knew I'd slow down once I reached the Alps, but since I lacked any expectation of success, and didn't even know if I'd finish the race, my unreachable 300km target seemed no more or less impossible than making it to Çanakkale. I'd aim for whatever town I had said I'd reach, and as the race drew on I'd fall shorter and shorter.

My plan would see me finish the race in just over twelve days. I dithered over the hubris of booking accommodation for my arrival (and wasting money when I turned up several days late), and compromised by reserving a hostel bed thirteen days from the start. The finishers' party, which all but the slowest and fastest racers were aiming for, was a day later, and I entertained simultaneous fantasies of screeching into whatever bar it was held in at the very last minute, still covered in sweat and dust, and of turning up so much sooner than expected that I had to beg the hostel to let me in a night or two early.

I didn't see the girl with the black hair again, but I did run into Jayne. We commiserated over the stress of pre-departure, knowing that, for each other, we were partly the cause of it.

It was a relief to assemble in the town square in the fresh evening air. The swarm of cyclists, with their fluorescent yellow vests and blinking red lights, was interspersed with family members, hugging and taking photos, and strolling citizens of Geraardsbergen, who regularly came out to watch bike races pass through their town, but seemed nonetheless fascinated by this one, which had no press caravan, no service cars and a finish line so far off that it was more of a direction than a goal.

I found Leo, who was volunteering this year, and would be driving one of the race cars across Europe, with Kate waiting for us at the finish, and we greeted James Hayden, who gave me a nod, but refused to shake my hand for fear of picking up an infection. Leo laughed at him, suggesting that he might have taken his professionalism a bit too far, but I could only marvel at his attention to detail. He had prepared for this race as meticulously as any pro team would for the Tour de France, knowing from the moment he'd quit the previous year that he'd come back to win. I had briefly aspired towards such dedication, but the mindset I admired in James and Mike (engineers both) was not one I shared. Much as I liked the idea of following a training plan, tracking my improvements, hacking and tweaking at my body to make it more efficient, I never seemed to get round to getting started. I was not a person who tinkered with her bike for fun, or who compulsively took things apart to see how they worked. My obsession was with the feeling I got *when* they worked, and I was grateful enough for that not to risk polluting it by trying to improve things or asking how it was they came about.

I could tell that many of the riders present had followed similar arcs to James, and I felt unworthy in comparison, worried that I was overconfident in my body's ability just to keep going, as soon as it was on a bike with a continent in front of it. At the same time I longed for the race to start, knowing that all of these doubts would be left behind me once I was riding.

The streetlights outshone the sky, and around us the spectators lit their torches. We clustered together in the square, fidgeted through a few minutes of speeches by the luminaries of Geraardsbergen, and then, finally, the town crier hollered out a countdown and we set off to the sound of his ringing bell, shuffling our way across the start line, swerving and faltering as the group gathered pace, then clipping feet into pedals at last and feeling the reassuring push of muscle into motion.

We rode a circuit of the town, following the race car at an easy pace and here and there introducing ourselves, exchanging bland small talk about what lay ahead, and how glad or afraid we were to have started. I was towards the back of the pack as we passed again through the town square, and watched the river of red lights rise up ahead of me towards De Muur, like lava flowing back to its source. At the top, between the ranks of torch-bearing spectators and through the cacophony of cowbells, I glanced back and saw the final glowing rays of the sun sinking below the horizon, then turned right at the chapel, and rode into the darkness.

For the first few hours the quiet roads were animated by our freewheels and flashing lights. We rushed through silent villages, converging at junctions and veering apart when our route choices diverged. At one point I passed Jayne going in the opposite direction, and spent the next twenty minutes trying to explain to myself how that might have happened. We weren't on a major through road when we crossed paths, so she wasn't necessarily riding in the wrong direction. I decided that the village we were in must have been adjacent to two north-south routes, and I was on my way to one, and she the other.

The group had thinned out by the time the colour crept back into the sky, and I remembered the surprising desolation of Northern France. The landscape felt bleaker than it should in midsummer, as I ground my way over its undulations, past endless fields of wheat, scanning motionless villages for signs of life. It was still early, but I had been riding for many hours, and wanted coffee as much for a change of scene as for the burst of energy it would provide. I drew within sight of another racer – a lean man in a grey jersey – and noticed that he slowed down just as I did whenever we passed through a village, glancing this way and that in search of a light and an open door. We eventually found a *boulangerie*, and bought lavish piles of sandwiches and pastries that we alternately gorged on or strapped to our bikes for later, but it was approaching midday before I reached a bigger settlement, found my way to the town square and spotted a café awning. Three well-loaded bikes were propped up nearby, and three racers shared a table, looking up with interest as I approached.

'I remember you!' said one, as I emerged with my two *cafés au lait* and pulled up a chair. 'I used to be a courier in London too – years ago now. Don't know if you recognise me?'

I frowned as I scanned his face, trying to ignite some spark of familiarity. He was tall, broad and unkempt, wearing a white jersey and a sleepy, good-natured expression. I had to admit I'd never knowingly laid eyes on him.

'Well, it was a long time ago. I'm Michał.'

'Nice to meet you, Michał,' I said, holding out a hand.

'Or Mike, if you prefer,' he said, shaking it.

We gratefully sipped our coffees, and exchanged identical tales of how long it had taken us to find them. One of the other men, whose name I had forgotten, but whom I believed to be Swiss, was looking at the tracker on his phone.

'Wow – the leaders are already a long way ahead!' He showed us the screen, where three or four blue dots were spaced out ahead of the main cloud of racers. 'I reckon they'll get to CP1 within twenty-four hours.'

Six hundred kilometres in twenty-four hours? It didn't seem possible. I wondered if James was in the lead again. I thought of him, and Kristof, knowing that to cover that sort of distance they'd have to ride almost constantly, and that, whenever I paused over the next week, to drink coffee, or sleep, or catch my breath at the top of a pass, they would still be pedalling. I knew non-cyclists regarded my own exploits with similar awe, and that to a civilian, there wouldn't be much to differentiate us, but riders like James and Kristof – and Mike, and Juliana – seemed to have transcended the limitations that held me back. I wasn't so naïve as to assume they'd found ways of avoiding pain and fatigue, but I was fascinated by their ability to carry on in spite of themselves. No matter how firmly I resolved that I would *not* stop for coffee, or that I would resist the successive temptation of petrol stations and their cold drinks, I always managed to talk myself into a short break when the opportunity arose. I should have ridden straight past this café.

Michał was scrolling through his own phone.

'Hey, looks like you're the first woman!' he remarked.

'Ah, that doesn't mean much,' I replied. 'You know what they say, if you're in the lead on the first day, you won't be by the end. Once people start sleeping, it'll all rearrange, and someone'll probably overtake me.'

He looked at the leaderboard more closely, and found out that I was also ahead of him, simply because I'd covered a greater distance to get to this café.

'You see? That means I'm a less efficient rider, because if I've done more miles, I should be further south than you. But clearly my route planning's not as good, and you've come a more direct way.'

'We'll have to see how it goes,' he said. 'It's still so early. I don't think anyone's even slept yet.'

Nods from the other two men confirmed that they hadn't.

'And now we won't need to.' I downed my final mouthful of coffee, and indicated the cups they were all still sipping. There was no sense in waiting for them, I realised, since we were technically in competition, and prohibited from riding together, so I said my farewells, told them I'd see them down the road, and got back on my bike.

Ignited by the caffeine, my mind returned to the mysteries of James and Kristof's resilience. Kristof was celebrated for his enigma as much as his achievements, because no one could quite explain why he was *so* much faster than any other rider, and he wasn't giving anything away. No one had heard of him when he'd won the first Transcontinental, but by the second race he was already famous for the astonishing margins by which he beat his competitors, arriving in Istanbul more than a day ahead of the second-placed rider and, in 2013, even beating the race car to the finish. He had had so much time in hand that when he arrived at the top of the Lovćen Pass in Montenegro, and was told that he'd made the mistake of taking the ferry across the mouth of the Kotor fjord (explicitly forbidden in the race manual), he was able to avoid disqualification by backtracking down the mountain, circling the bay, and reascending with an extra five hours and 1,000m climbing in his legs, race lead intact.

I had met him at the start. He seemed to know who I was, and introduced me to his wife and daughter, sharing a box of *tartes au poire* they had brought him. People walked past us with the awestruck glances normally reserved for Mike Hall, but Kristof, like Mike, seemed oblivious to his stature. We made small talk about how much we were looking forward to the ride, and quickly veered off into tales of outlandish camping spots and unexpected hospitality from our touring days. He had a dry, humorous way of speaking, and it wasn't difficult to imagine him as the physics teacher he was during term time. He was as tall and muscular as you'd expect – but then, so were most of the other men who milled around us, and it was likely that he'd beat all of them, and that even I would beat some of them.

What was it that set Kristof apart? Theories abounded, but no one could say for sure whether it was the obsessive efficiency of his logistics and route-planning, the volume of his training (he was said to have ridden over 12,000 miles already that year), or some unknown factor that meant he had a greater ability than anyone else to keep going through pain, cold, heat, exhaustion and anything else that might occur during a race. I suspected that, if scientists studied Kristof and managed to come up with a conclusive explanation for his excellence, it would turn out to be a lucky combination of all of these things – but still, he consistently won races with margins so generous that they begged a different explanation. People had begun to refer to him as 'The Machine', and to speculate that he was the only person who might be able to beat Mike. Or perhaps Mike was the only person who'd be able to beat *him*. At any rate, the two hadn't raced against each other, and quite possibly never would.

I wondered if the lead riders had made themselves any rules about stopping – whether they set an alarm, or planned their breaks in advance. I'd heard about one rider who'd decided to allow himself precisely five hours off the bike every day, to include eating, sleeping and disaster management. Presumably this meant that if he had a time-consuming mechanical, he would lose most of that day's sleep ration.

I would have set myself rules, were it not for my doubt that I'd be able to keep to them. My secret twelve-day plan, which I had already fully acknowledged to be over-ambitious, was as far as I wanted to go with plotting out my ride against the time in which I might complete it. I feared that if I set myself any more obligations the ride would shrivel into a series of deadlines, which I'd either fail to meet or end up renegotiating with myself, all along bemoaning the frailty of my resolve.

It seemed to come down more to sheer strength of will than I had previously realised. There probably wasn't much between the top riders in terms of fitness, I thought to myself. What differentiated them was their ability to keep going, and to minimise the disruption of tiredness, injuries, mechanicals and vacillating mood. Mike had told me once that, during his round-the-world ride, he had done his best to ensure that all emotional breakdowns took place on the bike, rather than at the roadside, and I had wondered what he meant, not quite able to picture him riding along in tears.

I thought back to Ventoux, and other rides from which I'd learned that, although I'll often feel unable to go on, and quite plausibly exhausted by what I've done, if I continue, the tiredness will pass. Understanding that energy comes and goes over the course of a ride, rather than draining steadily from 100 per cent to zero, was one of the most significant lessons I learned in my early days of cycling.

And that afternoon, as I rolled through France's golden-green fields and clusters of shady woodland, I resolved that I would keep on riding whenever I could. If I was tired, or if the pain in my already-sore feet got worse, I'd slow down, but I'd keep riding. I'd remind myself that those hours when the strength blazed in my legs would balance out the long afternoons when I despaired of myself, and crawled along just above walking pace. If I felt weak, I'd ride weakly – but I'd still ride. Anticipating the moments of panic I knew I'd experience later on in the ride, when I'd convince myself that I was a failure and didn't even deserve to be there, I told myself that, as long as I was riding my bike, however slowly, I was doing it, and I was on my way to finishing the Transcontinental, no matter how long that might take.

I arrived in Auxerre as the day's heat died down, knowing from the sprawl of car dealerships and shopping malls I passed on its outskirts that I was likely to come across a big supermarket. When I found it, I was even more pleased to see that there was a kiosk selling freshly baked pizzas at its entrance. I marched briskly through the aisles, emerging with an armful of pastries, salted cashews, cherry tomatoes, brie triangles and Orangina, then ordered myself a pizza topped with onions, new potatoes and slices of brie, sat on the pavement and deliberately ate myself into a stupor, knowing that the next hour on the bike would be difficult as a result, but wanting to fortify myself for a long ride into the night, and potentially another morning of fruitlessly hunting for cafés.

'Jayne's just 1km back!' tweeted a woman I'd stayed with in Santa Barbara six weeks previously.

I didn't feel the anxiety I'd expected, knowing that the competition was nipping at my heels. Jayne would stop for dinner too, and even if she set off before me, I had a feeling I'd ride longer into the night. Groaning with carbohydrate and cheese, I carried on south, plunging into the loose golden folds of the hills as if breasting through waves. All around me the shadows lengthened and the low, heavy sunlight was the colour of honey.

I wondered if Jayne would catch me before bedtime, but found myself unable to care very much if she did. It was so much further to Turkey that what either of us had accomplished so far was negligible, and we'd both lose much bigger chunks of time to sleep, wrong turns and other minor catastrophes. There was no sense in celebrating my position now – or even trying that hard to maintain it, since in doing so I might well tire myself out and affect the remainder of my ride. I remembered Josh Ibbett, the year before, biding his time, riding as well as he could, sleeping as much as he needed to, knowing that James wasn't, and that he'd eventually crack. Kate, who'd watched an exhausted James duct-tape his head into position at Checkpoint Four, told me Josh had been calm and efficient in comparison, pausing briefly at the checkpoint to charge his devices and eat, before carrying on to ride the final 1,000km.

'I know the route from here,' he'd told her. 'I know the bush I'll be sleeping in tonight, and what time I'll hit the towns. I just have to keep it together till Istanbul.'

Unlike James – and myself – he had resisted the urge to sprint through the night to distance himself from his rival. Instead he had moved at a pace he could sustain, knowing this had to include the time he spent sleeping and otherwise looking after himself. And that was all anyone could do, I realised. To sustain the fastest pace I could over a two-week ride, I'd have to factor in necessities like sleep and self-care. If it turned out that Jayne's overall speed was higher than mine, whether because she slept less, cycled faster or was more efficient in her supermarket shops, there was not very much I could do about that. My only plausible strategy was to ride as swiftly and sustainably as possible, and hope that that would be enough.

So I carried on. Just after nightfall I rode through a town called Clamecy, admired its medieval buildings and intricate church steeple, and felt momentarily dismayed that I had no reason to stop there. It was too late for a coffee, and I was keen to make the most of my energy, knowing that I'd been awake for over twenty-four hours by now, and that it was only a matter of time before my eyes began to close. Perhaps I'd come back here one day, I told myself, on a more leisurely tour, and spend some time sipping coffee beside the river and exploring the old town. And there would, I realised, be an abundance of pretty little towns over the next few days. I could afford to squander this one.

I eventually slept in a picnic area beside the road, under tall trees that soared upwards like a cathedral, the reflective stripes of another supine racer visible a few metres off when I swung my light in that direction. My alarm went at 4 a.m. and I set off into the darkness, careful not to wake the motionless man who'd unwittingly shared my campsite, and lavishly recalling those blissful seconds I'd enjoyed between lying down and passing out, as I pressed my stiff legs into motion, knowing that as long as I kept them moving, eventually their energy would return.

It was a slow start. My eyes kept closing even after the sky lightened, and every so often I would succumb to the temptation of a grassy verge or an opening in the trees, set my alarm for ten minutes, and guiltily lie down for more sleep. It was only when my dreams were punctured by the sound of a freewheel hub whirring past that I leapt up, spotted another cyclist vanishing over the brow of a hill and gave chase, convinced that this must be Jayne overtaking me.

As I drew level with the other rider, however, I discovered that it wasn't Jayne, but rather an amiable, bearded Belgian named Rudy. We followed each other for a while, careful to leave enough space between us to avoid accusations of drafting, and eventually descended into a large town spread across the confluence of two rivers, reassuring each other excitedly that somewhere this size would definitely be able to provide us with coffee and pastries.

Fortified, we continued, drifting apart as the morning wore on, but knowing we'd run into each other down the road. The landscape opened out around me, wooded slopes gave way to vast, flat fields, and conical mountains began to appear on the western horizon, partially obscured by the damp grey clouds that hung in the air. The countryside smelt moist and fruity and fertile, as it might after a rainstorm. It was close to 1 p.m. by the time I reached the outskirts of Clermont-Ferrand, and the steep green peaks that surrounded the city were ribboned with mists as the rain that had soaked the leaders the previous night evaporated past me, back up to the sky from whence it came.

Checkpoint One was full of surprises. I was the first female rider to arrive. Mike was still there, grinning when he saw me, but looking faintly flustered, since his car was supposed to be tailing the leaders, so should have left hours ago. I was told that Josh Ibbett had pulled out, citing back pain. And James Hayden was sitting on a bar stool in his

Lycra. He'd arrived in the middle of the night, he told me, shortly behind Kristof and Neil Phillips, but his ride hadn't gone as it should, and he'd realised that what he'd thought was allergies playing up was in fact a chest infection. So he'd stopped for the night, seen a doctor that morning, and wasn't sure what he was going to do now. Probably wait for the antibiotics to take effect and then carry on riding towards the finish, though the win he'd poured his heart and soul into all year was now beyond his reach. I felt bitterly disappointed for him, though he seemed philosophical, calmly watching the other racers come and go as he sipped his orange juice. I wished him luck, finished my sandwich and set off for the Alps.

Chapter Nine

The bottle of iced tea was far too small, and cost far too much, but was my excuse to spend half an hour at the wooden table outside this tiny roadside café in Slovenia, listening to the traffic roaring past and exchanging nods with the old men who came and went from the bar inside.

It was my eighth day on the road, though a dot-watching friend I'd been corresponding with insisted it was only the seventh. I was more inclined to trust his arithmetic than my own, yet several attempts to count up the days I'd spent cycling, delineated by brief slumbers in Alpine meadows and behind bus shelters, persistently yielded the number eight. And since it was on Day Eight that I'd come to grief the previous year, I decided that if I could get over this hurdle, I'd already have outdone myself. Beyond lay uncharted territory that thrilled me more than it scared me.

My early start, and the hundred miles I must have ridden

already, made it feel like late afternoon, although I knew it must still be before midday. I took a quick inventory of my condition. My legs were stiff and swollen, bulging fatly from the tight cuffs of my cycling shorts, and their joints were worryingly sore. I had always considered myself lucky to avoid the knee problems that so many other cyclists manage and endure, and was quietly concerned that, since I entered the Alps three days previously, mine had hurt with every pedal stroke. Getting back on the bike each morning, or even after a coffee stop, had become increasingly painful, and I was using lower and lower gears to try and reduce the pressure I put through them.

My lungs felt crusty and full of cobwebs. The night after the first checkpoint I had ridden till 2 a.m., up and down sweeping hills, noticing how the temperature dropped with each descent, and remembering the more severe temperature inversions I'd experienced when riding through Alaska two years previously. Eventually I lay down beside a river, and spent the next hour awake, too cold to doze off, but convincing myself that to stand up, walk a couple of steps to my bike and rummage for my thermal gilet and foil blanket would disrupt the sleep I felt sure was just around the corner. Eventually I gave in, stepped out into the chilly air and, after wrapping the blanket round my feet and the gilet round my torso, finally drifted off. But the cold woke me again before my alarm, and I rode out into the dawn, watching mist rise from the folds of the landscape, and finally realising what a fool I'd been to camp at the bottom of a damp valley.

An hour into the ride I hit a steep hill, my lungs began to protest and I coughed until my throat hurt, then noticed when I stopped for breakfast that my head was hot and throbbing. I told myself it was mostly down to lack of sleep, promised myself a guesthouse that night and decided optimistically that this would replace the pain in my feet (which had by now mysteriously dissipated) as my *malaise du jour*.

The cough had continued, mostly ignored and unremarked, as I knew that if I thought directly about it I would be obliged to admit this was a silly state in which to contest a bike race, that it might be better for me to stop, at least for a day or two. When I reached Checkpoint Three in the Dolomites, where Juliana was volunteering, she started when she heard what was by now a deep and throaty cough echoing all the way back into my chest, and asked if I was OK. I changed the subject quickly, not wanting to risk being told to take it easy, and set off up Passo di Giau, trying to force air in around what felt like the moss growing inside my lungs, stopping on every single hairpin to get my breath back. When I reached the picture-perfect summit, I gazed lightheadedly at its shining towers of rock and intricate Alpine meadows, as if they were some fabrication of my exhausted mind. I tweeted a selfie, marvelling that I looked no different from how I might normally; that no one, looking at my smile, would guess how feebly I'd crawled up this mountain, dripping with sweat in the afternoon sun and trying to pull enough of the thin air into my damaged lungs to keep myself going. At the fifteenth hairpin a carload of nuns had applauded and cheered me on, one of them leaning out of the back window in her black-and-white robes, and at various points I had been passed by fellow racers, soaring back down the pass to continue their journey south. I was told that a few – Kristof included – had continued north, following a route that, though longer, included only one more col before following river valleys and flatlands through Slovenia, and thus gave them a strong advantage over riders like me, whose legs were empty after three days of multiple mountain passes.

After Passo di Giau I had improvised a route that, rather than following the Piave Valley south, as I knew other riders would, took me up over one of the shoulders of raised ground overlooking the Venetian Plain, so that I could spend one more night breathing in the mountains, free from the maddening din of the crickets, the hot sticky night air and the risk that last summer's nightmare would engulf me once again.

But unlike the shrieking, sweltering inferno I'd feared, Northern Italy was relatively benign. I swept down the hill in darkness, scarcely seeing another vehicle until the pale pink sunrise began to animate the farmland, vineyards, industrial estates and quiet, red-roofed towns. I was too exhausted to put up much resistance, rolling passively along the flat roads, riding in the smaller ring, reminding myself that, no matter how incapable I felt, how empty my legs, if I just kept pushing the pedals gently round and round, I was still doing it.

I had promised myself a coffee break in Trieste: a brief interlude where I'd sit alone in a sunny piazza, forget I was in a race and romanticise to myself about the empires that have triumphed and tussled over this tiny strip of land between the mountains and the sea. But the southbound traffic thickened around me, its fumes scorching into my groaning lungs, and badly driven cars towing enormous boats forced me to swerve repeatedly onto the narrow grass verge. I decided I'd had enough, and started looking out for a café to stop in. And shortly, helmet and gloves off, iced tea in hand, I checked the map and found I had bypassed Trieste altogether – it was now behind me, and I had unwittingly crossed my own imaginary line between Romance and Slavic, pizza and bürek. A text appeared from Marija, who was excited to see that I was back in her country, and wanted to warn me about a storm that was due to hit Northern Croatia that night. She was on holiday with her family on Cres, she told me, otherwise she'd have come out to meet me.

My body blossomed with tiredness as I sat there. The last time I'd had a shower was in a hostel in Fribourg, listening to distant fireworks as the oblivious Swiss celebrated their national day, the night before I reached Checkpoint Two in Grindelwald and the night after I'd shivered sleeplessly beside the river. My skin itched with the restless discomfort of sleep deprivation, with the encrusted salt of three days of sweat, and with the pimples and insect bites that were beginning to pockmark my face. The white parts of my jersey were now grey and brown, the blue parts stained white with sweat. My hair hung lank and matted from my cycling cap, and I wondered if I would ever be able to get my fingers through it again, or if I would have to hack it off when I finished the race. I dug grimy fingers into my eye sockets and inspected the assortment of deceased insects that emerged, wondering if any had been visible to the woman who served me the iced tea.

I scanned Twitter, curious as ever to see what the rest of the racers (and the dot-watchers) had to say, drawing as much comfort from those who were thriving as from those who were suffering. Kristof had passed through Checkpoint Four and was in Serbia, following the route he had taken twice before: through the mountains into Bulgaria, then along the treacherous E80, towards the Turkish border. Riders from previous years recounted their experiences on this road with the theatrical dread I used to describe mine in the Po Valley. It was said to be pitted with potholes, strewn with roadkill alarming in both size and profusion, and frequented by unlit juggernauts that rattled past terrified cyclists with inches to spare. I had ridden this road five years previously, and didn't remember it being as bad as they all claimed. I wondered if it was that my years as a courier and long-distance tourer had increased my tolerance of traffic, or simply that the road had deteriorated since I was there. Perhaps a toll had been introduced on the highway, sending drivers back onto the old E80.

James Hayden was 400km ahead of me, somewhere in rural Bosnia and, to the surprise and unrestrained excitement of the dot-watchers, back at the sharp end of the race. He had taken thirty hours off at Checkpoint One, waiting for his antibiotics to take effect, then started again, now in 148th place and more than a day's ride behind the leaders, announcing that he intended to chase his way back into the top ten. I had reached Grindelwald before he did, but the following day he had breezed through the pack as most riders crossed Albula Pass. I was a long way north at that point, following a bike path through cornfields, little knowing that it would eventually become a gravel track, and then a hiking trail, along which I bumped slowly, swearing out loud at myself and almost weeping with frustration at my stupidity, knowing that at least a few people would be watching my dot diverge from the rest of the pack, zooming in to see what terrain I was covering, and speculating over why I'd made that particular routing decision.

I'd known that anger was a waste of energy, and that by letting anxiety quicken my legs I was only going to hasten my exhaustion, but I found I couldn't help myself – I'd take a deep breath, tell myself to calm down, then within moments I'd be sprinting again. At that point I was only five days into the race (which seemed like both a lot and a little), yet already I was at the mercy of my emotions as much as the weather or the hills. Shortly after breakfast I had rolled through the cornfields, watching the sharp rays of the sun filtering through the high mountains around me, and begun to sing, enjoying the brief burst of energy the caffeine had given me, and relishing the promise of another day's riding. The song was Corinne Bailey Rae's 'Put Your Records On', and although neither the words nor the melody held any particular significance for me, when I reached the chorus my voice cracked and I began to cry. This puzzled me – nothing had been going on in my head to lead to this emotional outpouring, and I scanned the words of the song, unable to find anything that could have triggered my tear ducts. I started singing again, and again, when I reached the chorus, I abruptly started to cry, as if someone had pressed a button. Amused, I tried it a couple more times – sang the first verse, reached the chorus, started to cry – and eventually gave up and continued riding, wondering if I'd ever come up with an explanation for what my subconscious mind had been doing in that moment.

But despite my detours, I was now a long way ahead of Jayne and the other female racers, and most of them had now been slowed further by a storm in the Alps. The most recent pictures of people passing through Checkpoint Three showed riders swathed in waterproofs, grinning bravely at the camera and displaying hands that were pale and wrinkled from their sodden gloves. I wondered if that was the storm that was due to hit me that night, and redoubled my resolution that I'd sleep indoors. Lee responded to my complaints about swollen knees with a suggestion that I take ibuprofen to reduce the inflammation. I followed her advice and by the time I reached the Croatian border both the swelling and the pain had disappeared, as if by magic.

By sunset I was inching my way up a steep single-track road, past wizened trees and low-lying scrub, the pale karst rock of the Adriatic coast emerging everywhere from the undergrowth, as though mere flora could not contain it. To my right, the landscape fell away towards the sea, now shimmering white and silver in the dying light of the day, the islands of Krk and Cres silhouetted against its brilliance. I sent Marija a text, told her I was waving at her, and carried on cycling, concerned that I was riding further and further from any place populous enough to contain a guesthouse, and regretting that I hadn't followed the example of a German racer I'd met an hour or two previously. We had parted at a junction, where he descended in search of a hotel, and I carried on climbing up into the hills that towered over the coastline.

But before the sun had left the sky I found a tiny village called Donji Zagon, nestled into the hillside, its grey-white walls and red tiles glowing in the rich resinous intensity of the evening light. On its outskirts was a two-storey house with a sign that announced a room to rent, and a middle-aged man called Drago ('like dragon!') introduced me to his wife, ushered me into their spare room, and warned me, when I told him of my 4 a.m. departure plan, of the impending storm.

I wallowed lengthily in the bathroom, laundering my clothes in the sink and guiltily helping myself to a handful of Drago's wife's conditioner, then watched in fascination as a hairball the size of a rat gathered at the bottom of the bathtub. By the time I was clean the sun had set and the landscape sunk into two dimensions, the blazing colours I'd ridden through reduced to dust and ashes. I fell asleep immediately, but was awoken shortly afterwards by the wind howling outside, shaking the trees, rattling the windows and hurling the patio chairs across the terrace. And then came the rain, the steady sizzle of droplets on leaves, eaves and dry soil, the syncopated rhythms of water dripping from branches and gutters, and the sudden crescendos as rogue gusts of wind threw handfuls of water directly at my window. I dozed for a while, remembering rainy nights in my tent on the Qinghai Plateau and in a soggy playing field near Fukushima, reawakened when the cracks of thunder began, then drifted off again, satisfied that I could not have made a better decision about where to spend the night.

I packed myself into my jacket and gloves and overshoes before setting off the next morning, but the storm was already blowing itself out, and the gusts of wind that hurtled across the hillside were mostly dry. The road quickly deteriorated into gravel, a quick check of the map told me that a detour would involve too much backtracking to be palatable, and I stumbled on through the twilight, loose stones rattling under my feet and dust and debris whirling through the air around me. The wind felt directly personal and I attacked it with an anger that hovered about my head like a swarm of bees, searching pettily for an object. For the first time in over a week I remembered the torturous subplots of my recent heartbreak, and seethed with the same indignation and disbelief that had weighted my thoughts for most of that summer. Now though, they imbued me with a crazed energy (at the back of my mind I knew a night in a bed had also done its work), and I battled on, tilting at the wind, furious with everything, wrestling the air and the bike and the gravel as if I were a drunk being ejected from a bar.

After an hour of pedalling and pushing, as dawn broke around me and grey light filtered through the lingering clouds, the track dipped down and rejoined the main road at the apex of a large switchback, and the German rider

I'd met the previous evening was riding up towards me. We greeted each other with sympathetic grins. The coastline of Croatia at this point was nothing but an enormous hillside, rising out of the Adriatic and segregating the coast road from the rest of the country like a prison wall. Philipp, as his name turned out to be, had slept lower down and ridden uphill to reach this point, whereas I had kept my height, though sacrificed a lot of speed to the gravel.

We spent the rest of the day leapfrogging each other. Twice I emerged from supermarkets to see him pull up at the entrance, and once I walked into a tiny village café to find him sitting at the bar, sipping an espresso and eating a packaged croissant, to the genial hilarity of the other patrons. Both of us were in a holiday humour, though whether that had to do with the proximity of another racer or with the relief of a relatively undemanding topography I had no idea. I had explored Croatia's coastline and islands before, and traversed the interminable suburbia of its eastern wing after quitting the previous year's race, but I had never visited this region and I was instantly in love. I rode through rippling green fields – the wind by now having died down to a gentle breeze – through lush woodland and past tidy brown-and-white houses in various states of completion and habitation. Above me the sky was a symphony of blues and greys, and the temperature was more reminiscent of a Welsh summer's day than a Balkan one. My early-morning fury forgotten, I rolled placidly along, planning the conversations in which I'd tell all my friends to come and cycle through Croatia.

Occasionally I'd remind myself of the previous afternoon, remembering the sense of bicycle and knees creaking as I'd hauled myself up a stiff urban climb in Rijeka, fat drops of sweat oozing from my face as if I were being wrung out. I'd stopped in yet another café, for yet another iced tea, anticipating the frozen weight of the can, not so much for the brief refreshment it would offer as for its assurance that coldness could still exist in the world. As usual I'd sat as far away from other drinkers as I could, hoping to conceal the stench rising from my body and clothing. But the storm had swept all of that away, and today I swam blithely through the cooler air, dancing like a swallow along the quiet roads, still filthier than I'd ever be at home, but satisfied that the previous night's frenzy of washing had restored me to social palatability.

Towards the end of the day the road skirted a range of hills, and I gazed out over the turquoise lake that filled the broad valley to my left, and the striated grey mountains rising up beyond it. According to my secret twelve-day plan, this was where I should have spent the previous night, and I felt pleasantly surprised that I was still less than a day behind the schedule I'd thought was over-ambitious. I'd assumed the Alps would slow me down more than they had.

A flurry of text messages arrived. My family were assembling in Wales, to celebrate my brother's thirtieth birthday around a campfire in the field, and I sent them a smiling selfie as I rode along, a blue-and-gold sunset visible over my shoulder, my eyes unfocused and the skin around them crumpled like a paper bag – a foretaste of wrinkles that will be a permanent feature in a decade or two. I stopped to fix a puncture and as I got back on the bike I was engulfed with a wave of tiredness so powerful that I felt drunk with it.

I'm surprised that ultra-cyclists haven't had more conversations about the various flavours of tiredness. I had heard talk of the Sleep Monster, who stalks the exhausted rider on long dark nights, and had hounded me through the cold early mornings of this race, before I shifted my sleep pattern to awaken with the dawn. But there were times when I thought of nothing but sleep, yet could still ride (albeit slowly) all day and night without stopping. Was I less tired in these moments, or just differently tired?

Tiredness expressed itself in so many more ways than simply the urge to sleep. For the last few days I had bemoaned the soft emptiness of a body that felt it had nothing more to give – and yet I'd continued to cycle, somehow drumming more power out of muscles that felt spent. Occasionally I'd have a surge of energy as strong as those I'd experience on Friday afternoons when I was a courier, and for an hour or two everything would roll along nicely, save for the tinnitus buzz of exhaustion in the background – it was always there, never fully disguised.

Tiredness could emerge as clumsiness, or the inability to make a decision. I had rapidly evolved my supermarket shops so that I no longer needed to – everything was in the same place in Lidl, no matter what country I was in, and I'd march through the aisles, collecting orange juice, cherry tomatoes, bread, cheese and salami, and whatever the local pastries happened to be, almost without breaking stride. If any of these things were out of stock, or not where I'd expected, I'd stare at the shelf for several minutes like a stalled engine, trying to compute what was missing, what a palatable alternative might be, and where I might find it.

There was the tiredness that attached itself to every buried emotion, and floated them to the surface like a life-buoy. I didn't know why I had started to cry a few mornings ago, when at that moment I hadn't been thinking about anything more cumbersome than how pretty the light looked as it peered from behind the mountains. I told myself my subconscious mind was probably too tired to keep everything in order – like an overworked librarian, who has left books piled up on the tables and shelved willy-nilly, P. G. Wodehouse rubbing shoulders with *Jude the Obscure*.

There was the tiredness that slowed and weakened me, turning the slightest incline into a mountain and the lightest breeze into a gale, so that I cursed in disbelief at my sluggishness. During these ordeals, I'd remember the times I've ridden along trying to prevent my eyes from closing, and I'd tell myself that *that* was tiredness, that what I was experiencing now was merely weakness, either of the body or the spirit, and that I had better keep going, rather than prove to myself that I was inadequate. This was the tiredness that would drain my resolve, and see me stopping at every service station or café-bar I passed, despite repeatedly vowing not to.

But now I had no choice but to stop. In the small part of my brain that still functioned, I understood that I was powerless against this flood of exhaustion, and that the only possible reaction was to find myself somewhere to sleep as quickly as possible. I was approaching a town called Sinj, and although I'd planned to ride longer into the night, when I got there I headed for the first hotel I found on the map. The tiredness was syrupy, intoxicating and almost irresistible, and I muttered instructions to myself as I navigated carefully around the junctions towards the hotel. I passed a bakery and made the excruciating decision to stop, knowing that I'd need food before I slept and food when I woke up, and marvelled distantly at how adeptly I was looking after myself, despite the imminent danger of losing consciousness.

The hotel had a wedding party in full swing, the whole building reverberating with dance music. I waited for two intolerable minutes in the echoing marble lobby for the receptionist to book me in, twitching with the urgency of my tiredness, resenting anything that stood between me and sleep and knowing that I'd pay whatever sum he demanded. He didn't raise an eyebrow when I proposed taking the bike upstairs, either seeing that I was in no fit state to argue, or wanting to offer some gesture of apology for the noise, and I cut him off in the middle of his explanation of breakfast timings. I would be long gone by then.

Never has a hotel room felt so anonymous. If you asked me to sketch the layout, I couldn't – I was aware of the corridor alongside the bathroom where I leaned my bike, the beige shower curtain, and the single bed nearest the door. The rest of the room remains a mystery, and I couldn't tell you whether the other bed was a single or a double, what size and shape the window was, or even if there was a window.

I resisted the impulse to lie down fully clothed, without showering, remembering that I'd only be setting myself up for saddlesore the following day, fumbled through the most cursory of washes, and then sprawled naked and supine, my splayed legs propped up on pillows, with the dual purpose of draining the acid from my muscles and airing my crotch. My final thought was what a horrendous view someone would get if they stumbled into this room in the dead of night.

When my alarm went I was still in the same position, my knees so stiff that they felt rusted into place. I and they both groaned when I tried to move them, so I took two ibuprofen, set my alarm for another twenty minutes and then got up to face the day, pleased with myself for finding a solution that had also enabled me to sleep for longer. When I left the hotel the wedding music had stopped, but the streets and bars of Sinj still heaved with people – pretty young women with long hair and short dresses, and tanned men in jeans and pressed shirts. I bought my breakfast in a bakery clearly catering to drunken carbohydrate-seekers, got back on my bike and headed for the border.

Chapter Ten

My second breakfast that morning was from a roadside bakery in the border town of Imotski, though I dimly recalled stopping for an espresso at around 5 a.m., and watching a lurid music video as I speculated about the couple who sat wordlessly at the next table, the woman younger and smaller than the man, and clad in full wedding finery. The day was grey and windy, and when another racer joined me outside the bakery, I found my tongue was too heavy to make conversation. All I could do was stare at him, trying to approximate a smile to show that I was at least friendly. His name was Stefan and I hadn't expected to see him again after Checkpoint Three, where he'd pulled ahead of me as I struggled breathlessly up Passo di Giau, and then followed a more sensible route down towards Venice, rather than working in one final col, as I had. But here he was again, and we set off towards the border within sight of each other, though a few minutes into Bosnia I quietly stopped and let him pull ahead. I was too tired to match his pace, and didn't want to endure the struggle of trying to keep up, or the humiliation of watching him retreat further and further up the road ahead of me.

'Today is going to be an exercise in keeping going,' I told myself, and tried to think about how much worse it could be. I had no saddlesore, to my amazement. My back was still supple, and the blazing agony that had assailed my feet for the first few days of the race had settled into a gentle smoulder. My cough was slowly drying up – what two days ago had felt like boulders moving around in my lungs had reduced to some polite hacking every twenty minutes or so. Nothing was that bad.

'I've just got to stay awake', I thought, 'and stay on the road, and keep turning the pedals, and not worry about going fast, just keep moving.'

As I rode into Bosnia the tree-lined road opened out into a plain and I repeated this wisdom to myself, dismayed but unsurprised by how little difference it made. Despite knowing that a few hours of energy might lurk ahead of me, I was unable to summon them any closer, or to believe that this all-consuming tiredness could ever have an end to it.

Bosnia felt unfriendly. I had chosen a route that took me north of the coast, and yet south of Mostar, where many other riders were going, and the road offered little diversion, passing through a series of hamlets that never quite coalesced into a town, and across long stretches of dull farmland. The houses I saw were often uninhabited, pockmarked with bullet holes or missing chunks of masonry, and this only added to my lingering gloom. After a few hours the landscape tightened around me and I found myself following a rocky canyon that funnelled the wind towards me, concentrating and strengthening it until I felt more like I was swimming into a strong current than riding a bike. I felt unequal to this wind, and rather than returning its anger, as I had the previous morning, I feebly submitted, dropping into lower and lower gears as I shuffled up the gorge. I marvelled that this shallow incline could prove such hard work, and resented every person in the occasional cars that passed me, imagining them sniggering and heckling at how pathetic I looked, and wondering why I didn't either give up or speed up.

On one of my frequent roadside rest stops I checked Twitter and discovered that Kristof had arrived in Çanakkale, finishing the race in eight days and fifteen hours. The tweet was accompanied by a black-and-white portrait, in which he leant against a stone wall, his shrivelled eyes staring off into the distance, and his skin, even in monochrome, many shades darker than it had been when we shared *tartes au poire* in Geraardsbergen.

'Brutal, just brutal,' he had exclaimed on arrival, and I tried to imagine how much worse his suffering might have been than mine, pushing harder and sleeping less, but yet again found it an imaginative leap as insuperable as when I tried to reassure myself of how much stronger I would feel in the future. It was impossible to picture the calm, humorous man I had met at the start grunting with pain, or struggling up a hill too long and steep for him. Even in the photos I'd seen of him during the race he had looked inscrutable, sitting at an ornate wooden bar I now recognised from Checkpoint Three with a pint of coke; pausing on a mountain pass to don a jacket for the descent, the thin yellow fabric whipping away from him in the wind. Unlike the other men, he had remained clean-shaven throughout the race. I couldn't picture him wasting time in front of hotel mirrors, but the thought of him brandishing a razor as he cycled along was equally implausible, and his smooth chin only added to the mystique with which everyone was so eager to invest him. Although he told us of his difficulties, he did not display them.

> *Pain – has an Element of Blank –*
> *It cannot recollect*
> *When it begun – or if there were –*
> *A time when it was not –*

I had occasionally turned Emily Dickinson's lines over in my head when I caught myself veering towards superlatives to describe whatever hardship I was going through. I was suspicious of the ease with which I'd declare 'this is the toughest day I've *ever* spent on the bike,' reminding myself that I'd thought that numerous times before, that in fact I had doubted myself on those occasions too, and pondered the handful of days I'd decided were the 'toughest', no longer able to remember precisely what it was that I had felt to be so tough.

There seemed to be a veil of amnesia between the moments when cycling was so difficult that I couldn't conceive of a way to keep myself doing it and the rest of the time, when it reverted to an activity I found enjoyably challenging, and sometimes even easy. When I was struggling I regarded my own encouragement ('Nothing lasts forever! You'll come through this and feel strong again!') with the utmost scepticism, unable to believe it except in the most academic sense – much as, all of that summer, I had assured myself that my depression would lift, that despite the hopelessness I felt, I would eventually fall in love with life again, just as I always had before. I could never quite make myself believe it.

And yet once I was on the other side of the veil, my struggle resolved itself to glory, and even the grim tussles with my own psyche took on a heroic glint, dooming me endlessly to repeat them. When I had sat at my desk and plotted mountainous detours into my route, it was with a sense of disbelief that, when I finally got there, I would be suffering so much that I couldn't muster a few ounces of energy to go and explore.

Why was it, I wondered, that in spite of my long experience, I failed to recognise the full extent of my suffering unless I was in the midst of it? And, conversely, why, when I felt as exhausted and weak as I did currently, couldn't I believe what I'd many times proved to be true – that I'd eventually come through it and feel strong again? I rode slowly on up the canyon. Maybe on some level I did believe it.

The landscape opened out as I descended into a broad valley and cowered on the windswept forecourt of a garage for a few minutes, eating a box of chocolate biscuits I'd picked up in the bakery before crossing the border, since it had seemed unnecessary to carry Bosnian money when I only had 130km to ride in the country. Riders like Kristof and James Hayden would go that far without putting a foot down, I scolded myself, concerned by how rapidly my stockpile was disappearing.

I followed the road up the side of the valley, passed by a couple of men in an old car, but otherwise alone, realising that, since I saw Stefan outside the bakery that morning, I hadn't had any interaction with another person. The family who ran the garage where I'd eaten my biscuits had stared across the forecourt, but not approached me. At the top of

Running towards my bike at the start of the Strathpuffer twenty-four-hour mountain bike race.

Sarah Outen comforts me with tea at the end of a long hard night on the bike.

Mike waits to lead the racers around Geraardsbergen
at the start of the Transcontinental.

The racers set off, by sunset and torchlight.

Passing the time of day with the locals in Montenegro.

My cockpit, loaded with food, drink and navigational devices. The more accessible everything was, the longer I could ride without stopping.

An unknown racer rests in a bus shelter, somewhere in Ireland.

(previous page) Enjoying the Durmitor National Park, en route to Checkpoint Four.

Resting on the ferry between Eceabat and Canakkale,
minutes from the end of the race.

Sharing tiramisu with Kristof the evening after finishing.

Descending into the Elan Valley with Mike, the last time we rode together.

the hill an enormous dog bounded out of a gateway, snarling and snapping, and the only thing that saved me was the road, which mercifully bent downwards at that point and meant I could pick up speed. I rode on, shakily, thinking about the people who had nodded at me from their stone-walled garden, but done nothing to help.

I reached a bare junction, surrounded by windswept heath, and remembered from my route planning that this was where I took a minor road across the border into Montenegro. I had painstakingly scanned the satellite map, to assure myself that the road was surfaced and passable, and thought no more of it until reports started to appear on Twitter of some of the race leaders taking an 'unconventional' route towards Checkpoint Four. A photograph of Neil Phillips showed him summiting what looked like a hiking trail, with a shimmering lake behind him, and accompanying debate as to whether this more direct route was a good idea, given that it included 10km of gravel, or whether Neil would have done better to save his legs and tyres, and go the longer way round. One commentator speculated that he might get into trouble when he tried to leave Montenegro, given that he had passed no border crossing and received no entry stamp.

What had appeared to be a crossroads on my map was in fact a T-junction, and I rode up and down the north-south road, cross-referencing my Garmin with my navigation apps, in search of the road that would take me east. My heart sank when I realised I'd been in the right place after all. The faintest trace of tyre tracks led up the bank from the main road, and a dusty farm track spooled off towards the rising hills that marked the border. I followed it tentatively, through the bleached grass and pale scrub, picking over my various options. I could continue along this track, and see if it improved, or became tarmac further along. Or I could go back, detour north or south, and take a more reliable route across the border. But I hated to turn my bike around once I'd started to ride in a certain direction, and both of those options would mean many more hours of pedalling.

The track hardened, and then all at once I was riding on tight, newly laid tarmac across the valley, breathing a sigh of relief that I hadn't been put off by the initial roughness of the track. The road descended gradually as I neared the edge of the valley, towards a small cluster of red-roofed houses, tucked in at the base of the hills. And then the tarmac ran out, and my heart sank again as I bumped along a dusty track, the stones sliding and rattling under my wheels. I toyed once again with the decision to turn back, but I was even further along now, and still moving forward. I decided to keep going. There would only be about 10km of gravel, probably leading up to the pass Neil had crossed, and then down into Montenegro, and I knew I'd spend the extra hours on tarmac wishing I had had the courage to endure it, rather than slowing my progress still further. It was interesting, I noted, as I stood on the pedals to navigate the bike round a steep bend, that in contrast with my constant and often irresistible urge to stop riding, turning back still felt like a taboo I couldn't break. Somehow, I had managed to plait the necessity of forward motion so tightly into my will that to transgress it felt like sacrilege.

The road, with its loose, dusty stones and steep, winding climbs, was a difficult one, and it took all of my strength and focus to ride it. But I spent that afternoon in the same trance I've entered in other remote parts of the world. The brief panic that I was losing time, that I was making a terrible mistake and everyone must be watching my dot get steadily more and more lost, that I might even fail to make it through to Montenegro, and end up retracing these kilometres and losing even *more* time, all wilted away in the face of the rushing, roaring glow of excitement that flared up to replace it.

The road pulled me off into the hills, higher and higher, further and further away from the busy traffic of Bosnia and Croatia, past small hamlets, where occasionally a lone person or dog would watch my progress, themselves as motionless as the landscape, up into the trees, and up again out of the trees, on and on into a wilderness whose end I couldn't foresee and whose length I wasn't sure if I had it in me (or my food pouches and water bottles) to traverse. Something about this road inflamed me, igniting reserves of energy I thought I must long ago have plundered.

For hours and hours I forgot about tiredness, and all of the itches and aches that had been plaguing me. I even forgot about the race, my mind instead filled with the resounding chord of fear and excitement I've felt on previous journeys, in Qinghai, in Iceland, in Alaska, when I pressed on into heat or cold or wildness that my deepest instincts feared might kill me, even though reason insisted that it wouldn't, that this was after all a road, and that it would lead somewhere, eventually, and that if I could just keep going, I'd reach safety.

At the top of the pass, just as my phone pinged to let me know I was crossing a border, I found a small graveyard, filled with headstones of polished marble that seemed out of place among the unkempt trees and shrubs. I wondered who was buried here, on a remote international border, suspected it might have something to do with the Balkan War, and concluded reluctantly that I didn't have time to find out.

It was not then downhill all the way into Montenegro. The road rose and fell repeatedly, leading me further and further into the hills, and I battled on, with a creeping background fear that, even if this road *did* connect to the highway I wanted to be on, there was a chance the border area might be patrolled, that I wasn't supposed to be here, and would be turned back and sent on a lengthy detour to an official crossing.

Here and there I'd discover a strip of concrete spread across the gravel, usually close to some homestead or hamlet, and on one heady occasion I found myself back on tarmac, on a narrow lane winding upwards through a tunnel of deciduous trees, reminding me so closely of Mid Wales that for a few seconds I forgot where I was. But the gravel resumed, and I left that mysterious strip of tarmac behind and continued down into a long valley, lined with soft grass and tiny Alpine flowers. As I thundered round a hairpin, my front tyre deflated with a sudden loud hiss, and I stopped in dismay to find an inch-long slash in the rubber, the white sealant leaking out like spilt milk. I took the wheel off and got out my spare inner tube, anxiety humming at the back of my head that both my water and my energy were going to run out eventually, and that I still had no idea when this road would lead me back to civilisation.

The inner tube was too small – a skinny remnant from my courier days – and no matter how much I pumped, I couldn't get it to fill my 28mm tyre. I saw that this could be the end of everything. My options were few, and none of them easy. I could walk, for as long as it took to reach a bike shop in this under-populated country. That might well be several days, although there was a chance a kind local might offer me a lift. I'd passed no vehicles, but I'd seen jeeps and ancient cars parked outside houses. Finishing – let alone winning – the race was probably now beyond my reach: there was a rule that, if you had to accept a lift in an emergency, you were obliged to return to the point where you'd stopped riding, and continue from there. The practicalities of this, as I sat stranded in this valley, not knowing when I'd next encounter a human being, or how many hundreds of miles it might be to wherever I could acquire a new tyre, were too daunting to contemplate.

Well, you have to sort this out somehow, said a small voice in my head. *And there's no point in panicking – that'll just waste energy, and you'll end up exactly where you started. So what'll make a difference? Food? Water? Sleep? Have something to eat.*

I unzipped my frame pack, and pulled out the malt loaf I had been hoarding as an emergency food stash. Sitting on the grassy bank that overlooked the blond gravel and my injured bike, I devoured it in just a few minutes, remembering the malt loaf I'd eaten at the summit of Ventoux the previous year, listening to the wind roaring around Marion and Kevin's camper van. And then I looked into my frame pack again, wondering if by some implausible stroke of luck I had happened to bring another inner tube – and there, tucked in behind where the malt loaf had sat, was a brand-new 28mm tube, rolled up and fastened with an elastic band, reassuringly plump. I remembered, faintly, throwing an extra tube – the thin one – into my seat pack as I fretted away the last hour before catching the train to Dover, thinking that, as I had space, I might as well fill it. I had had what I needed all along.

And now it was with calm contentment that I unfurled my Leatherman to cut a strip from a bag of Lidl cashew nuts, carefully positioned it between tyre and tube, and reached for my pump. I'd been carrying this pump for four years, ever since a friend sent it out to Japan to replace one I'd worn out on my long ride across Asia. Steff had died shortly afterwards, passing away in his London flat as I battled through a storm in Akita, and every time I used this pump I thought of him, grateful that his generosity had got me out of yet another tight spot.

Tyre reinflated, I carried on along the gravel, now attentive to its sharper flints, and aware that only one of my bottles had anything left in it. At the top of each hill I stopped for a sip, and when I occasionally saw a house in the distance, usually at the end of another imposing gravel track, I debated whether to go and ask for water. For now, shyness won out, though I knew this would change as my desperation mounted. When I eventually came to what passed for a village – a handful of buildings clustered quietly together on an open plateau – I spied a police jeep parked outside the first house, and feared that this might be the moment I was apprehended, turned back or at the very least held up by a lengthy monolingual interrogation about passports and papers. Through the open door, as I approached, I could see a pair of uniformed legs, and I knew that my fate would depend on whether their owner was asleep, looking in the opposite direction or busy with something on his desk.

Pedalling lightly to hide the sound of my freewheel, and carefully choosing the smoothest part of the road to avoid disturbing the stones, I stole past the building, and looked in to see a tired, dark-haired man sitting on a plastic garden chair and holding an ancient firearm. His eyes met mine with no expression whatsoever, and his head turned to follow my progress as I rode past.

I continued, watching the clouds flush delicately as the sun sank behind them, at once fervently hoping that I would reach the tarmac soon and reassuring myself that I was capable of riding this gravel road in the dark. I had survived a lot worse. Tangled amongst my ambivalence was an elusive sense that I didn't want this to end. The difficulty of this road had forced me to muster all of the physical strength and mental concentration I could, and for all of that afternoon I had become, in a slightly different way from how I had on Ventoux, a creature composed entirely of will. Nothing remained but the necessity of moving forward, and the exhaustion with which I'd toiled through Bosnia that morning was forgotten. Peripherally, I was aware that my forearms were shaking, that my thirst was rising, and that coiled deep within me was the gnawing insistence that I lie down and sleep. I knew that eventually my fire would die down, that I couldn't possibly sustain this energy for the rest of the race, and that I'd have to give in once again to tiredness. I both longed for that moment and dreaded it, wishing I could hold on to the purity of my naked will, but knowing that strength, of whatever sort, must always fade.

Just before dark I rumbled my way down a final vertiginous switchback and was back on tarmac, the bike suddenly floating forward as one's arms will float upwards after putting down heavy bags. I descended for an hour along that dark, empty valley, drifting downward like thistledown, still longing for the road to end, still longing for it to last forever. And then another junction, and down below me a carpet of bright lights. This town was not on my route, but I descended into the valley anyway, riding through the kindly aura of yellow light cast from porches and kitchen windows, and finally found a grocery store, moments from closing. I paced the aisles, unable to reconcile my overwhelming hunger and thirst with the specifics of choice. Then the small voice in my head spoke up again:

You just need food. It doesn't matter what. You need bulk, so buy bread. You need protein, so buy a tin of fish. You need snacks for the road, so buy nuts. There's no way you can overdo this, so buy whatever sweets and biscuits take your fancy. Don't worry if it doesn't feel right. It will do.

And I lolled on the forecourt with my unlikely picnic piled between my legs, tearing off chunks of white bread to scrape tomato sauce from a can of tuna, interspersing it with mouthfuls of chocolate spread, and emptying a litre of fruit juice and two cans of iced tea down my throat. The shopkeepers turned off the lights, closed the shutters and nodded at me as they got into their cars. Once I had reduced my pile of food to a quantity I could fit onto the bike, I set off back up the side of the valley, pedalling slowly into the night.

Chapter Eleven

Twenty-four hours later I was slumped gratefully on the white cotton of a hotel bed, still feeling filthy after my shower. No amount of soap and water could reduce the prickling of sunburn on my skin, the grey tide marks that blended with my tan lines, and the cuts and sores that were appearing all over my body, especially on my face, where excessive sweating had caused spots to form around my mouth, and excessive cycling had refused to let them heal. I had developed mouth ulcers from all the sugar I'd been eating, and every time the tip of my tongue touched my front teeth I felt a sharp sting and tasted blood. My hair, which I hadn't had the energy to wash, still held the dust and salt of the last two days.

But I was happy to be where I was, as clean and comfortable as I felt I could reasonably get at this stage. All four checkpoints were behind me, and most of the mountains, and now I would spend a few hours in this hotel room, gathering my strength for the final push. I was managing myself well. And in contrast to the previous day's push through the gravel, I had spent this evening descending from Checkpoint Four's 1,500m eyrie back to sea level, feeling the landscape warm and blossom around me, the air moisten and the traffic thicken as I approached Podgorica, Montenegro's tiny capital city. Hotel Oasis was a smart five-storey building near the Albanian border, and when I arrived yet another wedding party looked like it was in the process of winding down.

There is an unavoidable tension to staying in hotel rooms when you're racing. For starters, you've shelled out for a whole night, yet will only be using the room for a few hours, leaving before breakfast is served. Every time I've stayed in a hotel I've felt guilty about the money I'm wasting. Then the intention of getting what passes for a proper night's sleep is disrupted by the conflicting need to make the most of the privacy and running water the room also offers. Cleaning body, hair and clothing takes time, and there's the temptation to loaf about before going to bed, texting friends, checking social media. It wasn't until the latter half of the race that I began to notice a new flavour of relaxation – that of the person who has spent every single minute of the past few days in public space, always aware that she may be observed or approached, whether she's drinking espresso in a roadside café, peeing behind a hedge, pedalling past an indifferent policeman or lying unconscious in her bivvy bag. To sit and do nothing much, behind a locked door, knowing that there was no chance someone might notice me, watch me or come and ask what I thought I was doing, was as refreshing as the shower and the clean sheets.

So I propped myself up with all the pillows in the room, admiring the white band about my thighs where my tan lines ended, and demolishing the final slice of the two pizzas I'd ordered at Checkpoint Four. I chewed with my mouth open, dropping crumbs onto my bloated stomach as I scrolled through my phone.

Neil Phillips had reached Çanakkale, winning the race for second place which, given the impossible bar set by Kristof, had been invested by the dot-watchers with as much prestige as first. And James Hayden, quite incredibly, was now within reach of the Turkish border, racing a Canadian rider for fourth place. Behind me, Jayne had been overtaken by a woman called Johanna, and both were battling with the headwind on the Croatian coast. There were a few quips about the photos that had been posted of me with my two pizzas at Checkpoint Four. And a tweet from a man I didn't recognise, that said, 'I hope Emily Chappell knows what she's doing!'

He included a screenshot of the tracker, in which a line of numbered dots streamed eastwards from Montenegro into Kosovo and Macedonia. And beneath them, a long way south, was the lonely number seven – mine – sitting on the Albanian border, many miles from any other rider, or any plausible route to Turkey. I had fucked up.

In an instant, all of the satisfaction I'd felt at a day well spent and a hotel well chosen drained out of me, and I flushed with a rising tide of panic. It had been too good to be true after all. I had advanced so well throughout the race, steadily extending my lead over the other women, just by keeping my head and riding my bike, and now, with one idiotic wrong turn, I had thrown it all away.

I scanned the map again, hoping to find some way of quickly putting this right. But there was no shortcut, no way back onto everyone else's route without either back-tracking up all the hills I'd descended that afternoon or finding a way through the mountains to the east of me, which looked as remote as the borderlands between Bosnia and Montenegro. Everyone watching my dot could see the mistake I'd made, and the futility of trying to put it right.

And this wasn't an unintentional detour. The previous year, when the fourth checkpoint had been at Lovćen on the Montenegrin coast, this was the route that most riders had taken to the finish, avoiding Kosovan landmines and Bulgarian trucks by swerving south, through Albania and into Northern Greece. Leo claimed to have made this decision principally on the basis of preferring Greek food. I had intended to ride through Bulgaria, but the southern route included significantly less climbing, and took me through the major cities of Tirana and Thessaloniki, where I could find bike shops if the damage to my tyre worsened. At Checkpoint Four I had made the decision, loaded the route and set off towards Podgorica. On the outskirts of Žabljak I passed the junction with the road I'd come in on, leading back up into the mountains, and out of the corner of my eye caught the silhouette of a cyclist descending towards the checkpoint.

I stopped the bike a few metres on and looked back over my shoulder, wondering if this was another racer, if they had seen me, if it was anyone I knew. The cyclist stopped at the junction and I saw a dark grey jersey and knew it was Stefan: Stefan who had drawn ahead of me in the Dolomites, and with whom I'd failed to hold a conversation outside the bakery in Croatia. Here he was again, now apparently a few hours behind me. Wordlessly, I raised an arm. Wordlessly he raised one back, and with that we both turned back to our handlebars, one of us bound for the comfort of a checkpoint, the other for the finish line. It was the last time I'd see another rider for three days.

Stefan must now be a long way east, following the river of riders flowing across the Balkans towards Bulgaria. And here I was, stranded by my own folly on the border with Albania, with not a single other idiot to keep me company. I fought for a few moments with my panic and the lack of a plausible solution to this mess. I had no appetite for quitting the race – that would be an acknowledgement of my error, and if I kept going, I might find a way at least of mitigating, if not fully erasing it. I wished I could stop the hordes of people from watching and commenting on my progress, that I could hide for a while, or persuade them to devote their full attention to people like James Hayden, and Jayne and Johanna, and ignore me.

The voice of reason spoke up again:

There's no point worrying about this now. There's nothing you can do tonight, and everything's always worse when you're tired. Go to sleep. Put this off till the morning.

And I did. My body reliably lost consciousness the moment I turned the light out, and four hours later, as I examined the maps over bread and chocolate spread, I saw I had just over 1,000km to go to the finish.

That's three days' ride, I told myself. *It'll be three long days, and you'll have to ride well, avoid stopping and remember that you're doing this to save face. It'll probably be harder than what you've done so far. But if you could do all of that, you can do this too.*

It was early on Tuesday morning. If I managed to ride 300km a day, I'd arrive in Çanakkale on Friday, the day before the finishers' party and, quite incredibly, still only a day behind my secret twelve-day schedule. It was still within my reach.

But I knew now how likely I was to lose sight of this resolution a few hours hence, in the heat of the afternoon, when the urge to stop and rest swelled to such proportions that it would obscure any other intentions. Plus, I was about to enter Albania, one of the few countries whose bad reputation was confirmed, rather than dispelled, by cycle tourists. I had never been there, and after hearing all the stories of filth, crime, dogs, potholes and terrible drivers, I didn't want to. Rationally, I knew I was unlikely to encounter anything worse than I'd already survived in various deprived pockets of various countries across the world. But this would not be a day during which I'd make much progress, and all along I'd know the others were racing along their sensible route through Kosovo, Serbia and Bulgaria, drawing closer and closer to Çanakkale, and further and further ahead of me.

The road to the border was deserted, and I was waved through by muffled guards who seemed half-asleep.

Here we go, I told myself. *If anyone can do this, I can.* Nestled in amongst my fears, I sensed a steel edge of resolve and determination. I let it sit there, on the periphery of my awareness, afraid that to turn my full glance on it would be to reveal it as a chimera. Alongside my conviction that I was attempting something far beyond my abilities, that things would eventually go wrong – and in fact, that they now *had*, which was no more than I should have expected – ran a subtle parallel knowledge that I was in my element. Throughout this race and that of the previous year, I had listened to the other riders' complaints about heat, wind, saddlesore and exhaustion with slight surprise. It was as if they hadn't expected it to be difficult, or had believed that their meticulous preparations, their well-planned kit lists, their expensive gadgets and bike-fits, should have obviated any suffering they might experience during the race itself.

Was it simply that my years of battling through London – then limping across Asia – had accustomed me to hardship? Or was it something less noble than that, a passiveness that meant that once I was into a situation I'd meekly continue to push myself through it rather than face decisions like whether to turn back, reroute or give up? A day or two before I reached the gravel road between Bosnia and Montenegro, one of the top ten riders had started along it, then turned back and attempted to detour south, then changed his mind and turned north, each decision traced out like a trident by his blue line on the tracker. Eventually he had withdrawn from the race, and I wondered what had been going through his head at that point. Did he quit because he had by now lost any hope of a podium place, and felt the struggle was no longer worth it? Was he as embarrassed as I was, that his errors were seen and commented on by countless online observers? Or was it that his wanderings had frustrated his single-minded push forward, that in turning this way and then the other he had accidentally extinguished the will to go on, and now saw no point in continuing?

I was glad I'd kept going along the gravel, and I kept going now, into Albania, confident that, no matter what difficulties it held, it couldn't possibly be the worst place I'd ever cycled. And anyway, the race had been going better than I expected so far. Here, at last, came the challenge.

As the daylight gathered force I sped through acres of farmland, orderly green fields and verdant gardens surrounding large, red-roofed villas, not all that dissimilar from Northern Italy. I was wary as the warming air began to waft the scents of the countryside towards me, remembering the reports of squalor I'd heard from other cycle-tourists. But what reached my nostrils was the warm, sweet scent of caraway, and I drew in long breaths, trying to detect whether this emanated from some small bakery I might be approaching, before realising that it was the crops on either side of me, gently toasting in the early-morning sunshine. A few miles on the smell changed – this time it was a greener, more piquant flavour, which I recognised but couldn't put a name to, and I peered at the blooming fields on either side of me, trying to make out the shape of the leaves as I sped by.

A few hours in I spied a petrol station that looked like it had a café, or at least a shop attached, and I stopped to see what I could do about breakfast. I was met by a slender man with soft, dark hair, who apologised falteringly for his lack of English, then magically seemed to rediscover it.

'Now,' he said, 'please come and sit. I will make you coffee.'

It was that 'now' that amazed me. Underneath his diffidence, he spoke English with the fluency and flourishes of someone who rejoiced in the language, whether he'd picked it up from an anglophone circle of friends or a few years spent in London or Birmingham. I wanted to talk to him more, but he placed my espresso in front of me and retreated behind the counter with a shy smile. A few minutes later, as I paid for my coffee and a small handful of packaged cakes for the road, I asked him the word for 'thank you' in Albanian.

'Faleminderit,' he enunciated carefully.

'Falemin – derit?' I repeated. He nodded proudly.

'Faleminderit.'

'Faleminderit.'

I waved goodbye and continued south.

I had dreaded the Albanian cities, anticipating fumes, crowds and unruly traffic, but Shkodër passed me by in a slick succession of well-surfaced roundabouts and tree-lined streets. The words, on hoardings and shopfronts, were in a language strikingly different from any I knew, or from the juicy consonant clusters of Croatian and Montenegrin. I savoured the novelty of Albanian's Qs and umlauts, pleased to have discovered a corner of Europe that still felt foreign.

The road south was flat, fast and raised from the landscape around it, giving me a view of the acres of green crops, the avenues of poplar trees, the parched riverbeds and the dark green mountains to the east. And, enlivened by my coffee and the relief that Albania, at least for now, was nowhere near as difficult as I'd feared, I was flying, whirling along the road as if blown by a gale. For once my body settled gladly into the bike: the saddle cradled my bones; my hands felt sure and solid on the drops; my legs wanted to do nothing so much as turn the pedals; and my excitement at this compulsive forward motion translated itself into little bursts of acceleration, like fireworks. The road rolled away beneath my racing pedals as I relished the glowing thread of pure intent that connected mind to muscle, muscle to motion. I remembered those elusive afternoons when I was a courier, when for reasons I could only guess at, I'd overcome all of the usual impediments to speed – tiredness, stiffness, traffic, my sagging chain – and whirl through the streets like a dancer through a dance, riding so fast that I seemed to reach beyond motion and become still again.

On these occasions, or when pelting along Clerkenwell Road on a Monday morning, just as the caffeine took hold and the jobs started coming in, I'd revisit various fantasies, fond and foolish and familiar, of lives that might have been, or that might yet be. I'd inhabit various cyclists I'd seen or read of, I'd chase Bahamontes' wheel up Pyrenean cols, or, in my favourite of all, I'd win a stage of the Tour de France, hearing the roar of the crowds around me and the thundering of thousands of hands on the barriers as the finish line drew closer and closer. I'd imagine watching the footage afterwards, seeing a stocky, dark-haired woman sprinting along the finishing straight to the sound of Phil Liggett's voice, hoarse with excitement:

'And Chappell takes the lead! No one can catch her now! I don't believe it, Emily Chappell, a cycle courier from London, wins her first stage of the Tour de France.'

And as I crossed the line, teeth bared, the cheers reached such a pitch that they drowned out Liggett's voice and became a huge distorted roar that filled my senses like fire sweeping through a building. And I'd realise I was now standing in one of London's cycle cafés, gawping up at the screen with everyone else as I crossed the line in triumph, caught up in the web of noise and emotion with all of my friends and colleagues.

Racing along that sunny road towards Tirana, faster than anyone has a right to go after ten days in the saddle, I tried to revisit that fantasy, but couldn't hold on to it for long enough. I switched to one where I was at the head of a race, in one of those lone breakaways I'd always admired, where a single rider sprints ahead of the pack for many hours and, just sometimes, manages to reach the line without being caught. I was midway through assembling the fantasy's discrete parts (the other women in the peloton, the moment when I'd attacked and no one had followed) when it occurred to me that I *was* in a race, that I *was* miles out from the rest of the pack and that, if I carried on like this, I still stood a good chance of winning.

I laughed out loud as the story I'd been telling crumbled around me. I hadn't expected to approach my fantasies so closely that I began to recognise them in my ordinary life. I would have to find some new ones.

I recalled the sparse accoutrements of winning the Trans-continental: the finish line portraits I'd secretly coveted of exhausted faces in black and white, emblazoned with sponsor logos; the picture of Kristof and Juliana, back in 2013, standing side by side in their dark-grey winners' jerseys, embroidered with the number of days, hours and minutes they had spent on the road. Then I let all thoughts of winning blow away behind me, and thundered down the road towards Tirana, where I spent an hour lost in a maze of busy traffic, roadworks and sharp urban climbs. The roads that took me through the city were in the process of being resurfaced, and I bumped along them for several kilometres, tempering the panic and frustration I felt at all of this wasted time with reassurance.

Nothing's actually going wrong here – you should know by now that it always takes longer than you expect to get through cities, and that you'll balance that out by going faster elsewhere. Remember how long it took you to ride into Istanbul in 2011? Remember Taiyuan?

Taiyuan was a Chinese city where I'd spent a night in 2012, during my frantic dash to the ferry port in Tianjin. I'd been riding furiously for eight days, and the night's sleep had done nothing for me: I'd felt as exhausted when I started pedalling as I had when I got off the bike the previous evening, and it took me all morning to find the road that took me eastwards out of the city – four hours of wrong turns, false flats, billowing fumes and torturous conversations with people whose language I didn't share, and who invariably sent me off in the wrong direction. It was midday by the time I rode out of the city, my rising panic augmented by the knowledge that all the time and energy

I'd expended trying to escape Taiyuan was irrelevant to my overall goal, that I'd only made things harder for myself.

Tirana was nowhere near as bad, and I carried on towards the city limits with the calmness of one who has been here before, and knows it won't last. The morning was heating up, and unlike the previous days, there were no clouds to protect me from the glare of the sun. I sweated along the tangle of main roads that left Tirana, already nostalgic for the dawn hours and the early morning, when I knew I'd have done my best cycling of the day. For now, at least until sunset, I would be slow, hot and reluctant.

I stopped for coffee in the gardens of a stone-walled house beside the road, and watched an extended family having a party at the other end of the terrace. I stopped in a tiny grocery store next to a bridge, eying dusty vegetables as I spent all the Albanian money I had on ice creams. I stopped partway up a long, leafy climb to buy a bag of blackberries from four young boys who had pursued me for several minutes, and were happy to accept euros. I stopped just over the brow of the hill and briefly despaired as I saw the road I wanted to take swooping down the other side and disappearing into a tunnel – I didn't harbour even the slightest hope that bicycles would be allowed in there.

I checked the map and found a smaller road leading south, though its twists and turns suggested that there was no way I'd avoid climbing up over the green mountains that now soared around me. Half an hour later I stopped again, this time because my amazement at my surroundings had grown so overpowering that I had to savour the moment at a standstill.

The road rose gently ahead of me, ranging across the wooded hillside in a series of switchbacks. All around me the insects sang, and the mountain breathed out the scent of pine needles and toasting grass seeds. Sweat washed comfortably over my skin as I stood there, and when I pushed myself back into motion, the gradient seemed exactly proportional to the strength of my legs and the space in my lungs. I watched my lean, brown forearms, their muscles twitching in alternation as I climbed, and smiled.

I had been dreading the temperatures of Southern Europe, and hadn't been able to imagine a scenario in which a long exposed climb, in the searing heat of a Balkan afternoon, was anything other than hellish. And yet, here I was. This felt nothing like a race – rather, it recalled the leisurely afternoons I'd spent winding along the Adriatic coastline five years previously, watching clear blue water glowing through the pine trees and basking in the warmth that reflected off the pale grey cliffs.

And when I reached the top of the climb, it got even better. The road emerged from the pine forest and rolled languorously along a high ridge, rising and falling at just the right frequency that my momentum from each drop in the road carried me buoyantly up the following ramp. And, with something like disbelief, I found I was surrounded by mountaintops on both sides, an endless parade of summits stretching off into the blue-green distance beneath me, as I swooped southwards, surfing the curves of the road as an albatross might the currents of the air.

Eventually the road took a downward turn, and another luxurious set of switchbacks swept me down the eastern side of the ridge, towards a broad green valley, speckled with tiny houses that grew larger as I slid round each hairpin. A young couple appraised me curiously as they sped past on their moped, slowing for each bend so that for a few minutes I gained on them, and almost drew alongside them again, before the road straightened and they buzzed off through the olive groves towards the base of the mountain.

I cruised through Elbasan and began the long, slow climb towards the border, exuding contentment and having it exuded back at me by the people I passed. The road crept slowly upwards along a leafy valley, overlooked by damp greenery that was far more reminiscent of Mid Wales than the parched hillsides of the Balkan coastline, and I pedalled myself calmly onwards, enjoying the sense of sufficiency borne of a good morning on the bike, followed by a better afternoon. The day didn't owe me anything else; I could drift towards sunset knowing that I'd done enough, that nothing remained but to enjoy myself. The drivers gave me a wide berth, and a few of them hooted their horns and gave me a thumbs up as they drove past. In small towns and hamlets along the way I was greeted with smiles and nods, and when I stopped to investigate a water fountain halfway up the climb, a nearby group of truck drivers eagerly reassured me that it was drinkable.

'Faleminderit!' I called out to them as I rode off.

As evening fell I reached the end of the valley and began climbing more steeply upwards, surrounded by busy Albanians who shared my own instinct to rush outdoors in the hour where day becomes night. A dozen young men in football kit jogged past me, older couples promenaded through the villages and the ubiquitous car wash stations were all busy, sheets of water trickling across the tarmac as men and boys hosed down everything from brand-new Mercedes to fully loaded trucks.

The road leading up to the pass was smooth and broad, but I struggled against the gradients, my breath loud and coarse as the noise of the valley sank beneath me. By the time I reached the top it was dark, and the villages I'd passed through were a constellation of lights, far below. Here on my left was a large square building, topped with red letters that read 'Hotel Odessa', and with very little hesitation I enquired about a room. I could have gone further – night had only just fallen, and the next few miles would be mostly downhill – but to continue felt less like an urge, and more like an obligation that was easily ignored.

The hotel looked modern from the outside, but inside it seemed a lot older, and I was led along a gloomy corridor to a high-ceilinged room full of heavy wooden furniture, and with an antiquated bathroom that refused to give me any hot water. I relished its eeriness, amusing myself with a conviction that it must be haunted – or even that the hotel itself was a mirage, and in the morning I'd find myself huddled in my bivvy bag beside the road.

The air was chilly, and I found a thick duvet in one of the wardrobes, snuggling into its warmth with amazement that I could have found such comfort in a country I had expected to be inhospitable, and a region I had assumed would be inescapably hot at this time of year. I set my alarm for a generous five hours, elevated my legs on a pillow and instantly fell asleep.

I left the hotel long before daybreak and woke up another set of border guards on my way down the hill towards Lake Ohrid, struck by the fact that I had crossed into Albania just twenty-four hours previously. The day I spent there had been intense and vibrant, set apart from the other days I'd spent riding, stopping, eating and drinking. 'I'm having a holiday within the race,' I'd tweeted the previous afternoon. And now, I thought, it was back to school. I skirted Lake Ohrid in the dark, only aware of its presence from the chill that rose from its waters, and the way the lights of distant towns shaped themselves round the contours of its shoreline. I had been hearing about the beauty of this lake for years, but this was no time to stop and stare. By the time day broke I was marooned unhappily in a petrol station, a little way inland, making repeated trips to the counter to buy more food, partly as an excuse to stay there a little longer, partly in the hope that filling my stomach would warm me up and stop my shivering. I eventually forced myself out into the tentative morning light, knowing that my stiff limbs would loosen as the rising sun warmed the air around me, and set off up the hill without a backward glance.

Chapter Twelve

When I look back through the photos I take during races, I find they're mostly of myself – my weary face, my tan lines, my scars – or my food. I rarely bother to record the magnificence of the landscapes I pass through, partly because I am usually more preoccupied with drinking in the wonders than stopping to photograph them, and partly because I already know that the vistas I behold will make a greater impression on my mind and memory than they ever would on Instagram. Everything looks smaller on an iPhone screen.

Whereas, when I slouch in the corner of a café, or sprawl beside the shopping trolleys outside a supermarket, chewing my way through baguettes and chugging litres of orange juice, I have nothing better to do with my time than get out my phone, and take pictures of whatever happens to lie before me – usually my lunch or my legs.

Kate was waiting with Leo at the finish, and I sent one of these pictures to her from a supermarket car park on the outskirts of Thessaloniki. It included half a cucumber, the stalk of a tomato, a cheese pastry, a bag of cashew nuts and two bottles of juice. Evidently, I had been too hungry to photograph the feast in its entirety before tucking in.

'My skin shivered all over when I bit into that cucumber,' I told her. 'It was lovely.'

For too long – in fact only a day, but in the strange, concentrated, elongated timeframe of racing it felt like an eon – I had been following crisp, sunny Greek roads that passed through absolutely no settlements. The small sustenance I'd found had been from petrol stations, which stocked nothing but junk food, and my previous meal had consisted of a chocolate bar, a sesame snack, a can of fizz and a bag of heavily flavoured 'bagel chips'. I had rejoiced when I saw the sign for Lidl towards the end of the afternoon, with its promise of fruit and veg, freshly baked bread, yoghurt, juice and unflavoured nuts. Still reeling from my hours of famine, I went back into the supermarket after I'd finished eating, and bought as much food as I could squeeze into my various bags and pockets. My appetite had waxed and waned over the course of the race, but for now my stomach was a furnace, instantly burning anything I put into it, and constantly ready for more.

I was within reach of the finish now. More than a day's riding remained, but far less than two, and the distance was beginning to feel navigable. Kate and I were in more regular text contact, as she ceased to be an abstract figure, existing outside my immediate concerns along with everyone else I knew, and floated into focus as something I was aiming for. She had clean clothes waiting for me, and we planned to celebrate my arrival with the biggest Turkish breakfast she could find in the local cafés. The prosaic details of arriving in Çanakkale had begun to fall into place, though the overall import of finishing this race still felt like a fantasy.

I considered various scenarios as I rolled out of Thessaloniki, towards the flat road that would lead me through the night to Kavala. I pictured myself as I had been the previous afternoon, storming along singing 'Don't Stop Me Now' at the top of my voice. The race car would probably come out to meet me, I thought, if I really was the first woman to arrive. I looked forward to performing my jubilation for them – to showing them that this didn't have to be the story of an exhausted, broken hero, and that I was still far more animated than the weary men who had been collapsing off the ferry at regular intervals over the last two days. I even spent twenty minutes riding along with my hands off the bars, practising an air guitar version of Brian May's solo, knowing how much that would amuse the dot-watchers if it was captured on film.

Or perhaps I would be overcome with the emotion of it all, I thought. I might speed into Çanakkale, throw my bike down and burst into uncontrollable sobs, releasing all the emotions I'd carefully guarded over the past fortnight. The assembled men would shuffle their feet awkwardly, and my black-and-white finisher's portrait would show tear tracks through the grime on my cheeks.

I might be more restrained than that, I thought, imagining myself skidding up to where the race crew were waiting, calmly swinging a leg over my bike and announcing 'well, that's that then', or something equally understated. Perhaps I'd just give a satisfied nod, as if to say 'job well done'.

I wondered if I'd arrive to an ecstatic crowd or – as seemed more likely if I turned up in the middle of the night – a couple of yawning volunteers, who'd quietly stamp my brevet card and note my time down on a clipboard, then disappear back to their hotel rooms.

Would the triumph dawn immediately? Or would it be delayed, accompanying a rush of congratulatory emails and text messages like the one that followed my Ventoux ascent the previous summer? Maybe I'd find a more subdued reception, with people disappointed that my ill-thought-out Albanian detour had effectively added a day to my overall time. I knew from Kate's texts that it was a topic of discussion among the finishers in Çanakkale.

'They're like, but what's the *strategy?*' she told me. And then, with a little eye-rolling emoji, 'Boys.'

Her overnight shift would finish at 8 a.m., she told me, and it would be best if I aimed to get there around then, so that we could proceed with our breakfast plans. I ignored the text and carried on riding. I wasn't close enough to start estimating arrival times, and her assumption that I could felt slightly jarring.

I rode for most of the night, and reached the coast road in time to see the sun rise – a huge glowing beacon that made the landscape blush and dazzled me so strongly that I felt my eyes closing again and had to lie down on the dusty verge between the tarmac and the open sea. The road stretched plainly ahead of me, overlooked by a thorny cliff on one side, and overlooking the glistening water on the other. Other signs of civilisation were sparse, although they would not have appeared so to anyone passing this way in a car or truck. The world was too big for me, and Kavala still far too far away.

The day had taken hold by the time I rounded a head-land, sped down a long hill and finally saw what I'd been looking for. The bakery had a coffee machine, a toilet and a shady terrace where I drank my two coffees and ate my two pastries with practised relish. The fresh-faced women behind the counter were delighted with me when I went back in for a second helping.

I found a wifi signal and checked my route. The ferry port at Eceabat was just over 300km away. I could cover that in twenty-four hours.

And all at once I knew that I was going to make it. All that remained was a distance that I had ridden many times before, by day and by night, in winter and in summer, in high winds and driving rain and baking sunshine, and on almost every day of this race so far. It would be hard, I told myself. I shouldn't consider this a done deal. But then, I understood in that moment, all of the hardships that might come up – all of the heat and hills and headwinds; all of the punctures and insect bites; all of the physical soreness and stiffness, the emotional torture, the crises of motivation and momentum – all of these were challenges I had already survived multiple times. There was very little the next 300km could throw at me that I hadn't already endured, in the Chinese desert, in the Yukon winter, in the streets of London and along the highways, steep mountain switchbacks and meandering gravel tracks of the Transcontinental itself.

I texted Kate, and made a date for breakfast the following morning. Then I took one of the bottles from my bike, and locked myself into the bakery's small bathroom. I filled the bottle, sat down on the toilet and carefully poured water into my lap, before drying myself with paper towels and putting on my clean pair of shorts. I scrunched the pair I'd just taken off into one of the back pockets of my jersey. The next time I washed them would be in a laundrette in Turkey, or maybe even at home in Wales. I filled the bottle again and gulped down water until my stomach would take no more. It would be a hot day, and no matter how assiduously I drank, I'd be dehydrated by the time I arrived. Best to get ahead while I could. Standing in front of the mirror I washed my face, armpits and torso. When I shoved my arms back into my jersey, the familiar weight of my phone, wallet, spare shorts and assorted pocket food settled it easily onto my shoulders, like a ceremonial robe. I was a knight preparing for battle.

And then, as ready as I'd ever be, I set off through the streets of Kavala, along the cobbled waterfront with its palm trees and tourists, up the hill, over the cliffs and off into a bare landscape where the shrunken grass struggled to cover the earth beneath, and the mountains trembled behind a haze of heat, as if evaporating into the vast blue sky.

I pressed on, through avenues of trees that never seemed to cast their shade in my direction. The day crackled and simmered with heat and I tried to calculate – without wasting effort by rummaging in my pocket for my phone – how close to midday it must be, when the furnace was likely to reach its zenith.

It was reasonable, I thought, to pause for half an hour and sleep in the shade. I had been up most of the night, and I was unlikely to cover any serious miles now. As I slowed the bike, examining the verges for shady corners where I could lie down, I felt the heat surge up from the tarmac and understood why my shoes had begun to hurt me again – my poor feet were hovering just a few inches above the surface of a grill, being slowly cooked as I rode.

I pulled into a car park, beside what appeared to be a deserted hotel, and lay down in the narrow strip of shade next to one of its walls. Although I'd felt too sleepy to ride any further, I realised after ten minutes that I wasn't going to lose consciousness, and might as well be riding, so I got up and slowly carried on.

The afternoon stretched on as I followed the road into what I remembered, from my long-ago route-planning, was some sort of national park: a fractured shoreline of lakes, inlets and wetlands. There were no towns here, and at one point the tarmac stopped and I bumped along a dusty track for a few miles, pretending to myself that I was enjoying it, and trying not to panic over the minutes and hours I was wasting. I shouldn't have spent so much time on Twitter over lunch. Excitement was mounting over my approach to the finish line, and although I was still likely to be the first woman to arrive, Sir Wobbly announced, with some relish, that Johanna was now only 150km behind me.

That's only a hundred miles, I thought. If Johanna was feeling fresh, she might cover that in six hours, and I could easily squander that amount of time sleeping, or staring into cups of coffee, or following this meandering line along the coast, rather than taking the highway that most of the other racers had chosen. My legs quickened in spite of the heat, and I noticed my breathing becoming shallower as I sped up and down the endless hills. I tried to draw it out, counting a slow one-two rhythm as I concentrated on inflating my torso, and then slowly squeezing it flat, but within a couple of breaths I'd find myself panting again.

'Keep it together, Chappell,' I said out loud. 'Keep it together. You've got this.'

And then, because it seemed to work, I carried on talking, more and more freely, and less and less coherently, lulling myself with the sound of my own voice, weighting the air that flowed in and out of me, so that it moved more steadily, and so did I.

'You're doing fine. You know what you're doing. All

you have to do is just keep on riding, keep on keeping it together. You're going to make it. Just need to keep calm. Keep *calm*. Keep. Calm.'

I had never been here before, never heard myself talking out loud like this. All of these mantras and affirmations were for other people, and even in my solitude I felt embarrassed by the self-help gibberish with which I was holding myself together. But the meaning of the words was more or less irrelevant. I slowly breathed in air, and slowly breathed out incantations.

I pictured Johanna chasing me down in a fury, scenting victory as she realised I was half a day's ride away, and wasting time by following this jagged coastline. Perhaps, by the time I reached the Dardanelles, we would be neck and neck, as I had been with Zara in the Strathpuffer, neither of us in any state to conceal our exertion, both tasting the sour dread of being the first one to drop back.

Keep calm. Keep calm. Keep calm.

I could see from the screen of my Garmin that the route I'd planned was about to dive south, only to swing back north a few miles later. I stopped and checked the map, hoping that there would be a road that took me across the third side of this triangle, but there wasn't. I crawled exhaustedly up the long, straight hill into a village called Maroneia, even the panic no longer enough to fuel me. Before turning back north I stopped at the village shop, bought an ice cream and sat on the shady step as I consumed it, scouring my phone for sympathy. Twitter followers were more interested in egging on the conquering heroine than commiserating with her struggles, so I sent out a few plaintive texts to friends, and waited to see if anyone would bite.

Lee immediately started talking sense into me.

'Johanna's nowhere near you,' she retorted. 'And she's not slept for ages. She's clearly about to crash.'

She sent me a screenshot of Johanna's time/speed graph from the tracker website. Sure enough, although there were around ten points where the orange line went flat, showing when Johanna had been stationary for a few hours, for the last day and a half there were no gaps at all, suggesting that she was riding almost constantly.

I sent a screenshot of Sir Wobbly's tweet, perversely wanting him to be right as a justification for my panic. Lee didn't rise to the bait.

'Nah, it's more like 400km,' she said. 'You're doing fine. You've put in the hard work, now you just need to nurse this home. Finish your ice cream and get back on your bike.'

I did as I was told.

Eventually the road curved back in from the coast and rejoined the highway that would lead me to Alexandroupoli – the last town in Greece, and the point at which I knew I would be 200km from the finish. I paused in the shade of some trees, and became aware of my own blossoming stench as the air settled around me. My skin prickled with exhaustion, filth and heat, and the overripe smell of rotting vegetables hung in my nostrils. My crotch was beginning to burn, and I cursed myself for not washing my spare shorts that morning.

'Go on, send me a selfie. I want to see how bad you look,' urged Lee.

I looked even worse than I expected. My skin had a clammy, greenish tinge, the sores were clearly visible around my slack mouth and the edges of my eyes slumped downwards, as though the muscles could no longer hold them up. My blue jersey was decorated with white streaks of salt.

Another flurry of texts arrived from my family, who

seemed happily oblivious to my plight. I resented their absorption with anything other than me, though I smiled grimly when a photo came through of my one-year-old niece, mouth wide with delight under a lopsided helmet as she rode on the crossbar of her father's bike for the first time. Even in my exhaustion, I couldn't help but be amused by the contrast with the photo I'd just taken of myself.

I didn't want to carry on, but after a couple of minutes large flies began to nibble at my sticky skin, and my only option was to ride away from them.

Another racer passed me as the road curved upward, back into the hills. I instantly forgot his name, remembering only that he was Italian, tall and muscular, with a bright yellow jersey and a small backpack. We exchanged pleasantries – or attempted to, in my case – and he sped off confidently, eventually disappearing around the side of the hill at a pace I couldn't match.

If I hadn't gone through Albania I'd be a day ahead of him, I told myself as I watched him go. But I had gone through Albania, and now I was behind him. I pedalled on up the hill, my legs throbbing indignantly.

It was dusk by the time I arrived in Alexandroupoli, fidgeting as I descended through the outskirts of the city, trying to find a position that would relieve the hot prickling that felt as though I were sitting on a handful of nettles. I parked my bike next to another racer's outside the first supermarket I came to, hoping that whoever it was wouldn't want a touching reunion or a long conversation, and glumly prowled the aisles, trying to remember what it was I'd want to eat if I still had an appetite.

I eyed the glass-fronted pharmacy across the road, wondering if I dared sully it with my filth, and also whether they sold Sudocrem. The immaculate young woman behind the counter smiled as I apologetically tiptoed into her haven, and understood immediately what I was trying to ask for – as if she could tell from the way I walked that I was suffering the worst nappy rash of my life. I slunk out, embarrassed, and went off looking for a public toilet where I could put a handful of clean white cream down my stinking shorts. It only occurred to me long afterwards that I might not have been the first saddlesore cyclist to limp through her door that day.

I saw more racers as I rode out of the city and into the night. For the first few miles the quiet road was lined with streetlights that gave it the feeling of a stage set – off to our right and our left was empty darkness; all that remained was the dance we were playing out on the floodlit tarmac. I passed a couple of slower riders, but mostly was overtaken by eager men who had caught the scent of the finish line. One of them slowed for long enough to tell me that his wife was waiting in Çanakkale, that they had a flight from Istanbul the following afternoon, and if they didn't get on the bus at 8.30 a.m., they'd miss it. He hared off into the darkness ahead of me, and I didn't see him again.

The streetlights disappeared as the Turkish border drew near. I freewheeled through a mess of gates, fences and dark, anonymous buildings, past cars full of tired families and lines of roosting trucks. In the middle of this no man's land was an insalubrious service station which I stopped to investigate, mostly just as an excuse to stop. In the hot, smelly toilets I spent a few pointless minutes rearranging my shorts and applying more Sudocrem, searching for a respite from the burning that was now so painful I wasn't able to forget it for more than a couple of seconds. Mosquitoes whined around my head and suckled greedily from my ankles and upper arms. The horrors of the Turkish border complex rapidly outgrew the horrors of continuing, and so I continued.

I still had 145km to go. That was almost 100 miles, and yet I'd been telling myself since Alexandroupoli that I only had 100 miles to go. Why was it taking so long?

I passed the first sign for Çanakkale shortly after making the last right turn of my route at Keşan. From now on it was just one road, all the way to the ferry. But the road was cruel. For a while it inclined ineluctably upwards – the kind of steady gradient that favours trucks, but slows cyclists to a pathetic crawl. I forced myself onwards, picking out landmarks ahead of me to reach before I'd let myself put a foot down, lift my weight off the saddle for a moment and check my phone to see how much further I had to go. I'd guess at what the current total might be as pessimistically as I could, hoping to surprise myself when it turned out to be less, but my estimates proved disappointingly accurate. After another hour of riding, my remaining distance was still in the high eighties.

The road descended briefly and then, with about sixty miles to go, tilted upwards again into what I knew would be the last big climb of the race. The map had seemed to crumple at this point, I remembered, and I had drawn my red line over a sharp fold in the landscape, across a low-lying plain, and then most of the way down the tongue of land that thrust south-west towards the Aegean Sea, separated from Çanakkale by the narrow channel of the Dardanelles. The journey could be held in mind in its entirety now – and yet the possibility of arrival seemed as distant as ever.

Almost all of the long bike rides I'd done had ended with a final sprint – no matter how many miles I had ridden, how exhausted I'd felt, I'd hit some magical tripwire in the final miles and soared into the finish with a smile on my face.

But sometimes I hadn't. The day I rode into Esfahan, four years previously, I had been pushing myself into a head-wind for over 100 miles, and even as I entered the outskirts of the city, all I wanted to do was stop. I even debated with myself whether it wouldn't be better just to pitch my tent next to the sign that said *Esfahan 5km*, and ride the remaining distance into the city the following morning. I suspected the final stretch of this ride might be the same.

I battled on up the hill, wincing – and sometimes openly whimpering – as I rose out of the saddle, felt my compressed tissues blaze as the blood rushed back into them, then, after a few pedal strokes, had to sit down again. I'd lower myself reluctantly, shifting and shuffling as I gradually released my weight onto what now felt like raw flesh, trying to find a part of me to rest on that didn't yet hurt. I thought about the engineers who had set the gradient of this road, the contractors who had decided on the quality of the tarmac, and the local government officials who hadn't got round to filling in the potholes. Why hadn't it occurred to these callous people that a saddlesore cyclist might one day ride over the surface they had created?

Fifty miles to go, I thought as I began the descent. But the rush of cool air forced my eyes to close and my head jerked time and time again as I yanked myself out of sleep. I squeezed the brakes, hating to waste the downhill, but knowing I was in imminent danger of tumbling over the handlebars or collapsing into the verge.

The drowsiness didn't abate when the road flattened out, no matter how urgently I churned the pedals to try and stoke myself into vigilance. Feeling like a failure, I stopped, hauled my bike over the metal crash barrier and spread out my bivvy bag in the dust. I set my alarm, turned my face up to the glittering stars, and breathed out. When I woke up, two hours later, the stars had gone and a rust-coloured dawn was breaking above me. The day's traffic had begun to rumble past, and I pushed my bike back up to the road and joined it. It would be hot again in a couple of hours, and Çanakkale was still miles away.

:::

In the months before I started my ride across Asia I devoured any book I could find that covered a similar journey. Quite quickly, I found myself abandoning them before the final chapter, losing interest just before the hero's triumphant arrival at his home, or the other side of the world, or whatever happened to be the designated end of the journey. Half a shelf of paperback books built up, each with a dog-earred bookmark protruding just a couple of millimetres from the back cover. I didn't understand why I wasn't finishing the books, and resisted trying to explain it to myself, wondering if I'd find the answer further down the road.

And as my own journeys progressed, I discovered a deep scepticism towards the endings other travellers described. I found that I simply didn't believe the emotions they recalled feeling, their uncomplicated joy and the resolution they implied by leading up to this moment and putting it at the end of a book. A lot of their stories followed a formula as clear as any thriller or romance novel, and after I'd read two or three, the homecoming scene rang as false as the happily-ever-after. Their writers, I told myself, were saying what they felt was expected of them – what they themselves had expected: that this was the greatest moment of their life, that they were happy, that everything had built towards this. I wondered if they were even able to admit to themselves that the template they'd spent however many thousands of miles moulding themselves into was false.

I had suspected that one of the race cars might meet me on the coast road, but it was only when I stopped my bike at the small ferry port in Eceabat that I spotted James Robertson the photographer, sitting on a bench among the commuters. He looked at me more as if he were a lost child than I a conquering hero, and responded only mildly to my greeting, before asking if I planned to buy a ticket for the ferry. I poked dumbly at the buttons on the nearby ATM, mustering the few words of Turkish I'd learned four years previously as I guessed my way through the process of getting money, only realising days later that I could have just pressed a button and translated the procedure into English.

Once on the boat I climbed up to the top deck and, with a vague sense of how a person ought to be behaving on such an occasion, took a photo of my swollen, crumpled face, with a background of white-painted railings and a watery horizon. I sent it to Leo, with the caption 'I'm on the fucking ferry.' I don't remember how I spent the twenty minutes it took to cross the Dardanelles. I may have slept, or stared at the sea and sky. I may have done what I always did now, whenever I had cause to stop cycling – check Twitter; see what the other racers were up to; see if anyone was talking about me.

The finish line was only a few pedal strokes from where we disembarked. I remember fighting through the traffic and wiggling self-consciously between bollards to get into the small square where they were waiting for me. An erect, white-clad figure standing with a knot of people at the end of the square turned out to be Kate, and she hugged me for a long time when I got off the bike. I returned the hug, relaxed my hold, then tightened it again as I realised she wasn't letting go. With my face squashed against her upper arm I wondered if she could smell the sour odour rising from my torso, wondered if she was making a point by hugging me for so long in spite of it, wondered why the intensity of emotion that clearly motivated this embrace wasn't able to bridge it.

'I'm just going to cut the tracker off your bag,' said someone. 'And if you could sign this, to confirm we've taken it.'

So that was one errand out the way – I wouldn't have to get round to packaging my tracker up and posting it back to Mike, as I had the previous year. This must be what finishing was like.

Mike himself was standing there, brandishing a camera. He shook my hand, and then hugged me.

James Hayden stepped towards me, his gait slightly bow-legged, handed me a can of Efes, and retreated to a bench, where he lowered himself down between two other racers. I recognised Nelson, and Stephane. They were both browner than when I'd seen them in Geraardsbergen, and their tired eyes seemed huge in their lean faces.

Kristof stood a couple of paces back, poker straight, arms crossed, as if on duty. He smiled when I caught his eye, and I detected a note of impatience. He had been here five days already, so his recovery would be more advanced than the rest of the men, who were draped about the benches and masonry of this small urban square like a pride of lions in the midday heat.

Kate and I laboriously formed a plan whereby I would leave my bike at the hotel, get myself cleaned up and follow her to a café for our long-awaited breakfast. In the end I let her tell me what to do, and listened meekly as she enunciated my instructions, with an affectionate smirk at how slow and stupid my tiredness had made me. I sat for a few more minutes in the square, finishing my can of beer as some of the assembled racers drifted off in search of their own breakfast and others remained on their benches, perhaps keeping me company, perhaps just too tired to think about moving. Looking down, I saw a chalky smudge on the front of my shorts, where the excessive quantities of Sudocrem I'd applied the previous night had begun to emerge.

It was only when I was standing under the warm shower in Kate and Leo's cramped hotel bathroom, having used my hands to hoist each stiff leg over the side of the bathtub, that I realised I had lost the sense of urgency I'd worn like a mantle ever since Geraardsbergen. My enjoyment of this shower need no longer be loaded with haste, and I cast my eye luxuriously around the bathroom, looking at the cracked tiles above the sink, Kate's toiletries arranged along the edge of the mirror, my Lycra limply piled on the floor and the folded cotton T-shirts on the toilet seat. Time rolled away ahead of me in an abundance both fearful and seductive. I no longer had to grasp at it. I could let it go.

Those of us who'd finished the race moved in slow motion around the town that weekend, our tan lines peeking out from the sleeves of the cheap T-shirts we'd bought from market stalls, often pausing to sit down, or lean against walls and catch our breath. The flight of stairs up to Mike and Anna's control room on the first floor of the hotel might as well have been K2, and as I paused to assess the height and depth of each step, and the number I'd have to climb before I reached Advanced Base Camp (the landing), I'd often encounter another racer, hobbling studiously downward, gripping the handrail and smiling ruefully as his eyes met mine, companionship easing our decrepitude from a concern into a joke. Much less than a week ago, I had sprinted up an external flight of stairs at the haunted Albanian hotel, carrying my loaded bike. It bothered me that I had proved myself capable of this so recently, yet couldn't muster the resolve to do it again.

Kate took me to a hammam on the morning of the finishers' party, and I lay like meat on a slab of marble as motherly women scrubbed at my hair and skin with a bar of soap. When they threw buckets of warm water over me to rinse me I could barely breathe, and felt as though I'd suffocate with every wave. My hair dried like wire.

My winner's jersey didn't fit well, and the pale-grey merino it was made from strained across my broad chest when I did it up. Clearly the sponsor had assumed that a woman capable of winning the Transcontinental would be smaller.

Johanna arrived in the early hours of Sunday morning, and by the time I was up Mike told me she had already found a tattoo parlour and commemorated the race by emblazoning its logo on her upper arm. I sought her out in the town square, to hand her a ceremonial can of Efes, admire her new ink and congratulate her on her finish. She and her husband, who had driven down to Turkey in their van to meet her, were planning a few days' holiday along the coast. Her second-place jersey was dark green and looked a lot better on her.

Jayne arrived in Çanakkale on the ferry I was due to depart on that night, and I failed to find her in the crowds, though I'd left another can of Efes for her with a race volunteer, and instructed them to give her a hug from me.

The journey home was as long and hard as I'd expected, and again I had the sense of trying to hold myself together. I had dismantled the bike and packed it into a cardboard box that threatened to fall apart as I dragged it through the crowded airport. The neat and efficient unit we had formed over the last two weeks was now exploding, its pieces moving farther and farther apart, back into chaos.

Shell was on the same flight as me, his green-and-yellow jersey replaced by a baggy linen shirt, and we waited together at Excess Baggage in Birmingham, gently exchanging race stories and tales of our families. I was preoccupied by my right foot, which had been as swollen as the left one since I finished the race, but during the flight had expanded even more. When I flexed my toes in an effort to keep it moving, a sharp pain appeared in the middle of my foot, and now even to touch it with my hand was excruciating. I struggled through the conversation with Shell, exhausted by standing for so long, trying to ignore the pain, and wondering why my bike box was taking so much longer than his to arrive. Several times I told him he should leave me to it, that I knew he'd want to get home.

'No no, I'm happy to wait with you,' he insisted.

'I'll just go and have a look at the main luggage,' I said, as everyone else on our flight had long gone by now, 'in case they sent it there.'

I'd said this nonchalantly, as though walking to the other end of the arrivals hall was no big deal, but it was a long and difficult journey, and an even longer one back to Shell, with the heavy bike box that *had* been there all along.

His wife and my sister were waiting for us, and Shell introduced me to the former with an air of ceremony, so I knew that that was the reason he'd insisted on waiting for me, so that we could walk out together and she could meet me.

On the train I googled the symptoms of deep-vein thrombosis, laughing anxiously when it appeared that I had all of them. When we arrived at my parents' house I had to be lifted out of the car like a child. The out-of-hours doctor offered me an appointment at 2 a.m., and to my dismay I had to submit to a lift from my father, who told me that cycling would be stupidly dangerous, and a taxi stupidly expensive. I set an alarm for 1.30 as I went to sleep on a mattress on the living room floor, unable to make it up the stairs.

A kind doctor assured me within seconds that I didn't have DVT, and after poking and flexing my foot, listening to me cry with pain, suggested that it was probably a fracture, and that I should make an appointment for an x-ray the following day. The x-ray showed nothing conclusive, and within a week the foot was more or less back to normal.

I spent that week sitting like a hungry ghost in the corner of the living room, voraciously attacking any food I was given, too helpless to fend for myself. I felt fractured. Fragmented. Doubtful.

Chapter Thirteen

Mike and Anna moved to Mid Wales that autumn, renting a remote schoolhouse an hour's ride up the hill from me. I was initially apprehensive when he suggested a weekly ride, worried I'd disappoint him by failing to keep up, and feeling daunted by the prospect of riding as equals with someone whose legend had grown steadily as he won more races, and picked off more records. But within minutes of leaving the house, as we tucked into the steep climb that led up out of the Severn Valley, he was caught out by my acceleration and rose out of the saddle for a few strokes to keep pace with me. We glanced towards each other and continued side by side, both breathing heavily, an agreeable note of surprise humming between us. Perhaps this was going to be more fun than either of us had expected.

We had set out later than planned. 'I need to catch up on sleep,' Mike had cautioned me by email the night before.

'Not sure whether I'll be able to get my arse in gear. On the other hand I may wake up early again.' And when he arrived at my house, he wasn't in a hurry to set off, gladly accepting the cup of tea I offered and welcoming the cat onto his lap. I glanced at the bike I'd serviced the evening before, standing it in the corner of the kitchen so as to be ready to ride the moment Mike turned up, and recognised my own habitual reluctance to leave the house. Anna was away in Cardiff, and I got the impression he had let himself go in her absence, staying up too late, sleeping in too long and lacking human contact in their isolated house in the hills.

'I bet it'll be good to have her back,' I remarked, envious of the ready comfort and company that couplehood seems to guarantee.

'Yeah.' He smiled, and then hesitated. 'Well, actually. Umm, I think we're probably going to split up.' My envy melted into a curious disappointment that the companionship I guiltily craved had turned out to be an illusion.

'Oh, I'm so sorry to hear that!' I said, with genuine sorrow, and then, plucking at the only obvious means of comfort, 'Do you want another cup of tea?'

There was just enough left in the pot, and Mike seemed to take this as confirmation that he could speak his mind.

'Yes. We've been having trouble working together,' he said, splintering another of my illusions. 'It's been pretty hard the last few weeks, and I think when she gets back from Cardiff, that's probably going to be it.'

Only the other day they had announced the checkpoints for the 2017 race, via a slick teaser video on YouTube and an endearingly shambolic live broadcast from a sponsor's headquarters in Italy, hundreds of would-be racers watching remotely as Mike fumbled through his desktop to find the slides, then revealed checkpoints of increasing magnitude.

First, a German castle perched on a lofty crag.

Then over the mountains to Monte Grappa, overlooking the Venetian Plain.

Then we'd cross the Alps again, this time heading north for a checkpoint in the High Tatras.

'And Checkpoint Four – well, it was really a matter of "when" rather than "if'," he remarked, with a nod to the fans who'd campaigned for certain iconic or notorious climbs to be included.

He'd changed the slide, to show yet another serpentine road, wriggling up a mountain even larger and bleaker than those we'd already seen.

'Transfăgărăşan.'

This line of Romanian tarmac, like many of cycling's most fabled climbs, had been commissioned by a dictator, to consolidate his powers, with little consideration of the hundreds of workers who lost their lives during its construction. I had yet to decide whether our athletic celebration had the effect of redeeming or effacing this brutality.

The race would end in Meteora in Greece, among monasteries perched on high columns of rock.

'It'll be the best finish yet,' Mike told me, sipping his tea and gently detaching the cat from his beard. 'There's quite a stiff climb at the start of the *parcours*, and then the last bit's downhill, and you'll actually be descending in among the rock formations. It's pretty special.'

But as the rest of the community celebrated and conspired, Mike had slunk back to Mid Wales alone. He told me how he and Anna had argued bitterly over the launch, and begun to realise that this might not be a situation they could redeem.

We followed a route of mine that took us rapidly from the leafy valleys of the Severn up into the barren landscape of the Elenydd, where rolling grasslands that had been golden a few months ago now glowered sullenly at us like a tarnished mirror. Often we rode side by side, carefully arranging our breath around the clauses of our sentences as we climbed, and even – I had never done this before – sympathetically withholding a question for a couple of breaths, until the gradient lessened, or stringing out a response to give the other person a chance to inhale, twining our conversation like a melody around the steady beat of legs and lungs, and the crescendo and diminuendo of the landscape. On the descents I would hang back, he would shoot forward and we'd resume our conversation on the exact word where we had left it hanging at the top of the hill. Other than on the downhills, we were well matched. He didn't outpace me on the climbs as I'd feared, and indeed, sometimes I'd press and puff my way to the top to find he'd been directly behind me, sitting on my wheel.

We climbed up into the Cambrian mountains as daylight admitted defeat and slowly submitted to gloom, and both of our phones suddenly rang out with alerts, having found one of the few patches of signal in this lonely part of Wales.

'Oh, Anna's been trying to get hold of me. I'd better – do you mind?'

He stood a couple of metres ahead of me, one foot on the verge, one still clipped into his pedal, and I tried to shrink back down the hill to give him privacy, as the phrases that floated back to me, and the rising agitation in Mike's voice made it increasingly clear that things had come to a head.

'Look, I really don't want to get into this now. I'm out with Emily, and it's getting dark, and we're standing by the side of the road getting cold. Let's talk about it when you get back.'

The call ended, our eyes met in acknowledgement of

what had just passed, and we carried on up the hill into the dying light. There wasn't much to say, and whatever else might be on our minds, both of us were preoccupied with the long gravel descent that connected this road through to the Claerwen Reservoir, and the picturesque Victorian dams of the Elan Valley. We'd planned to be home by night-fall, but the day had run away with us.

There was a ford to cross shortly before we began the descent, and I let Mike go first, planning to follow his line, and then improvising my own as he hit a rock, put a foot down in the icy water and swore gruffly.

'Do you think you'll be in Wales long-term?' he asked as we clattered down towards Rhayader, eyes trained on the flints and potholes of the track, and the reservoir lying beyond the aura of our headlamps, perceptible only through its chill.

'Not sure. I moved here as a bit of a stopgap – I knew I wanted to leave London, but I didn't know where I wanted to end up, and I thought this would be as good a place as any to call home while I figured that out. I don't know – I'm still not sure if there's enough going on here.'

We stopped in Rhayader, each waiting with the bikes under quiet streetlights as we took it in turns to go into the Spar (him for milk and chocolate; me for a tin of custard to go with the parkin I'd carried all day) before heaving our way up the final climb to his house. We ate our pudding immediately as the kitchen slowly warmed up, then Mike constructed a shepherd's pie and I huddled in a borrowed jacket and drank another cup of tea.

'We should do this again.'

'We should.'

It was a novelty to have a friend in Wales, and a comfort to share my days with someone else who still felt the sting of a breakup. Alongside Mike I discovered lanes I'd never bothered to explore before, and we traced a new skein of memories across the roads we both felt familiar.

'I'll always remember coming up here with Isla. She was on her singlespeed, and just dropped me when we got to the steep bit. I guess she had to attack the climb, or she'd have ground to a halt.'

'Ah – I brought Paul Errington up here once. I think he'd underestimated how far we were going; he totally bonked halfway up.'

And still, every time I climb out of Llangurig towards Cwmystwyth, I see Isla ascending rhythmically ahead of me, while Paul Errington flags and wavers in Mike's slipstream.

I found riding with Mike curiously devoid of my usual ego and insecurities. He didn't seem to mind, or even react very much, when I got up a hill faster than him, and on the occasions when he had to wait for me at the top I joined him placidly, without any of the fears I'd usually harbour, that my riding partner despised my slowness, resented having to wait for me, or was pruriently noting my display of weakness.

But his speed and strength increased as the months wore on. He was back in training, preparing for a new race across Australia – the Indian-Pacific Wheel Race – founded by racers who felt their continent needed an ultra-distance event of its own, and were assembling a start list to make the world pay attention. Juliana had already signed up – having raced the inaugural editions of the Transcontinental and the TransAm, there was no way she was missing this one. Perhaps she was also making up for lost time – what with the previous summer's RAAM debacle, and her knees giving out during TCR the year before, she hadn't completed a race in two years, let alone won anything. As well as the Indian-Pacific in March, her name was alongside mine on the start list for the TransAtlanticWay Race around Ireland in June, and when I asked if she would enter the Transcon, she said, 'Well, that route looks too good to miss.' It would be a big year for both of us.

But the real showdown would be between Mike and Kristof, whose involvement was announced early in the year. Dot-watchers were already speculating about this clash of titans – a convergence of the twain that some had doubted would ever happen. I admired the audacity of the two men. Both had the reputation of being unbeatable, but they'd line up at the start knowing only one of them could win. I couldn't imagine Kristof, The Machine, cool-headed and cleanly shaven, coming in second. But for Mike to lose his crown was similarly unthinkable.

I watched him curiously that winter, knowing I'd have to defend my own title the following summer. I was now a known quantity, welcomed by race directors and eagerly followed by dot-watchers – and any woman entering the race this year would have me in her sights.

Mike displayed none of the anxiety I'd have felt over such a showdown, or if he did, it was through the medium of obsessive preparation. He was approaching this race differently from his others, and during our mid-ride coffee stops I was treated to long discourses on his methods, as he tested hypotheses and chewed over what had gone wrong in past races.

I realised how much I had learned from him over the years. My own racing strategy, such as it was, included a cultivated conviction that it was time spent stationary, rather than slow riding, that made the difference, and Mike's throwaway remark that 'if you're not riding or eating or sleeping, you're wasting your time' had become a checklist I'd applied several times a day during the previous summer's race. Likewise, a comment he'd made years ago about making sure that everything, even major emotional breakdowns, happened on the bike, rather than beside the road, had morphed into my strategy of riding more slowly when my mood dropped in the afternoons, but not letting this become an excuse for stopping.

'It's very convenient for me,' I told him, 'you doing a race four months before mine. Means I can watch your training, and just follow what you do.'

He chuckled at this, and I suspected that his gratification was only partly in response to the implied compliment, and he was pleased to have a second opportunity to see how effective his methods were, not to mention someone to discuss them with, and help him fine-tune this approach even further.

We both rode fixed-gear bikes that winter. ('Come over to the dark side,' he said. 'I was already there!' I protested.) Mike had a theory that doing hill reps on 48x18 would build muscle mass, and counter the inevitable wasting effect of two or three weeks' cycling without recovery time. I wasn't entirely convinced of this, and I suspected he wasn't either, but there was no denying that his strength was growing week by week. On hills that we'd previously charged up side by side, he would now pull further and further ahead of me, or let me start first and then calmly overtake me halfway up, his legs pumping an absurdly high gear at a cadence I couldn't hope to match.

His silhouette was diminishing even at close quarters. Though in the past he had scorned the carb-free diet of some fellow racers, he now adopted a variation on this, and was in the process of convincing his body to rely more heavily on fat than sugar, perhaps wanting to bypass the occasional digestive woes of the long-distance racer, and to alleviate the stress and time-wastage of seeking out supplies in remote areas. Being several kilos lighter would also undoubtedly make a difference.

'I'm going to try and get through the Nullarbor on nothing but fats,' he announced one day, only slightly ruining the effect by tucking into a huge slice of chocolate fudge cake as he spoke. Like mine, his resolutions waxed and waned, and although his will power seemed feeble when faced with anything involving chocolate or double cream, he managed to enforce this new nutritional regime simply by keeping his pantry frugally stocked. I once sent him into a small panic by arriving in a state of near-hypoglycaemia, an hour before dinner was due to be ready. In the end he found a very old pack of crackers at the back of the cupboard to tide me over, but it seemed that any other snackable foodstuffs had been either eaten immediately or piously avoided at point of purchase.

I listened to his expositions with fascination and a certain indulgent scepticism, realising that these monologues were more exploratory than didactic, that all of this was a work in progress. The grovelling honour I'd expected to feel, witnessing the workings of such an innovator first-hand, quickly dissipated into a collegiate curiosity. I challenged him on occasion, smiled affectionately at his slips and hypocrisies, and began to review the way I myself would ride over the next few months, though I was still far from anything I could realistically call a training plan.

I liked Mike's idea of riding fixed to build up muscle specifically because that was already how I preferred to ride. Friends laughed at the doggedness with which I stayed in the big ring, grinding my way up hills rather than ever

admitting defeat and slipping down to the lower gears, and
those who coached, or followed training plans themselves,
were always telling me that riding at a higher cadence in a
lower gear would reduce my fatigue, improve my efficiency
and save me significant amounts of energy over a two-week
race. Mike's theory offered me a different solution – if I
built up an extra inch of muscle on each leg, I could continue to squander my energy by riding hard, knowing that
I'd have that much further to go before I inevitably weakened. Perhaps next summer I'd be able to cross the Alps
without having to nurse my creaking knees through every
pedal stroke.

And I enjoyed the sense of legacy from my courier days.
For several years I had perfected the curiously specific skill-
set of riding at speed through moving traffic, and every
couple of minutes having to sprint from a standing start
after stopping at the lights. I had initially assumed that this
physical fluency was non-transferable, aside from the basic
facts of muscular strength and cardiovascular fitness, but I
now began to notice subtle ways in which couriering might
have prepared me for the Transcon. Getting on the bike
every morning did something to affirm my purpose and
personality, especially at those times when I'd had nothing
else holding me together. I was, I began to understand, a
few steps further than I'd thought towards Mike's aim of
cultivating a 'craving' for the bike.

Indeed, perhaps I was already living proof of his theory.
I had turned out to be stronger and faster on climbs than
anyone might have predicted, and although it was more
obvious to attribute this to the long tours I'd done across
Asian and North American mountain ranges, I suspected
that my years as a courier had been building layers of
muscle all along, like the rings of a tree trunk, as I scraped

my way through each exhausted Thursday afternoon, then spent weekends in orgies of sloth and recovery.

Above all, I liked the self-sufficiency of Mike's new approach – more than ever before, he was cultivating his body (and encouraging me to cultivate mine) to ride for as long as possible without needing to rest, refuel or otherwise submit to the tentacles of the outside world. As a courier, I had become more and more self-contained. My radio and phone holster were lined up across my chest, so that I could answer both while riding. In winter, I learned to affix my lights to my body and bag, rather than the bike, so that I didn't have to remove them when I parked up to go into buildings.

For the Transcontinental I'd ridden a bike with a dynamo built into the front wheel, so that I no longer needed to stop to charge my phone and Garmin. And even during the race I had tweaked and refined my packing system. Pouches on either side of my stem held a water bottle and whatever snacks I was working my way through, and between my bars was a tightly stuffed dry bag, with an extra pouch on the front for more food. I'd reasoned that the more snacks I had accessible, the longer I'd be able to ride without stopping, and I had bribed myself up long climbs, and through sleepy afternoons, by filling the pouches with fresh fruit or chocolates.

The frame pack between my legs, I realised, was best for those items I might want to access while still astride the bike, though not while pedalling. So over the course of the race I shifted my waterproof jacket, overshoes, knee warmers and gloves from my seat pack to the space just behind my head tube, so that I could get them on without fuss, putting my left foot down and reaching for the zip the moment I felt the first raindrops.

In the thinner pocket on the other side of the frame pack was my passport, the brevet card I had only remembered about when needing to get it stamped at checkpoints and a few plastic strips of pills. As well as the ibuprofen I had been taking every few hours by the end of the race, my doctor had prescribed a drug called norethisterone, designed to postpone periods. Mine had been due to start a few days into the race, and aside from the obvious challenges of stomach cramps and heavy bleeding, I knew that dizziness, weakness and occasional nausea would be an intolerable drag on my resources.

'You'll need to start them three days before you're due,' explained Dr Smith, 'and then take one three times a day until you've finished the race.'

It was a neat and satisfying solution. I set my alarm for 6 a.m., 2 p.m. and 10 p.m., and my line across Europe was punctuated by this thrice-daily ritual, where I'd reach into my pocket to quiet the alarm, then either continue through whatever long descent or busy traffic I was navigating, reminding myself anxiously to take the pill as soon as the going became easier, or immediately drop my left hand to the zip beneath my top tube, cock my knee as I fiddled the package out of the pocket, bend it around the pad of my thumb to pop a pill into my mouth, and then stuff the pills back into my frame pack for the next eight hours.

In Çanakkale I had let go of this rhythm, along with the impulse to keep going and the necessity of washing my chamois every day, and after forty-eight hours my heaviness and exhaustion had seemed to concentrate in my womb, making me faint and dizzy as all of my remaining vitality was pulled into a hot clenching mass at the base of my spine, and then drained out of me in globs of thick dark blood. Normally I'd feel refreshed and revitalised after my period, but this one had felt like the final stages of my disintegration, the cramps menacing me like the roaring thunder that had disturbed my sleep in Croatia, and the blood that streamed out of me one more symptom of my loss of control. Next year, I resolved, I'd keep taking the pills until I was safely home. But I doubted I could escape the crashing despair that accompanied the blood – the sense that, in the space of just a few hours, I had fallen from the height of my powers to a state of helplessness where I could no longer control my own body.

'That's one of the reasons life's so hard right after you've finished a race,' Mike said. 'You've just done this thing that's more than you've ever done before, and everyone keeps congratulating you on your achievement – but right there, as you are in that moment, you're knackered; you're not physically capable of the thing people are congratulating you for. It's why I think a lot of us have these self-esteem crashes. We can't live up to what we were during the race.'

I told Mike about norethisterone, suspecting that he'd appreciate this further way of refining the human body, adapting its processes to smooth the way for racing. I didn't tell him about the week that followed the race, where I'd felt, more literally than ever before, that I was falling to pieces. Fragments of memory and aspiration flitted about my swollen, sluggish body, as it bled, and flaked, and oozed, and I cast myself back to that beautiful morning in Albania where I contained myself fully, where the present moment became so great that it subsumed fantasy, and obscured memory. I wished myself back on the Montenegrin gravel, where my body and mind had focused so purely on their task that no space remained for extraneous thought or doubt, for anything but what I had right there. I longed to be the person who had made it up Ventoux after riding 1,000km in three days. I wondered where I would find myself again, and what it would take to get there.

Chapter Fourteen

Mike was twenty minutes late, and I had already drunk most of the pot of tea I'd timed for his arrival. It was usually an hour's ride between our houses – often less for him, either because he was faster or because there was more downhill – although a few days previously I'd taken three, not knowing till I climbed up out of the valley that the higher roads would be shimmering with ice, and being by then out of mobile signal, so unable to warn him I'd be late. Concerned that I might have crashed, he found me on my way down the final hill, where the first feeble rays of the January sun were turning the ice back into mud.

But today the temperature had crept up and all of Wales was wet. The dark grey sky oozed a steady drizzle that now and then quietened into mist, or quickened into rain-fall. The dull fields squelched and glugged with water that had nowhere else to go, and even the hillsides were now waterlogged. A thin sheen of mud lay across every road, and a pile of soggy Lycra sat permanently in front of my washing machine. I had given up cleaning my bike, since this actually proved a disincentive to go out on it again, as I'd undo all my work in minutes.

I didn't remember winters being this hard, even when I was a courier. On the rare occasions when the clouds lifted, offering a brief respite from the dampness that seeped into my bones, the temperature would drop, mud would turn to ice and the brilliance of the winter sun held a frisson of anxiety as I knew my tyres might slide out from under me at any moment. I remembered the winter of 2010, when London had run out of grit, and for a few days the roads a mile out from the centre had become ice rinks, lethal to drivers, cyclists and pedestrians alike. I could still work on the cleared streets in the City, but was reduced to walking for much of my commute. One evening I'd kept riding onto the ice, which shone pearlescent under the streetlights, hoping that if I kept my body straight and my cadence regular, I might make it up the shallow incline of Court Lane towards my house. And all of a sudden I was lying on my back, laughing with surprise, the bike still between my legs, blinking up at the lampposts and the stars. I had no recollection of slipping or falling, and barely remembered hitting the ground. Perhaps this was what death would feel like, I mused, happily lying there on the ice for a few more seconds, contemplating my abrupt change of status. Perhaps for some people it comes so quickly that there's no time to notice it, and then no consciousness to remember it, or piece together what happened.

But knowing that the ice could pounce like this made me reluctant to leave the house, reasoning that a two-hour ride wasn't worth the risk of a broken collarbone, which would keep me off the road for at least four weeks. When Mike and I finally got going on our ride down to Hay-on-Wye the previous week, we had turned back a few miles into our planned route, which still had patches of ice between the hedgerows, and reluctantly headed south on the main road. He was unwilling to endanger his race, now just six weeks away, and we both bore the scars of earlier ice encounters, and were afraid our luck might run out. By the time we got to Hay my bare calves were encased in mud like concrete, and up the inside of each thigh was a white line, thicker than any of the sweat stains I'd created the previous summer. We both scratched our heads over it for a few minutes, then Mike suggested it must be the salt from the road, flung up by my wheels and washed towards my inseam by the heat that emanated from me as I pedalled.

We huddled in a café, among the well-to-do retirees of Hay, and ordered our usual chocolate cake (him) and scone (me).

'How's the diet going?' I asked.

He gave me a look.

'Not bad. It's alright when I'm at home. And I've been staying in, turbo-ing quite a lot lately, because of the ice.'

The friends we were meeting were still half an hour away, so after briefly discussing my own training plan (my latest theory was that I should put myself in more situations where I wasn't the strongest rider, to get myself psychologically used to losing) our conversation inevitably turned to Mike's forthcoming battle with Kristof.

'Presumably you've got a slight advantage,' I asked, 'since you've seen a lot of him during races? I mean, you've been right there in the race car and at the checkpoints, while he's going through whatever it is Kristof goes through.'

'Yeah, I suppose there is that,' he replied.

'And does he ever show any sign, you know, that he's struggling? I mean, do you have any sense of where his weak points are?'

I wasn't expecting much of an answer, but after a pause, Mike told me that Kristof, though meticulous with his route planning, was surprisingly slapdash when it came to details such as the checkpoint locations.

'You'd think he'd have learned his lesson in 2014, with the Kotor thing – you know, how he was meant to ride round the fjord, but he took the boat across instead, and ended up having to go back down and do an extra 80k.'

A similar mistake had occurred in the most recent race, when Kristof arrived at CP4 in a huff, because (like me) he'd got lost coming through Žabljak. It turned out that he'd had similar mishaps at almost every other checkpoint. Dot-watchers had been delighted with the vignette of him turning up at Grindelwald hours before he was expected, and waking the volunteers so they could stamp his brevet card, but Mike told me that this was because Kristof had thought the checkpoint was after the Grosse Scheidegg climb, and given an ETA hours later than his actual arrival. It was only good luck that he happened to spot the race car on his way through the darkened town – otherwise he'd have ridden straight past, and over goodness knows how many mountain passes before he realised his mistake. In Italy he had assumed the checkpoint would be at the top of Passo di Giau, and the volunteers waiting in Alleghe had watched him streak along the lakeside road without stopping. Mike, wrestling with his own policy of non-intervention, had decided to flag him down, reasoning that there might be some unforeseen ambiguity about the checkpoint location, which they wouldn't know for sure unless later riders also missed it.

'So that's when he loses his cool,' Mike concluded. 'When he makes an avoidable mistake like that and ends up behind his schedule. We saw it close up at Kotor. I had to explain to him that he had gone wrong, and I was all ready to suggest a solution – which was basically what he ended up doing: ride back down the mountain and back round the fjord the way he was supposed to. But he stormed off before I could say anything, and he was really worked up, pacing up and down, on the phone with his wife. Eventually he came up with the same solution I would have offered him. But he was really angry with himself. He gets angry.'

'It's amazing he didn't learn from that,' I remarked, 'and still made the same mistakes last year. Do you think he'll have it sorted out for Indy-Pac?'

'I don't know. You'd assume so.'

Neither of us could imagine that Kristof would fail to iron out any weakness in his arsenal, but then we all have our blind spots. I wondered what Mike's were.

'And what about you?' I asked. 'How do you react when things go wrong like that?'

'Probably the same way, if I'm honest,' he admitted, smiling sheepishly.

I remembered the final afternoon of last summer's race, and my frustration with myself as I pedalled frantically along the winding line I'd whimsically drawn along the coast, suspecting that Johanna would be wiser, sticking to main roads and drawing closer and closer. My fury had been turned fully on myself – until, that is, I ran into another racer in the all-night services in Keşan. He had greeted me warmly, but I'd had no appetite for conviviality.

'Do they have coffee?' I barked humourlessly at him, and then stomped off to look for a bathroom, irritated beyond measure by his friendly demeanour, though in another mood I might have fallen into his arms. A couple of days later, remembering our encounter, I had cringed with embarrassment at how rude I'd been.

I was glad that Mike and Kristof experienced the same frustrations, even though their higher overall speed suggested that they had better strategies for coping with them, or at the very least the ability to move more efficiently when things *weren't* going wrong.

'Mike, what do you think Kristof's secret is?' I asked. 'Why is he so much better than everyone else?'

Given the way Mike's mind worked I knew that he would have been turning this question over for as long as he'd known Kristof, and would at the very least have a plausible theory.

He gave me a conspiratorial smile, his eyes twinkling, delighted to have been asked. But just as he opened his mouth to respond, Gareth and Alex clattered through the café door, steaming with exertion as they unzipped their jackets and tugged off their neck warmers. Whatever answer he would have given me would have to wait.

And now, just a few days later, as I dithered over whether to save him some tea, or just finish off the pot and put the kettle on again, I wondered if we'd ever get to finish that conversation, or if Mike had ended up in a ditch somewhere. It was far more likely though, I thought, that he had just had trouble getting out of bed, or that he'd made the mistake of checking his email before he left.

Eventually the door opened and Mike staggered in, giggling to himself.

'Kristof won't be doing *that* sort of training!' he announced, bending over as he heaved an extraordinarily heavy courier bag from around his torso, and lowered it dramatically to the floor. 'Err, that was harder than I expected – sorry if I'm a bit late. I actually had to walk up that last hill.'

Inside the bag was a slab of rock the size of a tomb-stone, engraved with 'Strathpuffer 2017'. Mike had offered to bring it back to Wales for me, since he was driving down and I was travelling back by train a day later. I had assumed it would sit in his van until whenever he had reason to drive to my place, and wasn't sure whether he had decided to deliver it by bike as a training opportunity, to test himself, or to show off. But whatever his intention he seemed pleased with the result, glowing happily as he sat down with his favourite mug and submitted once more to the attentions of the cat.

'I've figured it out, by the way,' I told him. 'She's attracted to the sweaty cyclist smell. She has the same reaction to my backpack.'

Mike ducked his head to blow on his tea as Rags made her way amorously round the back of his neck, and I propped my trophy up next to the front door, wondering what other winners had done with theirs.

I hadn't expected to win the Strathpuffer, and had entered knowing I didn't stand a chance, assuming it would be good for me to try my hardest with no hope of distinc-tion. I needed to blunt that overpowering fear I'd felt as Zara and I climbed up the fire road the previous year, side by side, unable to veil our intent and our exertion, since I knew I was unlikely to lead by as great a margin in the next Transcontinental (if I led the race at all), and would need to get my head round the proximity of my rivals, the con-stant scrutiny of the spectators and the overall likelihood of failure. I had only found out I was soloing the Strathpuffer at the last moment, when Sarah Outen, who'd intended to race with me as a pair, had to pull out because of an asthma flare-up, and I was secretly pleased. Solo racing would suit me better – I could immerse myself in the dark cocoon of the forest and the trail, and although I knew I'd be one of the less talented mountain bikers on the course, I had no concerns about my ability to keep going for twenty-four hours, to ride through the darkness, and to handle the subzero temperatures that were forecast. Mike had spent the night in his van near the start, after riding a couple of laps to check out the course, and warned me that it would be faster than the previous year, when we'd floundered in axle-deep mud, but that there would be more and more ice as night fell, and the temperature dropped. He was also racing solo, though not trying to win, as it would be too late for him to recover in time for the Indy-Pac.

'It can take six weeks to get your top end back after a race like this,' he informed me, adding that he planned to take two hours off to sleep in the middle of the race, thereby, he'd calculated, reducing his recovery time to a mere fortnight. In the rush of setting up our base camp, I didn't get a chance to ask him how he had reached these figures.

We were sharing the pits with Zara and Jo, the women who had beaten me and Lee the year before. But this year we were all on the same side, as Lee had decided to try for the overall win, with a team of four women: the three Scots joined by Rickie, a short, loud, Welsh painter-decorator with whom everyone fell in love as soon as she opened her mouth, and who had twice come second in the 24-Hour World Championships. Our pitmates also included Naomi, the woman who had won the solo category the year before, now racing as part of a mixed pair. I remembered gazing at her in awe as she mounted the podium, smiling tiredly in a bobble hat and a down jacket.

Unsurprisingly, it was the presence of other people that

turned out to be my biggest challenge. Out on the trails I was mostly oblivious to anything but what lay within the beam of my headlamp. Mike passed me twenty minutes in, at the point where the route turned off the fire road into the first section of single-track, and remarked with amusement that he had drafted me all the way from the start without my noticing. Other than that, the racers were mostly wraiths who floated in and out of the darkness, occasionally shooting past me or panting along behind. But when I stopped at the tent to grab another pouch of food and accept a bottle of warmed-up Ribena, which would slowly cool and then freeze over the course of a lap, I'd encounter a microcosm of the world I was trying to escape.

The pit crew, and the other racers resting between their laps, were alternately firm and sympathetic, some greeting me with hugs and offers of tea, others turfing me back out into the cold with terse reminders of what I was here for. These were the finest twenty-four-hour racers in the country, I reminded myself, as I glimpsed Lee Craigie swapping stories with Mike Hall, Rickie Cotter darting back and forth with cups of tea for the mechanics, and Naomi Freireich scanning the white board on which one of the crew was keeping a tally of each rider's laps. None of them was racing solo, so they had time to lounge in their camping chairs, sharing jokes and passing hip flasks like some living breathing cyclists' hall of fame.

I would cower as I stumbled into their realm, embarrassed that I'd already worn down my buffer of pretence and exposed the trembling animal that lay beneath. And I cursed my weakness whenever one of them bounded past me on the trail, at far higher speeds than I had left in me, calling out a few words of comfort or encouragement as they disappeared into the darkness. At around 1 a.m., as I paused outside the glowing tent to shove half a flapjack into my mouth, Rickie came out to tell me that I was in the lead.

'There's another woman just behind you though,' she cautioned, glancing down at the lap counter on her phone. I noticed that she was wearing the down jacket that I'd left in my pile of clothing in the corner of the tent. 'In fact, she's *just* dibbed now, which means you've only got two minutes on her. So you'd better get going!'

'Oh no no no,' I quavered. 'No, I don't want to be in the lead. That just means everyone's going to be watching me, and waiting for me to fail. And I can't keep it up. I can't do it. I ...'

My whimpers faded as Rickie pushed me off and I carried on up the hill. There was nothing else for it – much as I hated the thought of defending a lead I was bound to lose, hanging around in the pits to discuss the situation with half a dozen more experienced riders was even less palatable, and the further into the race I got, the more dangerous it felt to stop. If I broke the cord of my momentum, my body would collapse into sleep and I'd be unable to get moving again. Exhaustion hovered at the edge of my awareness, like a pack of wolves slinking around a campfire's halo of light. And as the night drew on, and the air got steadily colder, the damp slabs of rock that lined the course began to sparkle ominously in the light of my headlamp, and I slipped and slid and frequently fell as I attempted to ride over them. Sections of trail I had shot through safely now threw me off, and the mental map of the course I'd built up over my first few laps had to be updated:

No longer safe to take that left-hand bend at speed. Try a new line next time. Remember those rocks are icy. Go wide; stay off the main trail. Stop using momentum to get you round that corner – you'll slip.

Within a few hours of nightfall I had crashed so repeatedly that each of my knees, hips and elbows was bruised, my right arm clunking alarmingly as I bent it, as though something had been knocked out of place. The trail was lined with gorse bushes, which flayed my bare calves as I veered through them to escape the icy rocks, blood running down into my shoes.

I walked most of my final lap. The sun had come up, revealing just how much of the course had turned to ice, and I was scared to take even lines that I'd ridden all night. My arms were so thick with exhaustion that I didn't trust myself to handle the bike through the more technical sections. Miserably, I stumbled down hills and through gullies, tearing my gloves and skin on the gorse I grasped to keep myself steady. A few of the other riders were in a similar state, though many more sprang past me, still full of energy and desperate to record a fast lap and push their team up the leaderboard before the race ended. There was still more than an hour to go when I got back to the pits, but I already knew I wouldn't – couldn't – go out again.

I wept with exhaustion, openly begging the pit crew to let me stay there, and not to make me do one more lap. Outen got a camp chair and sat me down by the side of the fire road, crouching in front of me with a mug of tea and a bacon sandwich and entreating me to consume them as I sobbed at her like a child. Rickie held my bike, insisting that I had it in me to go back out.

'Come on Chappell – you're so close now! Just one more lap and you've won. You've got this. Just get back on the bike. You're Emily Chappell – you can do this.'

'I can't, I can't, I can't, I really can't,' I wailed at her, and it was only after several minutes of this that Naomi came out with her phone to confirm that the woman in second place hadn't gone out for *her* last lap either, and there was no one else close enough to take the lead in the final hour. I had won, and I didn't have to do another lap.

Outen helped me into the tent, sat me down beside a heater and wrapped me up in warm clothing that she picked indiscriminately from other people's piles. I cradled my mug of tea, my tears slowing and softening as the relief of finishing flooded me with such force that I felt a physical glow spread through my body. It was over. Oh my god, it was over.

The other riders bustled around, repacking the boxes of food they'd brought to see them through the night and pulling down the socks and jackets and base layers that hung from every rafter of the tent. People congratulated me and I thanked them as I knew I should, though the fact of winning the race hovered a small distance from me – something I could understand and examine, but to which I'd thus far had no discernible reaction. The glow I felt derived solely from having reached the end of my ordeal, and from the knowledge that I expected nothing more of myself. I felt no more certain or deserving of my victory than I had at the end of the Transcontinental. Winning felt like a footnote; a minor statistic; an afterthought.

'How did Mike do?' I asked. Apart from running into him in the pits a couple of times I hadn't seen him since he overtook me on the first lap and, given his far greater strength, I'd assumed he would lap me at least once. I'd been looking forward to it – to the rare experience of sharing a race with him, to seeing a master at work, and to a brief glimmer of fellowship in the darkness of the long Scottish night.

Outen laughed.

'Oh, he went to bed, I think. He had some theory about sleeping for a couple of hours to help his recovery? But we didn't see him again. I think he probably got too comfortable, or decided it was too cold once he'd stopped.'

He was standing outside his van as we walked slowly down the hill to the main tent – me shuffling, Outen supporting – and seemed pleased to see me.

'Well done,' he said, meeting my eye and offering me the bottle of recovery drink that he happened to have in his hand. I was glad that he'd seen me win, that I was still maintaining the pretence that I was someone who could win races like he did. And I also knew that he, of all people, saw through this win, knew that it would be the thing everyone else celebrated while I struggled to fit it into the husk that remained of me.

We talked for a few minutes about how horrifying the ice had been, conversation stilted by my clouded head and rattling lungs. At one point I was overwhelmed by a hacking cough that rose all the way from my chest, as I felt something detach itself and rise into my throat. I held up a hand in apology, turned to the verge and spat out a lump of greenish phlegm the size of a snail. I turned back to Mike with faint regret, wanting to examine this gory evidence of my exertions more closely, but knowing that, although he'd unquestionably been in similar states himself, that was probably a step too far.

My moment on the podium was brief and bewildering. I was handed a metal trophy sculpted from bike parts, a bottle of beer and a bag of gifts from the race's sponsors, then had to juggle them in confusion and eventually hand them to the second- and third-placed women as I was presented with the gigantic slab of rock that was my ultimate prize. As I had seen the other winners do, I mustered every last ounce of strength in my throbbing arms to hoist it briefly over my head, then gratefully handed it to Outen, to be stowed in Mike's van for the journey back to Wales.

And now it sat on my kitchen floor, as Mike examined the dent it had made in his back, and I congratulated him on his effort.

'I've been a courier,' I said, 'so I'm probably one of the leading experts in carrying heavy stuff on my back, while riding fixed. And I can tell you I've never been more impressed.'

We were on our way to Newtown, an hour's ride down the Severn Valley, for a meeting of the local refugee council. I'd mentioned over the weekend that I was planning to attend, and to my surprise he had asked if he could come too.

'I think it'll be good for me to get involved in stuff happening locally,' he explained. 'Or I could end up getting quite isolated, living on my own. By the way, you know there's a cycling festival in Llandrindod?'

I had heard of it.

'Well, I went to see them the other day, spoke to a woman at the museum, and they'd be interested in having us there next summer, if you're up for it? I told her about you – she said she hadn't heard of you.'

I shrugged, embarrassed that Mike had already made greater inroads into the local cycling community than I had, and wondered what he had said about me. But within minutes we were immersed in an earnest discussion of what sort of event we might put together, and how each of our respective talents might contribute.

Eventually one of us noticed it was time to go. We drained our mugs of tea and reluctantly stepped out into the drizzle, Mike exclaiming over how much more enjoyable his courier bag was to carry now that it was empty, and me rolling my eyes afresh at his lunacy.

Chapter Fifteen

This was the year long-distance racing hit the big time. Everyone was talking about the Indian-Pacific Wheel Race, which began in March, when Australians with a summer of cycling in their legs would wield a distinct advantage over those who had struggled to train through a European winter. In June the Irish TransAtlanticWay Race would coincide with the TransAm Bike Race and the Tour Divide, as they crossed paths in North America. And the Transcontinental had a new rival in August – a race called the North Cape 4000, which took riders in the opposite direction across Europe, from Italy to Norway.

Almost a thousand people had applied for the 200 places on the Transcon, and Mike agonised regularly over the fairest way to allocate them. Women, race veterans and those who had volunteered on previous editions were guaranteed entry; a few riders who had the personality or reputation to illuminate the race were hand-selected, and the rest of the applicants went into a ballot. Many were disappointed, and I wondered if it wasn't a good thing that so many more races were springing up. None yet had the cachet of Mike's, which meant they were usually people's second choice, but the Transcon couldn't accommodate that many more riders without fundamentally changing its character. (I imagined long columns of bikepackers charging across the countryside like invading armies.) The proliferation of similar races suggested that this had become a movement – a new sporting discipline – that was far greater than any of us might have imagined, that sunny morning in 2013 when thirty cyclists lined up on Westminster Bridge to race across a continent.

Mike, of course, could pick and choose the races he entered and, following the Indy-Pac, his name was on the start list for the Highland Trail in June, and shortly afterwards the TransAtlanticWay, alongside me and Juliana.

'I was a bit surprised to see that you're down to ride Highland Trail *and* the TransAtlanticWay,' I remarked. 'Is there really enough time to recover between the two? I mean, if you set a new record in the Highland Trail, that still gives you only about a week, and I assume you'd still be a bit wrecked?'

'Yeah, if I'm honest the TransAtlanticWay's an insurance policy,' he admitted. 'You know, if something goes wrong, or I'm off my pace, I can slack off a bit, and save it for Ireland. But the Highland Trail's my main race, definitely.'

'I'm actually surprised you've not ridden it already,' I said. 'It's got your name all over it. I mean, it's the closest thing Britain's got to the Tour Divide.'

'I know! Yeah well, this is the year.'

I wondered, though didn't say anything, whether chasing

the Highland Trail record – one that was easily within his reach – was also Mike's insurance policy for the Indy-Pac. The effects of his training were remarkable. His body was now leaner than I had ever seen it, even midway through the Tour Divide, and I grew increasingly accustomed to the sight of his figure disappearing towards the horizon as he outpaced me on the hills. But he didn't seem to have identified the mysterious factor that would enable him to beat Kristof, and when I finally dared to ask him who *he* thought would be the rider to take second, he said, 'Me, if I'm honest.'

'Really?' I wasn't entirely surprised. The idea of Kristof losing a race – or even pulling out with an injury so that his opponent won by default – was impossible to reconcile with everything we knew of him. But then, I thought, my mind circling back for the umpteenth time, a race where Mike rode but did not win was equally unthinkable.

'And this is why this one's so exciting,' I told my mother, shortly before Mike left for Australia, 'because basically, unless one of them *dies*, only one can finish first. And they wouldn't let it be a draw – neither of them would do that. They'll fight right to the end.'

Mike was philosophical about his anticipated defeat.

'I think it could be good for me. Give me something different to get my head round. I've won a lot of races now, you know, I know the drill. I think it's about time I did something else with my life. It'll be more interesting than the usual post-race stuff anyway.'

'Fair enough,' I replied. 'You're probably right.' I recalled the adulation I'd received over the last few months, for a victory that – in its immediate aftermath – had felt like no achievement whatsoever. I had cowered behind my own façade as people praised me for something I no longer felt capable of, terrified of the moment when they realised that I wouldn't live up to my reputation.

This was probably a big part of why Mike and I had ended up becoming so close. We shared enough common ground that much of what we might have to explain to – or conceal from – other people was understood and taken for granted. I had little fear that Mike would see through me, because I assumed he had done right from the beginning, when two clinically depressed bike messengers conducted a halting conversation on a cold March night in Leicester Square, in the bleak aftermath of their respective odysseys. It was a relief to return to his company after standing on the Strathpuffer podium, or after one of the talks I was increasingly invited to give about my exploits, and to know that nothing more was expected of me than what I had to offer on any given day.

Although I suspected that Mike's prediction was in part an effort to brace himself for every possible outcome, and knew that he'd still stop at nothing to be the first to Sydney Opera House, I thought it *would* be good for him to step down from his pedestal, at least for a while. The hype surrounding the Indy-Pac had inevitably elevated him and Kristof to godlike status, and I knew only too well how lonely a position that could be. Remembering how isolated and hungry I had felt on returning from Çanakkale, I promised to get some groceries in and cook him a meal on his return, gratified by the way his face lit up.

'I don't know *what* I'll cook though. Let me know if you have any requests, otherwise you'll probably just get soup again.'

By the time he was home from the race it would be spring. Our rides would end in daylight, and rather than huddling in one of our kitchens, eating curries and stews as our waterproofs steamed on the radiator and one or the other of us dreaded the cold ride home, we could stay out and camp on hilltops, or drink pints in the pub opposite his house before I rode back down the hill through the sunset. We made plan after plan, as a way of holding winter's gloom at bay, or at least reminding ourselves that it would lift, and the year would open up before us. We'd announced a Transcon training camp in April, and would come up with something for the Llandrindod Cycle Festival. Between us, we'd source bikes for the refugees who were arriving in Newtown. He was planning a book to celebrate the first five years of the Transcontinental, and wanted me to contribute. I was planning a zine about my night on Ventoux, and wanted him to contribute.

We wondered if I would end up working with him on the race. It seemed an obvious conclusion, and had hovered obliquely in our conversations for several months. Mike asked me regularly if I knew when I would be ready to stop racing the Transcontinental, and all I could respond was that I wouldn't know until the moment came.

'If you can commit to not racing next year, we could drive back from Greece together,' he offered, as we sat in the café in Rhayader on the morning of our last ride together, eking out our coffee and eggs as raindrops battered the windows. Mike had brought along Max Leonard, another cycling writer from London, who had agreed to help put together the book about the race.

'Ha! Are you offering me a lift?'

'I mean, if you want to come over onto the organisational side,' he replied. 'That's when we pick out the checkpoints for the next race.'

'I know, I know.' I smiled in spite of myself. 'I'd really love to. It's just. Well. Let's see how I feel in a couple of months.'

I still wasn't sure. Working on the race would mean the end of riding it, and I was reluctant to bid farewell to the sublime moments of the previous summer, knowing that I'd pass them on to other racers, and already envying them their discoveries. But the thought of creating something with Mike, of carving out my own niches within the race, scouring the map of Europe for *parcours* and checkpoints, debating and fusing our ideas, painstakingly moulding this many-stranded, many-headed, many-mouthed beast into a beautiful whole, was too seductive to dismiss.

And yet I wondered whether the reality of organising a race – and working with Mike – might turn out to be less exhilarating. I was aware of how much time he spent answering emails, the sheer logistics of conveying 200 racers from entry to finish line, the teams of volunteers to be managed, the sponsor relationships to be negotiated, the accounts to be balanced, the endless human errors and irritations to be endured. Mike and Anna had ultimately found working together too difficult, and Mike's accounts of their struggles were far from one-sided. Whenever he salved his hurt by recounting unreasonable things she had said or done, he always included careful caveats that he himself mightn't have been the easiest person to work with, admissions that he struggled with giving up control and confessions that he hadn't always handled their confrontations as magnanimously as he could have. Mike and I seemed harmonious enough now, spilling over with ideas and projects, but the mundane business of turning fantasy into reality might be another matter.

But there was no hurry to make a decision. Mike would be occupied for the next few weeks, and after that the smaller projects we had planned could function as auditions. If the training camp went well, if we could come up with something for the Cycle Festival where I didn't feel my ideas were swamped and subsumed by his, then perhaps I'd say yes to the lift back from Greece. I wouldn't necessarily have to stop competing, I told myself – after all Mike had always entered at least one big race in the earlier part of the summer. I'd just have to find different events. None of the current offerings excited me as much as the Transcon, with its constantly evolving *parcours* and enormous chattering entourage, but all of them would evolve as this new discipline took hold. Being on the Transcon team, I realised, would make me part of this, a member of the family.

Eventually it became apparent that no one had enough left in their coffee cup to justify another round of conversation, and it was time to face the rain.

The three of us spent a couple of minutes admiring each other's bikes before we set off. Mike was on the same fixed-gear bike he'd ridden for most of the winter, and pointed out that he'd now fitted it with his carbon-fibre aero bars.

'Riding in that position means I can't put any force at all through my arms,' he told us. 'It all has to come from legs and core. And I think I've got myself to where I need to be.'

We left Rhayader and made for the mountain road that led over the northern end of the Elenydd Plateau towards Cwmystwyth, climbing up through bare trees towards a grey sky, our clothing already as waterlogged as the brown hillsides around us.

'I'll see you at the top,' said Max, who had already made his excuses, announcing that he wasn't pushing it today, and that he wouldn't stand a chance of keeping up with Mike even if he did.

We carried on upwards ahead of him, a rushing stream falling further and further away on our left, and a rocky hillside looming on our right, strewn with damp scree and boulders that had found their resting place there however many millennia ago. There wasn't enough of the scant, mossy grass to cover them, and I wondered whether, many years on from our particular geological moment, another foot of soil and growth would have entirely obscured the inner workings of the mountain, which as yet stood partially exposed.

I watched Mike's shape advance up the hill ahead of me, and then realised I was gaining on him, that today's configuration of legs and gearing was closer to matching his strength than I had been for a good few weeks. Enjoying the firm, slick sensation of bodily might converting to upward motion, I pressed harder to accelerate, and eventually drew alongside him, both of us panting quite audibly as we reached the steepest part of the hill. For a moment or two his eyes remained on the road ahead, as if this were a solitary experience that I just happened to be observing. Then he turned towards me, as if to say 'oh, there you are', and we carried on side by side for a while, lungs burning, suffering companionably.

He pulled ahead of me shortly before the summit and once again I watched him grow smaller, enveloped by the mists and raindrops, a fragile figure in spite of his strength.

We met with a nod, waiting side by side for Max to reach us, our breath easing and our skin glowing as fat raindrops soaked into our gloves and ran down our faces. All around us the heavy grey clouds hung low over the dull grasslands, swallowing the tops of the hills, obscuring the horizon.

'See you on the other side then!' I said as we parted ways back in Rhayader. I deliberately avoided wishing him good luck, partly out of an aversion to weighty goodbye rituals, and partly because any allusion to fortune seemed to diminish the extent and precision of his training. I

looked forward to watching him shovel in whatever nour-
ishing meal I managed to come up with on his return, and
hearing his post-mortem of the race between mouthfuls.
I wondered how many of his theories would survive the
testing ground of Australia, and how many of those I'd end
up adopting myself over the next few months.

Even before the race began, excitement over the Indy-Pac
exceeded anything the bikepacking world had seen before.
The racers mustered in Fremantle, and an image was circu-
lated of Mike and Kristof facing off across a dining table,
brandishing their cutlery as if they planned to eat each
other for breakfast, both smirking at the hilarity of the
situation. I thought once again how different they looked,
Kristof long and lean and cleanly shaven, Mike stout and
powerful, his wild hair and unkempt beard suggesting a
mad professor rather than an elite athlete. Kristof's skin
was a few shades darker, with a sharp tan line visible
beneath the sleeve of his T-shirt, and I wondered whether
he had done some warm weather training, or whether his
tan lines were now a permanent feature, like the gradations
of colour that remained on my thighs, a ghostly reminder
of the previous summer.

A similar photo appeared of Juliana and Sarah
Hammond, eyeballing each other across a café table with
knives in all four fists. An outtake, posted on Sarah's Instagram account, showed them collapsing into giggles, and
I remembered the hours Juliana and I had spent sitting
around in cafés before racing out of Geraardsbergen, gently
mocking each other as we filled ourselves up with the calories we'd burn over the next days. I wished I was there with
them all.

Juliana had, true to form, crashed less than a month
before the start, tearing a hole in her right knee that

required six stitches and a week off the bike to knit it back together.

'The main problem is, I've gashed it open so many times, there's no skin left to stitch it together if I crash again,' she remarked. I could sense her rolling her eyes at herself.

I was giving a talk in Sheffield when they set off from Fremantle, riding into the early morning air a world away from my overheated function room and the rainy night outside. Afterwards, two women came up to me.

'You probably won't remember me,' said the older one. 'I'm Shell's wife.'

'And I'm his daughter.'

Shell was now a dot on the map, creeping steadily through the eastern suburbs of Perth. We watched him for a minute, as the pack of racers slowly stretched out into a line, many still clearly within sight of each other. All of a sudden the people I knew seemed impossibly remote, as though, aside from our obvious differences in time zone and location, they had ploughed themselves into some hypnotic state that we non-racers could not hope to penetrate. Even if they kept in regular contact with those outside the bubble, Shell, and Mike, and Juliana, were now in some sense inaccessible to us until they emerged in Sydney, like divers breaking the surface of the water.

⁞⁞⁞

Everything seemed to burst into life that month. I travelled up and down the country, giving talks in places as far apart as Margate and Aviemore, still amazed that a crowd of people would turn up to hear my stories about cycling across a continent, and even more so when women approached me afterwards and told me they were planning to enter the Transcon the following year – or that, having heard my stories elsewhere, they'd signed up for this year, and would see me in Belgium.

In Wales the trees were still bare, but a bout of sunny weather dried the roads and brought out the daffodils. Finally it was spring, and my body reliably abandoned the sluggishness with which it had grumbled through winter, and fizzed with energy, begging to be let out to play. One bright Sunday morning I came in from a ride round the reservoir – a hilly loop that I'd assumed would calm me down and leave me able to work – realised that I wasn't remotely satisfied and set off again, up the hill towards where Mike lived. Up and up I charged, eating the air before me, stamping on the pedals, galloping over the hills, through the sparkling blue sky and past the bright ranks of daffodils. Three miles from Mike's house I turned left instead of right and carried on upwards, following an instinct that told me to get as close to the sky as possible, to put all of these hilltops beneath me. I followed a small single-track road I had never ridden before, and wondered if he had, and when we'd ride it together. My mind hummed with the potential of the long summer that lay before us, and I toyed with the idea of riding down to his house, sending him a picture of it surrounded by daffodils, and telling him to hurry back, that winter was over and he was missing the spring.

I was held back by the memory of his self-imposed isolation on the Tour Divide, when he had posted his phone home from the start to avoid both distractions and his own temptation to seek them out. Isolation was a little less possible on the Indy-Pac, given that Jesse had deliberately routed the race through Australia's biggest cities. A couple of days previously the lead riders had passed through Adelaide and videos had rapidly appeared of a bemused Kristof being greeted by the mayor of the city, a few dozen office workers in their shirts and dresses and a small peloton of cyclists who had met him on his way into the city and intended to follow him out. Mike had arrived – to a slightly diminished crowd – a few hours later, and Sarah after nightfall, appearing out of the darkness through a crazed blur of bright lights and roaring traffic.

Any other contenders for the lead had quickly fallen back or dropped out, and within a couple of days the race had resolved itself into the contest everyone had hoped for – Kristof versus Mike, with Sarah snapping at their heels. And in contrast with Europe's obliviousness to the Transcontinental, Australians couldn't get enough of the battle playing out along their highways, through their deserts and in their cities. The Indy-Pac, like no race before it, had instantly been elevated to the status of a national treasure. I watched on Twitter as cyclists and non-cyclists alike discovered the race, professed a rapid addiction to following it and reported overhearing strangers in coffee shops talking about dot-watching. Kristof had recently posted a photo in which a smiling family waved at him out of their car, patently delighted to have found him in the flesh. It was 'mindblowing,' he tweeted, how many people knew the race was going on, and he seemed to welcome the momentary distractions from heat and exhaustion. He admitted to having consumed six ice creams already that day, and was now in search of coffee.

The other riders were suffering even more explicitly, in all the usual ways and some less usual ones. Alongside the complaints of stomach trouble and saddlesore, one racer had apparently been injured by a kangaroo, and another ended up in hospital after a collision with a vehicle. Juliana initially made good time, but her dot had slowed alarmingly as she crossed the Nullarbor, and to my great consternation she had arrived at a roadhouse exhibiting much the same symptoms she had in Colorado the year before. Her race over, she had hitched a lift back to Perth and, after medical checks revealed an allergic reaction to painkillers, was debating her next move.

Mike's race had so far proved not to be the smoothest, though it could just have been that he was talking about his troubles for once, rather than keeping them to himself.

'Rough day at the office,' he had tweeted, of his first day on the road, and on the second day:

Made a few changes, things feel a little better but don't quite feel like firing on all cylinders. Meanwhile head is having a misfire

Legs seem to have joined the game after an impromptu Nullarbor bike fit session. Quick snooze and we'll see if the head wants to join em

And a day later, enigmatically:

Forget what I said yesterday

Of course, I thought to myself, the first three days of a race are relevant only as something to be got through. The rider's body needs to settle in (I remembered the debilitating foot pain I'd experienced early in the Transcon, which magically disappeared by the second week), his position in the race being dependent far more on who's resting when than on the actual speed of his rivals, and all anyone's doing is working their way into the state of tense sleep deprivation in which they'll complete the majority of the *parcours*. It was plausible that the numbness and lack of power Mike had complained of on the first day would turn out to be one of those seemingly insurmountable obstacles that he'd forget by the time he reached Sydney.

In a photo taken of him outside a petrol station, I noticed that he had shaved the sides of his head, which, together with his new leanness, and the aviator shades he had taken to wearing, gave him an unaccustomed loucheness. No matter how the race might be going, he was tackling it in style.

At the end of the third day, Jesse posted a short video they had filmed from the race car, of Mike riding along through the luminous twilight of the Australian bush, the last rays of sunset gleaming on the horizon behind him.

'Look at him,' remarked my father. 'Just look at that. His upper body's completely still, it's just his legs moving. Poetry in motion.'

We pored over the video, watching it again and again. Mike was bent over his aero bars, lean brown arms parallel to the ground, gloveless hands lightly wrapped around the extensions. The muscles of his back were visible through his tight navy-blue jersey, and his legs moved in the ceaseless rhythm that had already carried him over 1,700km. He blinked a few times as the car drew past him, but didn't spare a glance to the race crew or acknowledge them in any way. His look of careful focus suggested to me that he might be trying to avoid falling asleep, and sure enough, he tweeted a few hours later:

4hrs minimum at Border Village, I was dangerous on the way to here. I don't know how much of it all was real

He overtook Kristof a week later, having trailed him by 100km across most of the continent. I had speculated along with everyone else over whether this was a calculated strategy – hovering a few hours behind his rival, waiting for an opportunity to attack in the final days of the race – or whether Mike was clinging on, unable to move any faster and worried that the gap would grow. A couple of days previously he had referred vaguely to stomach troubles, and I wondered whether he had inadvertently made things worse for himself with his dietary experiments. But on 28 March, Kristof's dot faltered in the Australian Alps, and stopped for several hours on what appeared to be a narrow mountain road with no verges. There was no obvious reason why he should have paused there, and the dot-watchers fretted and theorised, as Mike's beacon drew ever closer. Eventually Kristof started moving again, but by now Mike's blue dot was rapidly gaining on his red one.

I was in London that day, giving a talk for *National Geographic*, and they had put me up in a hotel so stylish that I felt intimidated by it and couldn't relax, in spite of the towelling bathrobes and mounds of goose-down pillows. Repeatedly during that night I gave up my pretence of being asleep and leaned over to check my phone, watching as the two dots grew closer and closer, fizzing with excitement as they continued forward together. A very long way from me, Mike and Kristof were riding side by side.

I hadn't been sleeping well since the race began, my normal rhythms disrupted by my travels up and down the country, and my nerves held together with too much coffee and more alcohol than I was used to. Similar to during the Transcon, I sensed I was surfing a wave that eventually had to crash, that this level of activity and stimulation was unsustainable, and that eventually I would have to retire to

Wales, curl up among the hills and the clouds, and rest. My period was overdue, but showed no signs of arriving, and I suspected this was due to the same stress hormones that flood my system during long rides, though I had already been waiting for it for so long that I joked to friends that I was so busy my body had forgotten to menstruate, or that I might somehow have ended up pregnant. Glasses of wine in hand, we joked about immaculate conception, and exchanged far-fetched speculations as to how a person might be impregnated without even noticing. I did feel swollen and expectant, as though something unknown was gathering its forces inside me.

The Australians were in a similar frenzy over the latest developments in the race. Well-known athletes and politicians revealed that they were following it, and more and more people weighed into the online discussions of whether Mike would retain his lead, whether Kristof would overtake him again, whether Sarah, who was still only a few hours behind, would catch both of them. Teachers brought their classes out to cheer on the racers and the staff of a brewery tweeted a photo of one of them holding out a glass of cold beer as Mike sped past. The photographer had caught the moment where Mike's glance rested on the beer, with an expression of amusement and – most of us extrapolated – longing, and I wondered what was going through his head. Was he anticipating the beers he and Kristof would enjoy in Sydney a couple of days hence? Did he ever think about the sunny evenings back in Wales, when he and I would sit outside the pub in the afterglow of a long ride?

Juliana had restarted, announcing her intention to ride the route as an individual time trial. And it seemed, at long last, that she'd rediscovered her old talent. Within the first forty-eight hours of leaving Fremantle she had covered over

1,000km, and was barely daunted by a rash of punctures that rapidly consumed all her spare tubes. She eventually stuffed her tyres with clothing, and endured a bumpy ride to Border Village, where the truckers who had originally ferried her back to Fremantle were waiting with spare tubes. She posted a photo that morning of her standing next to a giant statue of a kangaroo on the state border. Despite the exertions of the past three days her expression was calm, satisfied and – perhaps only to me – held a note of mischief. I smiled when I saw her. If she kept this up, I thought, and if nothing else went wrong, she might well equal Sarah's time, or even beat her. In fact, given how close the three leaders were, there was even a chance Juliana might (unofficially) end up in second or third place, though she'd arrive in Sydney days after the race was won. This could be another James Hayden story, I thought.

Chapter Sixteen

Hello Mike – getting some unsettling news about an IPWR fatality, and just want to check you're alright. A lot of people worried, so please do give us a shout when you get this. Em x

I watched my anxious words turn into a little green bubble on the screen of my phone and settled down in the darkness to wait for a response. Scrolling back up, the last messages I'd received from Mike were from two months ago, the day I'd been held up by the icy roads.

Gonna come out and look for you, he'd said. I remembered how I'd caught sight of his now-familiar shape, coming out to meet me as I descended the muddy hill into his village.

A couple of minutes ago, just as I was drifting off to sleep in my sister's spare room in Manchester, a text had arrived from my friend Ian.

Em. Sorry to disturb you so late. There's been a reported fatality really, really close to where Mike's spot last pinged. It hasn't moved for 3 hours now. I don't have his mobile number, but trying to reach him would reassure a lot of people.

Ian was almost certainly overreacting. I reached for my laptop and opened the tracker, thinking once again how eager dot-watchers were to amplify a perfectly innocent stop to eat or rest into a crisis. I thought of all the times during my bike tours when well-meaning and paranoid loved ones had taken delight in scouring the news for any bombings, kidnappings or natural disasters that might have taken place within a thousand miles of where I was, and my own comparatively mundane experience of riding through small towns, absorbed in the prosaic intricacies of other people's lives, no more expecting these cataclysms to descend than I would had I been sitting in my own home.

'There's nothing to be scared of,' I'd told an assembled crowd of women at the talk I'd given that evening. 'You'll realise, as soon as you're out there, that your biggest worries are going to be boring things like wet feet, and punctures, and visa deadlines. If I was actually riding along in constant fear, thinking every man was going to rape me, and every truck was going to squash me, I wouldn't have kept doing this for so long.'

Mike's dot was indeed stationary. I watched it for a few minutes, as the map refreshed and everyone else's crawled slowly forward. Kristof was around a hundred miles ahead, and Sarah was rapidly gaining on him. Over on Twitter people were earnestly cross-referencing traffic reports, appealing for information from anyone who might be in the area. I tried not to get sucked into the speculation, knowing that I'd know what was happening before any of them did. I wryly recalled the worry that had preyed on my mind when he'd been late arriving with my Strathpuffer trophy, and how it had instantly been forgotten as he staggered theatrically through the door.

It was tempting to believe that something terrible had happened – there were reports on Australian news sites that a male cyclist had been killed in a predawn crash on the Monaro Highway – but there were so many other reasons Mike's dot might have stopped. He could have gone stealth, to confuse Kristof, or dropped his tracker without noticing. They were both within forty-eight hours' ride from Sydney now – there wasn't much further to go.

I checked my text messages again, in case he had replied and I hadn't seen it, wanting him to appease the dark knot of worry that I was trying to comb out of my chest.

Nothing. Just my own message sitting there, with no indication it had been read. Had he felt the phone buzz in his pocket as he rode along? Had he glanced at the screen, seen messages from me and no doubt many others, and decided, through whatever haze of sleepiness or paranoia or indifference, not to answer them right away? Or was he …

I couldn't let myself think of what might have happened to him, my mind blurring the images as decisively as a censor editing a particularly lurid news report. The closest I could get was to picture the cluster of police vehicles and paramedics I'd often seen in London in the aftermath of a crash, sometimes riding past with a plummeting feeling in my chest, sometimes puzzled by how little horror I felt, how distant this was from me. Somewhere in that blurred cluster was Mike's phone, with my message waiting for him. I hoped he would see it. I tried not to imagine the poignancy of someone else seeing it.

The phone buzzed in my hand and Lee's name appeared on the screen. She and Rickie had been giving a talk in Edinburgh that evening and, like me, had been alerted to what was going on in Australia just after they'd gone to bed. We stayed on the phone for a while. Neither of us knew what to say, but ending the call before anything was resolved seemed like an acceptance of whatever it was we didn't want to face, not to mention that then I'd be alone, sitting up in bed in the light of my sister's desk lamp, waiting for news that might not come for hours, and might be very bad when it did.

I checked the race's hashtag on Twitter as we spoke. Too many people were talking about the crash, repeating the same information, and I scanned desperately up and down, looking for something new.

'Oh. They're saying the cyclist was part of the race. I'm not sure if it's confirmed yet,' I told Lee, as another report was thrown into the arena, to be seized upon, wrestled with and amplified by the hundreds of anonymous voices who, I suddenly realised, would be sitting alone just like me, tense and fearful in darkened rooms all over Europe, and in offices and cafés in Australia, waiting for confirmation, wanting it not to be true.

'Let's hope it's just that Mike saw the crash and stopped to help,' suggested one person, only to be reminded by half a dozen others that it was now certain that the deceased cyclist had been part of the race. My mind – and no doubt everyone else's – once again veered illogically away from the obvious, trying to construct a scenario in which a rider further back in the race had sadly met their end, and that this separate incident had become conflated with reports of a road accident near Mike's position. It was improbable, but then, so is the fact that he's dead, I told myself, thinking of the countless times I've assumed the worst when a friend or family member runs late, and reliably been proved wrong when they turn up with an extremely dull story about traffic jams or phone batteries.

'We can't let ourselves jump to conclusions until they've announced who it is,' insisted Lee. 'We just don't know till then.' And a wave of hope swept through me. We don't know anything. It isn't true yet. All of the components are there – there's been a car crash, a racer has died, no one's heard from Mike – but until someone adds them up, it's just a hypothesis. Despite all signs to the contrary, this may yet not be true.

But a few minutes later Lee admitted 'it can't really be anyone else, can it?' and we realised that the only reason no official announcement had been made was that the next of kin had to be informed. I thought about Mike's mother, Pat, her immaculate house in Harrogate, a ringing phone, a bedside light. I couldn't go any further than that.

Eventually we ended the phone call.

'Are you going to be OK?'

'Well, no. But yes, I can cope.'

'Call me if you can't.'

'Will you be able to get to sleep?'

'I think so. I don't know. Call you in the morning?'

I spent the rest of the night awake, lying in the dark, trying not to think about Mike until all I could think about was him, and then sitting up and compulsively scrolling through Twitter, hunting for the voice that would tell me it was all OK, there'd been a mistake. Again and again I crept across the landing to the bathroom, listening to my niece's noisy breathing through her bedroom door, and wishing I could be as oblivious to this as she was.

They still hadn't released the identity of the dead

rider, but after a few hours no one could pretend any more that it wasn't Mike, and the hashtag dissolved into commiserations.

RIP Mike
RIP Mike Hall
RIP Mike ☹
RIP Mike. I can't believe it.
RIP Mike. You were my inspiration.
RIP Mike Hall
RIP Mike
RIP Mike. Ride In Peace.
RIP Mike. So sad.
RIP Mike Hall
RIP Mike. I'm still praying it's not true.
RIP Mike
RIP
RIP ☹
RIP Mike. You will be missed.
RIP
RIP
RIP

Eventually someone reported that Mike's dot was now moving along the highway towards Canberra at 100kph, and I had to stop watching after that.

Greeting my sister when she woke up, I felt the same disjointedness as when I queued for my morning coffee during the race, surrounded by ordinary people who had got up for work as on any other day, with no idea of the demons I faced in their streets and countryside while they were sleeping. My mouth couldn't quite fit itself round the words as I told her Mike had died during the night.

Everyone else's lives seemed to be continuing as normal. People who had been glued to Twitter alongside me in the dead of night were now posting pictures of their breakfast and opining on the day's news stories. My niece shouted and chuckled in her high chair, spreading her breakfast across her face and the floor beneath her. The sun blazed in through the French windows. It was a morning like any other.

I hadn't been prepared for the messages of condolence – but then, I hadn't been prepared for any of this. Email after email rolled in, some from friends I'd not seen for years, telling me they'd heard about Mike, they couldn't believe it, they didn't have the right words but they were thinking of me, they were so sorry for my loss, they were there if I needed anything.

I was grateful, and cried when I read some of them.

I was angry, wishing that people would stop talking about this and making it real, that we could remain suspended between doubt and certainty for just a little while longer.

I was numb, watching my inbox fill up as though it were someone else's, noting the words and sentences people strung together to convey their sympathy.

I was surprised. I hadn't realised so many people knew Mike and I were friends, or that he was anything more to me than the hero I'd initially expected him to be.

I was diligent, replying to each message with words that sounded most like what people would want to hear, pleased with how I seemed to be handling the situation.

Thank you. I miss him already.

Thanks. Don't worry, no one has the right words for this.

On social media people posted photos of themselves with Mike, from when they'd met him at a race or a bike show. Tributes and obituaries appeared as readily as if people had drafted them in advance.

There was little difference between a live hero and a dead hero, I thought, wondering whether someone had already got to Mike's Wikipedia page, to edit 'is' into 'was', now that the story was complete. And without a human presence to anchor him, people were free to turn Mike into whatever they wanted.

I hadn't replied to the last email he'd sent me – it was a query about the costs of self-publishing, to which I didn't readily know the answer – and now I could stop feeling guilty about that, I thought to myself, guiltily.

'Somewhere, Tommy Simpson is putting the kettle on,' remarked someone on road.cc, referring to the British Tour de France hero who had died on Mont Ventoux in 1967. I had passed his monument on that windy night two years ago, shortly after meeting Mike on his way down in the car.

'See you in Sestriere!' he had called, and I had marvelled even in that moment at this strange world we both inhabited, where running into a friend on a dark mountainside was as ordinary as nodding at your neighbour on the way to the bus stop. 'See you in Belgium!' I'd said as we said goodbye in Breckenridge the previous summer, wondering where else in the world our paths would cross over the years, deliberately and through happenstance. We had never bumped into each other unexpectedly in Wales, and that would surely have happened sooner or later, had he come back.

My face contorted suddenly, and a rush of sobs came over me like a fit of coughing, utterly beyond my control. I cursed whoever had written that about Tom Simpson. It was too neat, too wise, too beautiful an image – Mike being welcomed into Valhalla by another fallen hero – and I hated myself for drawing comfort from it, for thinking how Mike would enjoy meeting Tom Simpson, for the implication that there were ways of framing this that made sense of it.

Mike had been alive less than a day ago, pedalling through the Australian night as I wandered round central Manchester, buying cosmetics and chocolate and vitamin pills to put in a post-race care package for Sarah Hammond. As I arrived at the café where my event was held, chatted with the staff and helped set up the chairs, he had been riding, breathing, thinking. I clung to that proximity as to a life raft, not wanting to let go and venture out into the world where he was not.

I had heard of people brought back from the dead after being gone for minutes, occasionally even hours. I knew that the further we got from the moment when his breath stopped, the less hope there was of going back. Couldn't they have tried harder? His body would be cooling now, its electricity gone, more of his cells dying off with every minute that passed. The muscles he had sculpted with a seventy-inch fixed gear and the Welsh hills would now wither away. His hair wouldn't grow back. The scars and sunburn of the last two weeks would never heal. Had he had saddlesore? Or blisters? Had his knees hurt? Had his eyes itched? He won't have to deal with those problems now, I thought, and then I wondered who would wash and lay out his body, what they'd think of the stench and ingrained dirt of two weeks' cycling, which no one else was meant to see, and another fit of sobbing roared into me, like the wind on Mont Ventoux.

Helplessly, I watched the rest of the world building his pedestal – or was it his funeral pyre? – installing him firmly as a legend while I silently screamed at them to stop. I was too much aware of his declining presence in the world, the turbulence of his body moving through space, the air displaced by his legs as he pedalled, and pouring in and out of his lungs, now slowly swirling to a standstill. He wasn't fully dead yet. How is it that everyone else knows what to do?

My niece wasn't keen on someone else crying in a house where *her* tears usually ruled the roost. She responded with angry sobs of her own, which stopped abruptly when she was hauled onto my sister's lap, where she glared at me from the safe circle of her mother's arms as if to say 'You see? *I'm* the one who cries round here.'

I took the hint, and went out on my bike in the sunshine. I would get through this, I thought, with brief optimism. I could just sit out the difficult moments, remind myself that everything passes, and then get on with my life. I needn't even miss Mike that much. How many times have I lost touch with a friend, gradually or suddenly? It just so happened that Mike had gone away for a month or so, and that had now been extended. I could surely get my head round that. He hadn't even lived in Wales very long. I could just go back to how I'd been before.

I felt pleased with how I'd rationalised it all, and then another round of sobbing hit me out of nowhere, and I succumbed to it as helplessly as I had been floored by the icy corners of the Strathpuffer.

I still had to give a talk that evening, and I reluctantly included a picture of Mike at the end of my presentation, knowing that people would be puzzled if I failed even to mention him. I heard my voice thicken with tears as I spoke about what had happened, and thought how well, in that moment, I was embodying the persona of grief, knowing that most of the people sitting in the dark beyond the foot-lights would find a lump in their throat, and want to come up afterwards to express their sympathies and congratulate me on my bravery. I accepted and downed glasses of whisky with a sense of angry entitlement, then cycled back to my sister's as fast as I could, trying to get all my sobs out of me so that I could go to bed quietly, without waking my niece.

'I'm doing quite well with this,' I thought.

I set out the following day to ride back to Wales, think-ing to drown my sorrows in the motion of legs and lungs, remembering Juliana's decision to cycle round the world in response to losing her partner. It was a 100-mile ride, and would be just what I needed, to storm through my anger, and exhaust my sadness. Cycling would carry me through my grief in a way that was both helpful and true to the person I had lost. Like Juliana, I would plough my anguish into the road, use it as fuel for my eventual transformation. Perhaps, I thought, it was my destiny to pick up the baton Mike had dropped.

But as I left Manchester, I felt the warning rumbles of stomach cramps, like thunder on the horizon, and my period finally arrived, dissolving what remained of my energy, sucking it all into my throbbing womb. I wobbled along the A483 as far as Wrexham, my thighs empty and aching, my mind clouded, my lower back wracked by swelling waves of pain. No matter how I strived, I couldn't become the grim warrior, pedalling unrelentingly through her grief. I was weak, heavy, exhausted. I got on a train and huddled miserably next to the bike compartment, as it dawned on me that I didn't want to go home. Although I had known these Welsh hills my whole life, and Mike had shared them with me for a scant six months, they were now shadowed with his absence.

I heaved myself up the steep slope to the house, remembering the times we'd ridden it together, and with a sharp clench in my chest I realised that somehow I had missed the news about his death, because somehow, although it had hit me numerous times in the hours since I'd found out, I hadn't fully understood it until now.

⁜

The next day, Rickie and Isla came to take me out for a ride, following a route that a few of us had ridden with Mike between Christmas and New Year. It was a gloriously sunny day, and we passed other groups of cyclists on our way over the Staylittle mountain road towards Bwlch-y-Groes. Social media had told me that most of the world would be out on their bikes this weekend, salving their dismay with miles and companionship, uniting under the hashtag #RideForMike.

I wrestled with this privately. What did Mike care if we rode for him? Would he have cringed at all this adulation? Was this what he would want? And then, again and again, I'd remind myself that what he would have wanted was irrelevant now, since he wasn't around to care one way or the other. All of us who rode this weekend, or didn't, were doing it for ourselves and each other, to sustain an idea of Mike that drifted further and further away from what he'd actually been.

I resolved to avoid thinking about 'what he would have wanted', knowing that in doing so I'd only be colluding with this, constructing a hypothetical version of Mike, much like those police images that show what a child, kidnapped many years ago, might look like today. I'd stick to what I knew, what I remembered and what we shared, I decided, wondering all along whether I was getting this right. Perhaps everyone else's approach was healthier after all – they'd turn Mike into a story they could retell, mourn him, celebrate him, and then gently step away and get on with their lives.

Coming out for a ride had been a good idea, I told myself, since at the very least it would fill up some hours of the day, and offer me more distraction than I'd find sitting in an armchair, trying to make sense of this – or rather, trying *not* to make sense of it, since to rationalise the rupture of Mike's death suggested that it could be fitted into the grand scheme of things, that it was meant to be. I was well aware that to those who observed from a distance, there was a certain poetry to the way his life had ended. Perhaps this was the only satisfactory outcome of his long-anticipated battle with Kristof – we would never know who was the greater rider. Had they both reached Sydney, no matter who won or lost, there would have been a sense of anticlimax, of disappointment. One or other hero would have fallen. This was the only way both of them could remain unbeaten.

'How unoriginal,' I thought, furious with Mike for playing into such an obvious stereotype, and wondering if he'd have kicked himself, if he could have known a moment in advance that this was how things would turn out.

'Let's wait and see what *he* has to say about all this,' I decided, for the umpteenth time, before remembering that I wouldn't get to ask him. Why was it, I wondered, that my mind was so unwilling to swallow this simple fact, that it kept rejecting and regurgitating it, obliging me to stomach it over and over again? Sometimes I would simply forget that he was gone, and have to accept the news as though I were hearing it for the first time. Often I would retain the essential knowledge that my friend was dead, yet fail to understand its wider implications – that we wouldn't get to finish conversations we had started; that I had a gap in my diary the week of the training camp; that I no longer had to plan what to cook for him when he returned from Australia; that we wouldn't ride together any more. And a lot of the time the horror of it all sat a short distance from me, just out of reach, and I carried on with the ordinary business of life, offering Rickie and Isla coffee before we set off, discussing where we might stop for lunch and passing the time of day with the people we met on the road.

At the top of the first hill we passed the gateway where I had fixed an early puncture on our New Year ride, and Isla, Sam and Mike had passed around a hip flask, enjoying the warmth of the sun and gazing down over the thick white mist we'd just climbed out of. Today, to my relief, we were in the process of overtaking some other riders, our group of three swollen to five as we exchanged pleasantries before pulling ahead of them. From the corner of my eye, the gateway looked like any other.

A few miles later, we reached the point where Mike's keys had once flown out of his pocket as he sped down a hill and I, trailing behind him, had braked and swung round to retrieve them, instantly grinding to a halt as I remembered a moment too late that I was in my highest gear. But this time we were going too fast for the memory to stick, and I concentrated on following Rickie's line, readying myself to sprint up the following incline.

I already knew how this would work. Mid Wales was currently scattered with memories of Mike, like clues in a treasure hunt, hanging from the trees we passed, driven into the verges like stakes, traced along the white lines we followed. But I could plaster new memories over the top of them. Now, whenever I passed that gateway, I'd recall the convivial delight of running into friends. On the hill where Mike had dropped his keys I'd hold my breath, tuck my head and pretend I was Rickie Cotter, focusing on how fast I could speed though the right-hand bend at the bottom before the road rose up again, easing me through the transition from flying to grinding. There was no point turning every road into a shrine to Mike – people had already done that, piling up bouquets beside the Monaro Highway in Australia. It would be self-indulgent of me to dwell on what was gone. I'd let new memories eclipse the old ones. I'd move on. I was already moving on.

But by the time the russet hillsides closed in towards Bwlch-y-Groes I was tiring, struggling to keep up with Isla and Rickie's bright chatter, my legs hot and heavy. My intention had been to dance up the mountain ahead of them both. It seemed so obvious that the strength of what I was feeling could be converted into physical power, and sprinting up one of Wales' most difficult climbs, as I had watched him do, was surely a fitting tribute to Mike. But I flailed and faltered. Rickie took flight, and I watched her diminutive shape retreating up the road ahead of me. Isla sped up and fell momentarily into a rhythm beside me, but the thought that she might want to ride the whole climb together, to pace and comfort me, was as intolerably intimate as if she were a rival, pulling alongside to scrutinise me for signs of weakness. I stopped pedalling, put a foot down and let her go.

Just three months ago Mike had ridden away from me up this same road, out of the saddle, in the big ring, his yellow gilet billowing behind him as he ascended. Over to my right, the same twisted cliffs overlooked us, their strata of rock buckling under the unthinkable force of violence that was still underway, albeit on a timescale so much greater than our own that we could barely claim to witness it. Countless millennia to throw a single punch. A disaster so diffuse that none would mourn it.

For a long time I stood there astride my bike, hands still on the bars, bent over as if retching, my whole body clenching and convulsing with the gusts of grief that roared out of me. Mouth gaping and teeth bared, I watched snot and spittle landing on the sunny tarmac beneath me and listened to strange moaning sounds that I had never heard before, that seemed to emanate not from my lungs or throat or stomach, but from some darker place, wrenched up from the depths of me by the folded rocks, the rising road, the cruel bright spring air. I poured my pain out into the landscape, listening to it echoing across the valley, trying to empty myself out so that I could continue, and eventually the wave subsided and I carried on up the hill, on foot.

Isla and Rickie sat side by side at the top of the pass, gazing out at the mountains to the north, and I swallowed more tears and joined them for a nip of whisky. Rickie poured some out onto the ground for Mike.

'That's for you, buddy.'

We shared a slice of chocolate fudge cake at the café beside Lake Vyrnwy and I sat dumbly, unable to join in with either merriment or mourning. My gratitude at my friends' coming to take me out of myself dissipated into guilt that I had lost whatever dignity or denial was holding me together, and was now nothing more than a drag on their energy. We found our way back over the hilltops. I struggled feebly in their wake as we pedalled along the main road, and when we got home Isla sat me down at the kitchen table and took off my shoes and socks for me as if I were a child. I listened as they made plans for Rickie to spend the night at Isla's, in order to shorten her ride home, and watched them drive away, trying to figure out whether I felt more relieved or abandoned.

Chapter Seventeen

There is an all-you-can-eat Mongolian barbeque restaurant in Dublin, and I knew that was where I would find the rest of the riders. The following day a hundred of us were setting off to race around Ireland's rugged west coast to Cork, so now all there was to do was eat as much as we could physically stomach, and then sleep. Sure enough, a group of athletic-looking men sat around a table, heads bent over enormous bowls of food. I greeted them, followed a queue of people round an abundant buffet, piling my bowl high with every imaginable combination of meat, vegetables, noodles, spices and condiments, then watched, mouth watering, as the staff tossed it deftly on a grill for a few minutes, and handed the bowl back to me, steaming and succulent. When I rejoined the table, some of the men proudly informed me that they were on their fourth trip to the grill.

I introduced myself, instantly forgetting the names they mumbled at me, and suspecting uneasily that they'd remember mine. To my relief, we were all more interested in eating than talking, and no one exchanged any pleasantries beyond the usual ambivalent commentary – and exaggerated trepidation – about what lay ahead.

I hadn't been looking forward to this. For the last two months I had been avoiding social media, unable to stomach the constant references to Mike, the way his face would loom at me from someone else's tweet, the strangers lining up to expound on what he had meant to them. Seeing how many other people's lives he had touched somehow threatened to diminish the connection I had had with him, reminding me that he was far less mine than I wanted to make him. I could probably, if I thought about it, still count up the number of times we'd ridden together. I didn't think about it though. I handled my memories of him as I would an old and precious manuscript, knowing that excessive touching would eventually cause it to crumble, and wanting to ration out the treasures it still held. I wouldn't get any more.

But in amongst this reluctance was a thread of yearning, to be among people who had known Mike, and who shared the ineluctable puzzlement that he was no longer there.

'I keep expecting Mike to turn up and sort everything out,' remarked James Robertson, on the way back from the restaurant to Trinity College, where we all had rooms for the night. He had been engaged to photograph this race, and remained part of a team of friends and sponsors who were tentatively pulling themselves together to take over the Transcon, with Juliana at the helm. She wasn't in Dublin, and neither, of course, was Mike, although race director Adrian had introduced a 'Mike Hall King of the

Mountains' award in his memory, for the fastest rider to complete the five toughest climbs en route.

I intended to ignore this contest, as I tried to ignore the fact that Mike had become a motivational hashtag, captioning a series of selfies that people posted as they recalled the day they were lucky enough to meet him. For those who hadn't, Adrian promised that 'You will meet him in spirit on the road when you are hungry and tired, and you will meet him in spirit when the tears of desperation or joy (you won't know which) run down your cheeks.'

I resented this poetry, partly because I loathed the continual attempts to turn Mike into a messiah, and partly because the sentiment was a little too close to the conviction I sometimes felt that he was riding alongside me. Halfway up a steep Welsh lane, or as I swooped over the hilltops above his house, I'd look round for him, convinced he must be riding in my slipstream, or panting alongside me as we ascended.

Why aren't you here?

One April day, heading back over the hills after a weekend in Isla's workshop, I excitedly realised that I could divert to Mike's house and show him the new bike Isla and I had just built. He would be delighted, I thought, before stopping halfway up the hill and bawling for a few minutes, both from the shock of having remembered that he wasn't there, and the realisation – once again – that I could no longer ask his opinion on anything. There was no more to come.

Two days later I rode the bike behind his coffin, as a crowd of cyclists followed a slow hearse from Pat's driveway to the crematorium in Harrogate. This was my last ride with him, I thought, deliberately provoking myself to tears so that I could get them out of my system before the service.

I remember little of the funeral. Pat and Anna, two blonde women, following the coffin. The chapel bursting at the seams as people in bright Lycra and dark suits crowded the pews, stood in the doorways and sat in the aisles. Mike's father recalling him as a baby, howling in the night, then, as soon as anyone came to check on him 'he was all smiles, ready to play'. A tall, tearful man in a vintage jersey described a bike tour he and Mike had done when they were twenty-five, enjoying themselves so much that they had agreed to retrace their steps when they were fifty. He invited us all to join him in 2031, and to my horror I realised that this was one angle I hadn't yet thought of. We would all grow older, and Mike would still be dead. The eulogies went on too long, and eventually we were kicked out to make way for another coffin.

Afterwards, at a memorial reception to which even greater crowds showed up, I huddled on a sofa with Juliana, Kristof and James Robertson, taking it in turns to go to the bar for more whisky, and watching something between a dirge and a family reunion unfolding around us. People who had only ever seen each other on the road exclaimed and hugged, smiling and then wiping away tears. I wanted no part in this, and hoped that everyone would be too intimidated by the joint presence of Kristof and Juliana to approach us.

Juliana and I had met for dinner in Leeds the night before, and alternated between garrulous recollections of the times we'd spent with Mike and stuttering fury at what had happened. She told me how abandoned she and the other riders had felt as the race was called off and they were swallowed up in the well-organised memorial rides that ensued. I remembered the photo of a small knot of ragged mourners standing on the steps of Sydney Opera House, their backs to the camera, gazing up at the finish line that Mike never got to see. They wore the uniform of tan lines and crumpled T-shirts I remembered from Çanakkale, and I tried to imagine how they could have coped with Mike's death amongst the physical and mental collapse that follows such a great exertion. Maybe it was easier if you were falling apart anyway.

She had visited the verge of the Monaro Highway where he was hit, and met a man whose house was nearby, who had been first on the scene. The driver was young and terrified, he'd told her, sitting rigid behind the wheel as a woman's voice on speakerphone said 'go and see if he's OK – *go and see if he's OK*.'

I was glad she didn't tell me any more than that. I had occasionally attempted to think about the details of Mike's final moments, and found that I couldn't. My mind had erected a protective cordon around the scene, beyond which I could make out only the faintest outlines of what might have happened. A bump in the night, and Mike flying through the air into emptiness. He had died of a head injury – I didn't know if I had heard this or just made it up – so sudden and catastrophic that he wouldn't even have remembered hitting the ground. One moment cycling, the next staring up at the stars, no time for surprise or reflection. I tried to conjure up images of ripped flesh and twisted limbs, but nothing would stick except his face, pale and peaceful beneath his helmet, as if he were dreaming the whole thing.

It was then that I began to understand that my anger was irrational. It would have made sense to focus my rage on the man who had hit Mike, rather than those who joined me in mourning him. But I couldn't muster very much interest in the person behind the steering wheel, let alone the passion with which many other people were condemning careless drivers, poorly lit cyclists and the pressures of a race that meant riders kept going even when they were so sleep-deprived that they could no longer see straight.

Juliana seemed further ahead with her grieving than me, and I remembered she had been through this before, losing her sister in her late teens, and then her boyfriend in her twenties.

'I read something by Einstein,' she told me, 'about when his friend died, and he said the distinction between past, present and future is an illusion – for physicists, there's no such thing as time. We live in this dimension, and we experience it in a linear way, but in reality time's not linear, which means that everything that's ever happened – and is going to happen – is all happening now at this moment. So he's still out there riding his bike somewhere.'

Her tranquillity reminded me of the photo of her two days after she'd restarted from Fremantle – she seemed calm, but alive, energised, ready to go on. I still longed for this sort of transcendence, however fleeting it might be. I had previously joked that the solution to every problem I might encounter in life – be it depression, insomnia, writer's block or relationship woes – was to go out for a bike ride, but even now, a month after walking up Bwlch-y-Groes, cycling felt like a chore. My limbs were heavy and uneven when I pedalled, as if I were struggling into a headwind of my own making. After years of cycling through busy traffic without a care I now felt exposed, holding my breath each time I heard a vehicle looming behind me, hoping the driver had seen me, knowing I didn't stand a chance if they hadn't. I procrastinated leaving the house, and couldn't wait to return to it at the end of each ride, often thinking back to that glorious March morning when I had arrived home and promptly gone out again, dancing among the skylarks and the daffodils, eagerly awaiting Mike's return so that I could share them with him.

Why aren't you here?

Someone else was living in his house now – when I screwed up the courage to ride past, I saw unfamiliar plants in the kitchen, and a Lib Dems banner stuck to a window-pane – and the ice and mud of winter were long gone. The hedgerows blossomed and bustled, and the sunlight retreated up the wooded hillsides as I followed the valley towards Bwlch-y-Sarnau, wondering if I'd make it home before nightfall, still wanting to tell Mike about the scent of the wild garlic, and the swallows that were beginning to hurtle past my bedroom window as they returned home from their long journey.

'You should just tell him anyway,' said Juliana, who was more practised at these things.

I had longed for the TransAtlanticWay Race to start, for the relief of returning to my element and pushing the world to an arm's length, but as we streamed along the straight roads that led towards Derry, nothing felt as it should. My overshoes dug into my calves, rapidly scraping holes in my skin. My hands, still accustoming themselves to new handle-bars, were already sore. The rain began to fall two hours into the race, heavier and heavier, until the roads became rivers, and we pressed on into what felt like a solid wall of water.

Towards the evening I paused at the centre of Derry's Peace Bridge, fished a soggy brevet card out of my soggy frame pack and handed it to a soggy volunteer, then rolled off along the waterfront. The crew at the checkpoint had told me there were two women ahead of me, and I toyed with this fact, trying to figure out whether it accounted for my sinking mood. I didn't really care that I wasn't in the lead. The other women had probably trained and trembled for this race over many months, whereas I felt neither fear nor ambition, and was bothered by everyone else's assumption that I should.

I carried on along the coast, night falling around me. The traffic was thinning out, and the rainstorm had relented. Over to my right, a full moon rose above the hills on the other side of the Foyle estuary.

Why aren't you here?

Another racer caught me as we began what looked like would be our first big climb, up over a huge headland, the moon behind us painting a silver highway on the motionless sea.

His name was Paul, and he was much happier to be there than I was. He'd heard of me, and told me that I'd ridden alongside his clubmates in a Welsh event back in October. A minute later, as I struggled along a few metres behind him, he dropped back to tell me that they had texted him, joking that he must be sitting on my wheel, and I remembered once again that every metre of this race was under scrutiny, with a thousand armchair commentators monitoring my whereabouts, speed and direction. They'd be watching Paul's blue dot and my pink one climbing side by side, and wondering what we were talking about, whether we were grimly racing each other or jovially passing the time of day.

Once again I felt the weight of their expectation. I had no idea whether Paul's friends really thought I'd be pacing him up the climb, but here on the ground our imagined roles were very much reversed. He sailed upwards ahead of me, while I wrestled with my pedals, having already made my excuses for not riding alongside him, now just hoping I could keep sight of his lights as he rounded the hill and carried on upward.

I couldn't have told you what it was in me, physically or mentally, that was imploring me to stop. What some riders will glibly describe as 'pain' quite often isn't that at all – it's far more elusive: an all-pervading sense of discomfort; a reluctance that seeps through your veins like curdled adrenaline; the sense of something not quite being in place, though what that thing is, or what place it should be in, remains a mystery.

As I often do at these times, I conducted a physical and mental inventory, as much to distract myself as to try and pin down the location of this malaise. My legs were fine. They almost always were. They didn't particularly want to turn the pedals, but no part of them hurt, my muscles weren't any stiffer than usual, my knees weren't clicking or grinding. My feet were sore, but spinning in a lower gear helped, and when I focused on the soreness there was no sense of it forcing me to stop. My back felt as it often does on long rides – slightly stiff, but nothing that a quick stretch every couple of hours wouldn't handle. The edges of my hands still hurt from my new bars, but climbing was moving the pressure forward, so that pain wasn't in danger of stopping me either. My neck was fine. My stomach was fine. I had kept my fluids up. I didn't feel nauseous, or headachy, or feverish. It was the first day of the race, and I had slept for a good eight hours the night before. I should have felt OK. But I didn't.

'I'll just get to that next bend,' I told myself, then promptly put my foot down for a pre-bend rest, knowing that I'd end up stopping again as soon as I reached it, and then at the next bend too. Paul was now no more than a flickering light half a kilometre ahead of me, and since he could no longer see me I allowed myself to zigzag across the empty road, levelling out the gradient and reducing still further the amount of energy my reluctant limbs were putting into the effort. I tried to think about the times I'd sprinted up hills like this, recalling the delicious sensation of lungs filling, legs pumping, energy surging round my body as I pushed forward, in the hope that, since this difficulty had to be psychological, I might be able to trick my mind into sending different signals to my muscles.

It didn't work. I carried on plodding up the hill, feeling heavy and clumsy and useless. At the top there was a small viewpoint, where Paul and another rider appeared to be phoning their wives to say goodnight. I gave them a wave and carried on, knowing I'd be overtaken soon enough.

A few hours later I drifted into consciousness, having only briefly managed to escape it in the three hours I'd been lying down. Underneath me the concrete of the church doorway I'd camped in leached coldness into my muscles, and over to my left I could hear quiet footsteps moving towards me. It was unusual, I thought, that someone would be walking around a churchyard at four in the morning, especially in this tiny hamlet at Ireland's northernmost point, where the number of inhabitants probably didn't stretch into double figures.

A second later I realised who it must be. The click of a camera confirmed my suspicion, and I opened reluctant eyes to see James Robertson standing a few feet away. I had come to trust James, and grudgingly admired his portraits of me sleeping after the Transcon and weeping during the Strathpuffer. The previous night in Dublin I had given my consent for him to find my bivvy spots on the tracker and photograph me as I slept, particularly if I happened to have a slug crawling across my face.

I greeted him with an amicable middle finger as I emerged from my sleeping bag, then tried to ignore him as

I stuffed it into its dry bag, strapped it back onto the bike and hopped about trying to get into my overshoes. The rain had stopped, and it was already getting light. The north coast of Ireland was clearly further north than I'd realised.

'So you've started your stalking early then?'

James gave an exaggeratedly evil laugh.

'You guys are just making it too easy. There were five people around this church at one point.'

I remembered being woken up by the click-click-click of someone's noisy cassette, and opening my eyes to see another cyclist walking past, clearly regretting the fact that I'd nabbed the best sleeping spot.

'Sorry,' he'd said, and carried on around the side of the church.

I passed the cyclist again as I left, lying in his bivvy bag in the church's smaller front doorway, awake, but showing no signs of getting up. It was only when he caught me some-time later that I realised it was Paul, with whom I'd ridden the previous evening. He still seemed happy, and after a few minutes, realising that my conversation wasn't up to much, he accelerated off into the morning air. I envied his exhilaration.

The day wore on as I worked my way down the western edge of the peninsula, noticing as I reached Burnfoot that I was now less than ten miles from Derry, and wonder-ing whether I should just ride back there, announce I was quitting, check myself into a guesthouse and watch time suddenly slow down, the way it does when you step out of the current of a race. I was already twitchy and prickly with exhaustion, yearning for a hot shower and a few hours between dry sheets.

I had never thought so persistently about giving up. This was unlike my reluctant afternoons on the Transcon, where

I stopped for coffee or ice cream so regularly that it was hard to understand how I'd made any forward progress. On those days there was still, somewhere in my mind or body, a taut cord pulling me forward, a sense of necessity that would always eventually drive me up from whatever bench or chair I'd collapsed on, back to the bike and onwards down the road.

For my first few days in Ireland, the possibility of quitting the race sat at the forefront of my mind, beckoning to me voluptuously whenever I felt tired, uncomfortable or bored, which seemed to be most of the time. On the second night I arrived in a small town called Ardara and, knowing that the rain was forecast to start again before long, made the decision to put off Glengesh Pass till the morning. I had seen dozens of guesthouses along the road, each one offering me an escape route from this grimy, gloomy ride, and I knew I had chosen well when a motherly white-haired woman answered the door. Within minutes she had me sat at her kitchen table with a pot of tea and a plate of sandwiches, swathed in the dressing gown she insisted I borrow.

'I could just stay here,' I thought, as I warned Barbara I'd be leaving at 3 a.m., and listened to her effusive description of where to find my breakfast in the fridge. On our way down the corridor to my room she opened a cupboard, full of cosmetics left behind by other guests, and urged me to help myself to shampoo and conditioner.

'Take this one why don't you, it's more expensive. Will you be wanting an extra towel?'

The double bed, when I got into it, was stacked with pillows, and I arranged them around me until I felt like I was being cradled in someone's arms, momentarily safe from the storm that was beginning to rage outside.

The village was still sunk in darkness when I tiptoed out

a few hours later. I retrieved my bike from the damp garage and set off into wind and water, shivering past the silent houses towards the pass, wondering how long it would take to generate enough body heat to repel the chill that had settled into my bones.

Twenty minutes into the climb I remembered I'd left my bib shorts at the guesthouse, hung up to dry on the back of the bathroom door. My mood sank still further. To ride back down the hill and retrieve them was such a disheartening thought that I knew I'd end up burrowing back under the duvet and staying there, hiding among the pillows as I wondered what I'd say to Barbara when I emerged, and how I'd get myself back to Dublin. It was either that or abandon my shorts, and I chose the latter, wondering if I'd find a shop along the way where I could buy more.

The thoughts fell away as I ascended, sheets of rain and gusts of wind shaking me harder and harder as I became more exposed. I could sense hillsides around me, but my feeble front light only lit up as much of my surroundings as was useful, no more. With a sense of submission, I crept forward into the wavering tunnel of wet tarmac and raindrops, my breath rushing in my ears above the clamour of the storm.

By the time I neared the top of the pass I could make out a silhouetted horizon against the gradually lightening sky, and the wind was dryer, though just as strong. The bike jerked drunkenly beneath me and I realised, with another plummeting sensation of dismay, that my front tyre had punctured, and I had no choice but to fix it here, on this wide-open hilltop, at a moment when I had already been wishing that someone stronger would come and take this all away from me.

I sobbed out loud for a couple of seconds, conversationally, as anyone else in this situation might curse or groan. Then I found my way over to a flattened area a few metres up the road that looked, in the dim light, like a place sheep might be fed, removed the wheel and rummaged in my seat pack for a spare tube.

I had become used to crying, accepting it as one of the perplexing but inevitable functions of grief. Often, as I cycled, or sat at my desk staring up at the road that led towards Mike's house, I would burst into tears with very little warning, as though I had hit a tripwire in my mind, or ridden over a patch of black ice. My sadness heaved restlessly inside me, splitting the seams where I had hastily stitched myself together around my loss.

Sometimes it was the simple mention of Mike's name, or the sight of his face, that prompted these dissolutions. I'd find myself crying even before the memories ushered themselves into my conscious mind, as though both memory and mourning were happening of their own accord, on a level where I exerted no control.

Other times I'd sob my way up or down a hill, or find myself breaking into tears as I rounded a bend in the road and saw mountains or coastline unfolding towards a distant horizon. These feelings hadn't started with Mike, but they led me back to him, my mind scratching away at the surface of his absence, puzzled, still looking for him, trying to find a way of seeing this that meant he was still with me.

And sometimes it was nothing to do with him. I wept indiscriminately at sad films, happy endings, tragic news stories and photos of other people's weddings. I was in touch not so much with my own feelings as with everyone else's, a helpless conduit for all of the emotion in the world.

I fixed the puncture and rolled over the brow of the hill, ignoring my tears as I would a conversation that didn't concern me. The light rose and I descended easily, following the smooth ribbon of the road across a wide-open hillside with mountains rippling across the horizon like waves. Here and there I saw a black wound in the landscape, where someone had cut through the long grass, peeled back the turf and hacked out the peaty flesh that lay beneath.

I continued along the line that had been plotted for us, meandering down the coastline through towns whose names I recognised – Donegal, Sligo – but whose histories and topographies I had never bothered to find out. It hadn't occurred to me how much I gained from planning my own route for the Transcon. Here I meekly followed someone else's, barely caring what lay in store. I stopped looking at the map and rapidly lost sight of how far I had come or where I might be going.

A day and a night passed, and again I found myself struggling through the bleak acres of time that stretched out between daybreak and whenever I might find somewhere I could buy a cup of coffee and the excuse to sit down. I had left the coastline behind me, along with the bungalows that clustered about the road like barnacles, and was carving my way across a vast brown moor into a wind so strong that it felt as though I were swimming into a current, fighting desperately just to keep my place and avoid being swept back. The horizons were lost in cloud, and I braced myself grimly into the drumming raindrops, continuing only because there was no reason to stop, and no hope of comfort if I did.

Two hours in I saw a sign for a B&B – my first that day – and pulled over, hoping against hope that there would be someone there, that they'd let me in, be persuaded to serve me a cup of tea and turn a blind eye while I snoozed in an armchair. The lights were on and I peered greedily through all the windows at the staircase, the bookshelves and the dining table already laid for breakfast. It was just before 5 a.m., and no one was awake. I hobbled round to the leeward side of the house and sat with my back to the wall, facing up the road. Resting my helmeted head on my knees, I let my eyes close for a few minutes, awakened by the sound of a passing freewheel and the stare of a fellow racer, and then awakened again by the cold. Shivering, I got back on the bike.

It was after seven by the time I found a petrol station, having abandoned all serendipity, identified an establishment on the map that the internet promised me would be open and left Adrian's route in order to find it. I didn't know if that would automatically disqualify me from the race – I was missing a mile of the route, but adding to my overall distance – but I cared just as little about that as I cared about the two women who were apparently many hours ahead of me.

The petrol station contained not only a shop, but also a café with a pic'n'mix buffet of fried breakfast food and a machine that dispensed large milky coffees. I regarded this bounty with relief rather than relish. My appetite was still inexplicably absent, but the time it took to chew my way through a plate of food would be precious minutes away from the storm, and there was a group of three workmen at the only other table who seemed as though they might be good for conversation.

Sure enough, they looked up with interest as I slumped onto the banquette beside them and began fumbling my hands out of my wet gloves. The two outermost fingers on each side were useless now, numb and stiff, and beginning to curl in towards my palm.

'Where are ye off to?' asked one of the men.

'I'm riding the Wild Atlantic Way,' I replied, leaving out the fact that I was in a race, since that would provoke a barrage of questions I wasn't in the mood to answer.

They all sighed and nodded knowingly, and when I returned the question, told me they were on their way to work. They didn't say what their job was, perhaps assuming that I might guess from the thick, shapeless clothing they wore – combat trousers, heavy boots and hooded jackets. As far as I was concerned I looked fairly similar, stout and well-packaged in my layers of waterproofs, my bulky overshoes and my baggy high-vis vest.

We drifted companionably in and out of each other's conversations as I sat there, dripping water onto the floor, soaking the back of the seat and feeling the grease my breakfast was cooked in ooze into my mouth as I bit down on each morsel. I lost interest in eating halfway through, though this had as much to do with my aching hands as my reticent stomach. The few fingers that retained any feeling were now doing the work of all the others, and tiring quickly. I attempted to pick up my cup of coffee, accidentally stabbed at it with one of my paws, and knocked the whole thing over, watching with dismay as coffee flowed across the table, dripping down onto the floor on both sides and rapidly soaking into the front of my jersey and shorts.

The workmen, as embarrassed as if I had vomited or started to cry, wordlessly withdrew from the circle we had formed, turning in on themselves and ignoring my attempts to sop up the coffee with a napkin. I went up to the counter, paid for another coffee, gathered a handful of paper towels and returned to the table, trying to catch their eyes for a farewell nod as they stood up, downed their cups of tea and headed for the door.

I sat for another twenty minutes, sipping my second

coffee and forcing down the two hash browns I had unwisely served myself. A text message told me that Paula, the previous year's winner, had quit the race a few miles up the road. So now I was in second place, I thought to myself, wondering what Mike would have to say about that. It would be, I realised, the first time I finished a race without him at the end of it.

I rode into the wind and rain for another few hours, scraping my way across a landscape hidden by mist, though I guessed from the verges of the road that it was mostly bog and moorland. Eventually the ocean reappeared on my right and I followed the coastline down towards the bridge that would take me onto Achill Island, around which we'd ride in a figure of eight before returning to the mainland and continuing south. James Robertson's van sped past me, this time with Paula whooping and hollering from the window. They were waiting for me at the end of the channel, and although I knew James would want to get photos of me riding by, I couldn't resist stopping to talk. It was only as I dismounted and tried to stand up straight that I discovered how stiff my body was. Every muscle had been tensed since early that morning, as I fought my way into the wind, and I spent a few minutes by the side of the road, kneading the back of my neck and resting my feet one after the other on the crash barrier to stretch out my hamstrings. My ankles were swollen and the scabs raised by my overshoes a few days previously were embedded in my flesh like upholstery buttons. Beyond the barrier foamy white waves hurried across the surface of the sea, and great gusts of spray rose like steam between me and the folded green mountains of Achill. On the other side of the island I found tall jagged cliffs, battered by the seething ocean, with nothing beyond them.

It was not quite light when I started cycling the next morning, and a sign told me it was 90km to Clifden. *That'll do for breakfast*, I thought. A couple of hours later I reached the top of a small hill and found that I was surrounded by mountains – great green beasts whose tops were obscured by the ribbons of cloud that swirled among them. The road led down to the water and I skirted a vast fjord, dwarfed by the solemn peaks that glowered down at me from all sides. The particular way the rocks rippled and folded reminded me of Scotland, and I wondered whether these were the same mountains I'd seen on another coastline, wrenched apart long ago as the world turned beneath them.

All at once I felt Mike riding alongside me, as firmly and as unremarkably as if he were actually there. I didn't dare turn my head, and we carried on along the Connemara shoreline side by side. Between us, the damp morning air felt expectant, as it does the moment before someone breaks a silence.

Oh, there you are.

I didn't cry, and it was only when I reached the end of the inlet, and saw a hotel, and a gaggle of tired middle-aged tourists hauling themselves onto a coach, that I began to wonder at the delusion of the human mind, how it will so persistently conjure up someone's presence long after their departure. I understood now why so many people believe in life after death, or that the spirits of the deceased take a while to leave this realm. Was it presence or absence that was the greater illusion? Perhaps Juliana was right, and everything that had ever existed remained present, just more or less accessible depending on our perception of time. Or perhaps all that exists is absence, and our lonely minds translate longing into presence.

I often missed Mike with a tremendous ache in my

chest, just where my lower ribs joined, and was perplexed to be reacting so bodily, since ours hadn't been in any way a physical relationship. A few days previously I had tried unsuccessfully to remember if we even hugged when he left for Australia. It didn't seem very important whether we had or not. What I kept coming back to – what I missed so much – was the intimacy I'd felt as we'd ridden up hills side by side, or stood a few feet from each other at the top, catching our breath and waiting for our riding buddies to reach us. I usually found it unbearable to have someone else witness my struggles, to hear the ragged breathing that betrayed how hard I was trying, and sense my doubt that I'd be able to keep this pace all the way to the top. When I rode with other people I'd either make sure I was ahead of them on the climbs or gamely fall back and let them take the lead. Mike was the only person I'd allowed to see me as I was, and I often wondered why. Was it that I knew he'd been there so often himself? Was it that his status as the superior cyclist was so unarguable that failing in front of him wouldn't make any difference? Or was it that he seemed as willing to share his own inadequacies as he was to witness mine?

Clifden turned out to be a lot more than 90km away – I had forgotten that this race eschewed the more direct main roads, and baffled any forward progress by meandering around the coastline. At 10 a.m. I admitted defeat and, realising I had already been riding for seven hours, found an open pub and ordered the biggest breakfast on the menu. My appetite had finally returned.

I stopped early that evening, failing to reach Galway as I had planned. The road that led along the coast towards the city was the busiest I'd ridden for days; there was no shoulder, and it had started to rain again. For far too long I battled through the potholes, gasping as passing cars flung waves of gritty water over me and wondering how visible I was through the wavering headlights and raindrops. More than ever before I felt aware of my fragility, of how soft my flesh was, how delicate the mechanisms that kept me alive and pedalling. I threw my rage indiscriminately out at the traffic, the race, Mike (for dying), Australia (for not saving him), the builders of roads, the watchers of dots and the horror of the situation we had somehow got ourselves into, where Mike was taken away from us. When I saw a B&B up ahead I swerved towards it without even questioning myself, and gave up for the day.

The next morning I decided I'd quit when I reached Lisdoonvarna, recognising the name from a folksong. But with the infuriating logic of this maddening race, the route bypassed Lisdoonvarna, and eventually I checked the map and saw that it was behind me. I stopped immediately, in a pretty fishing village resounding with seagulls, ordered a bowl of soup in the first café I came to, and wondered unhurriedly what I should do. I could slow down and complete the remainder of the route at a holiday pace – which I was more or less doing already. I could stop riding altogether and find a bus or train that would take me back to Dublin. That might be the more sensible option, given that my hands were now so shrivelled that even gripping the spoon took a conscious effort, and I had to put it down between mouthfuls. Or I could stay here, in this sunny little town, and hold the world at bay for just a little longer.

I checked the tracker for the first time in a couple of days and discovered that the only woman left ahead of me had dropped out, along with many of the other racers. I laughed. Despite my reluctance, my all-too-frequent stops, and the previous night's eight-hour sleep, I had ended up leading the race. I might as well keep going. I left behind my half-formed plans at the café table and carried on south.

Later that afternoon I ran into Rudy, the bearded Belgian I'd followed through France on the first morning of the Transcontinental, wondering if he was Jayne. We continued side by side for a while, pleased with the sense of running into an old acquaintance, and discussed how our respective races were going.

'It's taken me a while to get my head into gear,' I told him, 'but I'm feeling pretty good now. Hands are a bit ...'

I grimaced and waggled one of them to indicate its lack of cooperation.

He commiserated, and we compared notes on the horrendous headwinds that had beset the first few days of the race. Neither of us had ever experienced such strong wind, or imagined it would be possible to ride into it. Racers I'd met during those first few days had often just laughed wordlessly at the absurdity of what we were trying to do.

But we had made it through, and for now the roads were dry and smooth, with no more than a gentle breeze wafting past us. In an hour or two we would reach Conor Pass, one of the race's five big climbs, and from there it was just over two days' ride to the finish. I knew from seeing the photos of riders further ahead that the road leading up the pass was hacked out of a bare cliff, twisting improbably along the side of the mountain, and I was looking forward to the views.

I stopped for snacks at a petrol station before the climb, allowing Rudy to draw ahead. The sky lowered towards me as the road ramped upwards, and the clouds ahead were a strong dark grey. The rain started again, and I reached down to turn on my front light as I realised that the hills ahead of me had disappeared, and that I was riding straight into a cloud.

I didn't see much of Conor Pass. All I was aware of was a damp cliff towering over me on one side, a low wall on the other and an unfathomable depth of cloud beneath. Headlights loomed out of the mist as drivers edged their way up and down, steering their lumbering vehicles into passing places hacked out of rock when they met someone coming the other way.

This road was most definitely not made for them, I thought, wondering why anyone would bother to drive over Conor Pass when all they'd see on a day like this was a metre of road ahead of them. I, on the other hand, was in my element, and used the opportunity of each car pulling in to dart past it before the other driver came by.

All of the heaviness and lassitude I'd felt since Dublin was forgotten as I charged up the hill, smiling to myself in spite of the raindrops running down my face and the thick grey mist billowing around me. I was a spark of warmth and light, enfolded in the air and the water and the mountain, my world at that moment consisting of nothing more than the wall of rock to my left, the unseen void to my right and what little I could discern of the road ahead. I pressed on with a sense of joyful submission, forgetting the pressures of progress and destination. Recalling the persistent tiredness that had nagged at me even in the earliest days of the race, I marvelled at how readily, how smoothly each thrust of my legs translated into upward motion. I had found my strength.

At the top of the pass I came out of the shadow of the mountain and was hit by a gust of wind so strong that it ground me to a halt and almost knocked me down. There was no shelter up here, just a small car park, from which, presumably, on a clear day I'd see mountains and coastline stretching away on both sides. Disinclined to linger, I got off the bike and pushed it down the hill until the wind died down.

The descent took longer than I'd have liked, and by the time I reached Dingle I was shivering uncontrollably, my hands so stiff that I'd been reluctant to pick up too much speed, as I could no longer grip the brakes firmly enough to stop myself. It was raining heavily, the clouds so low that it seemed dark, and knots of tourists hurried from shop to shop, muffled in Gore-Tex and hidden by umbrellas. I stopped outside a pub, leaned my bike in a dripping doorway and wondered what to do about my soaking shorts, gloves, shoes, socks, hair and cap. I was as wet as if I'd jumped fully clothed into the sea, and was reluctant to bring so much water with me into this warm, dry haven. But the need for shelter won out, and I settled myself into a corner of the pub with a pot of tea and a bowl of soup. It was a charming interior, wood-panelled and cosy, with three long shelves of whiskies behind the bar. I eyed them with a comfortable longing, knowing I wouldn't order one, but looking forward to finishing the bottle of Jura I'd started with Isla, Sam and Mike after our Christmas ride.

The water had seeped into the joints of my phone case, and I struggled to prise it open with my recalcitrant fingers, mopping the inside dry with a napkin as my sleeves were still sodden. I knew I wouldn't get any drier no matter how long I sat here, and that within minutes of stepping outside I'd be just as cold as when I arrived. The route now went west, looping around the peninsula, and passed through the town again before heading south. That seemed reasonable, I thought – I could use up the rest of the day with a few more hours' cycling, then find myself a hostel for the night. I could even book it right away, so I'd have a warm bed waiting for me.

But to continue riding felt quite impossible. My hands had lost much of their feeling and most of their dexterity. The last two fingers on each side had been numb for days, and my ring fingers curled stiffly towards my palms – I couldn't straighten them even if I pushed hard against the edge of the table. My thumbs and first fingers had lost so much of their gripping power that I had to clutch the spoon in my fist, like a baby. I cupped the teapot, hoping in vain that its heat might make some difference. Every other part of me, cold and damp notwithstanding, felt fine – better, in fact, than I had since I started the race. My legs felt strong, nothing hurt, and I was wide awake and ready to go on. But I knew that I wouldn't.

I toyed with this conundrum for a while, then paid for my soup, picked up my bike and pedalled through the soaking streets to the youth hostel.

Epilogue

My new hobby was giving up on things.

Two months after I stopped racing in Dingle I ground to a similar halt during the Transcontinental. Europe was buckling under a heatwave, and the racers I met at Checkpoint Two were variously shrunken and swollen and sunburnt. The checkpoint was a campsite near the foot of Monte Grappa, and I regretted my decision to sleep there rather than climbing partway up the mountain, where it would be cooler. All around me the crickets shrieked, the floodlights buzzed and an assortment of semi-clad racers snored on the dusty ground. We had been given tokens to use the showers, but the sweat carried on seeping out of my skin as soon as I emerged, and I wondered at how much more liquid my body seemed to exude than I was putting into it.

There weren't significantly more racers this year, but to me the crowds felt bigger. In Geraardsbergen everyone had wanted to talk to me, to commiserate about Mike, to tell me they were looking forward to following my race as they had last year. Marion took a photo of me with Björn, the winner of the Irish Race, and told us we were her predictions for first man and woman. I feigned flattery, and wanted to say that I didn't even know why I was here, that I had tried to rediscover the urge to ride, but now longed for the race to start only so that people would stop trying to engage me in conversation. I looked for Juliana, hoping we could retreat to a café together and ignore them all for a while, but she and Anna were busy coordinating the start line, fielding queries from racers and overseeing the new safety checks.

The race faltered less than a day in, with news that a rider called Frank Simons had been killed by a car a few hours after starting. Some riders stopped immediately. Some announced their intention to carry on, but at a touring pace. The lead group, after a brief conference at Checkpoint One, continued racing.

I was rolling along a broad cycle path next to the Saar River when I found out, and I watched my mind succumb to the horror of the situation. I wondered what Frank Simons had been thinking, standing in Geraardsbergen's town square as the sun went down, the torches were lit and we set off into the darkness I had longed for.

Then I pushed it firmly to an arm's length. I reassured my family that I'd continue to ride, but try to stay off main roads, and when I reached Checkpoint One I busied myself comforting other racers.

That night I was chased by a storm that swept across the rolling hills of Southern Germany, sometimes retreating to a distant rumble, sometimes roaring over my head as our paths converged once again. I slept in a graveyard, finding a tomb that had just enough of a shelter over it to keep me dry. Painted figures of Jesus and his apostles stared down at me as I lay on the flagstones in my sleeping bag, and twice during the night I was awakened by raindrops falling violently just a few inches from my head.

I had deliberately planned my route to include mountain detours, and as the sun set a few days later I was all alone on a tiny road in Italy that made no sense from the perspective of the race but was too tempting to ride past. It crept across the sheer mountainside at a steady ten per cent gradient, and I pushed painstakingly upwards, chasing the last of the light as the sun sank behind the mountains to the west, and the lakes and villages below disappeared into shadow. As I skirted each spur, I could sense the contentment I'd found on the gravel in Montenegro, retreating up the road away from me, now and then almost within my reach.

Why aren't you here?

At the top I met another racer.

'I know who you are!' he said, when we introduced ourselves. 'I watched all the videos of you in last year's race. It's great to meet you.'

We descended together into the heat and noise of the Italian night. People I didn't know recognised me at Checkpoint Two and asked how my race was going. My ascent of Monte Grappa the following morning was reported on social media before I had a chance to post anything myself.

'Busy on that mountain this morning!' commented Isla when I sent her a picture from the top. I sat up there for twenty minutes, enjoying the fresh air with a handful of other racers as a parade of dots marched up the road towards us. No one wanted to go back down into the furnace.

I stopped riding a few hours later. My head thumped and

boomed with the heat, the road swam in front of me and I had finally run out of sweat. When I tried to revive myself with a couple of cappuccinos, I instead felt the sharp tug back into sleep that I remembered from my exhausted morning in Slovenia two summers previously. As I leant my head back in my chair and closed my eyes I had the curious sensation that two cords were attached to the back of them, pulling my eyeballs back into my head, as though I were caving in on myself.

To ride on was impossible, so I staggered to the closest hotel, and once I'd slept and rehydrated I found myself in the same position as in the bar in Dingle, knowing that I wouldn't continue but not quite able to explain why. I phoned various friends, who alternately sympathised with my plight and tried to talk me into continuing. No one would care if I was now near the back of the race, argued Isla, and people would find my persistence inspiring if I carried on regardless. I didn't tell her that the very thought of that made my stomach clench.

The following morning I turned my tracker off, immediately relieved that no one knew where I was. And that night, just before midnight, I spread out my bivvy bag at the top of my fourth pass of the day, looking forward to whatever view might greet me when I woke up. I had covered 250km, ridden into the sunrise on the Italian plain, then turned north into the mountains and improvised my way through to Slovenia. At the top of the first pass I had stopped for a cappuccino, gazing tranquilly around me at the slanting lines of the mountains and enjoying the glow of caffeine, exertion and a decision well made. This leisurely break would in reality be no longer than my guilty procrastination sessions during races, but now the will to keep riding was an urge rather than an obligation. I rode on, surging with the excitement that had eluded me since the previous summer, and once over the border I took a left turn and headed up Slovenia's highest road, remembering a conversation I'd had with Mike once about the joy of riding up steep hills with no reason or purpose.

He would love Mangart Česta, I thought, wishing I could share it with him. The road was as steep as Ventoux in its lower stretches, charging up the side of a valley as if it intended to waste no time in getting to the good bit. I could make out the grey-white triangle of Mount Mangart ahead of me, and as I emerged from the forest that hugged its lower slopes a serpentine road led me in and out of the folds of the mountainside, higher and higher, up amongst the range of peaks that glistened in the sunshine all around, and whose near-vertical walls shielded me from whatever was still going on in the rest of the world. No one had any idea where I was.

This was a younger mountain than the ones I knew in Wales, and as I neared the saddle I saw crumpled masses of rock, their twisted strata still exposed, and bare pinnacles thrusting up towards the blue sky. The Alpine grass had barely had time to get a foothold here, and everywhere grey rock emerged from its scanty cover, as though it were a moth-eaten veil, hastily thrown over a pile of debris that no one had time to tidy away.

The road was scattered with debris, and it was only when I got higher that I saw the scree pouring down from underneath the peak, appearing to emit from a huge crack that crossed the face of the mountain. This landscape was still alive – every winter the snows would come in, the veil of foliage would be whipped away, and more rocks would be hurled down from the peaks and crags as they were assailed by the elements. Eventually, who knows, perhaps the great pyramid of Mangart itself would topple.

I stood at the top of the col for a while, gazing at the peak with its intricate tracery of cracks and fissures, like the lines of my hand, each one a small tale of friction and rupture and resistance and submission. Behind me was a drop of a thousand metres to the orderly fields and lakes of an Italian valley. A lone raven drifted lazily in the sunny air.

::::

A week later I sat on a stone wall beside Lake Ohrid, eating a kebab I'd bought in Elbasan a few hours earlier and wondering if I'd ever see this famed lake by daylight. A breeze blew off the dark waters, and my skin clenched with goosebumps, enjoying the novelty of being cold. No one was about – I hadn't seen a car for at least half an hour, the darkened houses suggested that all of Albania was asleep and the Transcon racers would be either tucked up in Meteora's hotels after the finishers' party or still fighting their way south through Serbia and Macedonia. James Hayden had finally won the race, beating Björn and dedicating his victory to Mike. I was happy for him.

After my jubilant flight into Slovenia I had spent a couple of days with Marija and her family in Škofja Loka then carried on towards the finish line, from which Juliana and I were planning to drive north, seeking out checkpoints for the following year's race. Still gleeful that no one knew where I was, I followed roads I'd taken before, sought out new ones and couldn't resist reprising my route through Albania where, despite my fears that I'd be proven wrong, the people turned out to be as unusually friendly as I had remembered. I was no longer racing, but still seemed to be at my happiest when riding upwards of 250km per day, and although there was time in hand, I found I had no particular urge to stay and watch the sun rise over Lake Ohrid.

I got back on the bike and headed south. The road was fast and flat, and a light tailwind hurried me through the darkness. The trees whispered gently alongside me, but otherwise Albania was silent and still, oblivious to my passage.

After a couple of hours I began to see the outlines of hills ahead of me, and knew that dawn was breaking. For once, I cautiously allowed myself to think about Mike's last hours on the bike. He had ridden through the night on a road very much like this. Had he looked forward to dawn breaking around him? Had he seen the darkness shrink to twilight as Australia's contours began to steal back into focus? I tried not to speculate. His thoughts were his own, and I was reluctant to put words in his mouth just yet, still hoping that I might get to ask him about it someday.

I sped on into the gathering day, wishing he was riding alongside me, but unable to sense his presence as I had that morning in Connemara, or on the days when I hurtled over the Welsh hilltops with him in my slipstream. A few hours later I would sob and howl my way along the beautiful *parcours* he had planned for us, down to Meteora where Juliana was waiting with a beer. But for now I felt my mood lifting, suffused with a strange sense of gratitude, though to whom, or for what, I couldn't say. Over to my right the distant hillsides flushed a rich earthy red as the rising sun touched them, and ahead of me the road curved gently upwards towards the Greek border. I didn't want it to end.

Acknowledgements

There are a lot of obvious parallels between writing a book and cycling across a continent. Both are difficult, interminable, and yet immensely rewarding.

One of the more obscure similarities is that, although writing is in its essence a solitary pursuit, you are surrounded by countless people who support patiently from the sidelines, or loom benevolently out of the darkness, in person or in presence, just when you thought you couldn't go on. Much like the morning I sat in a French café, with Ventoux behind me, it was only as I put together this narrative that I began to understand just how many people had been propping me up all along, and just what a wonderful community I had unexpectedly become part of.

The first – and perhaps the greatest – thanks must go to publisher James Spackman, who believed in *Where There's a Will* long before I did, who courted me patiently for over a year while I tried to convince him of all the other people who would do a better job than me, and who supported me in countless ways – professional, emotional, culinary and creative – during the long months it took me to produce a manuscript. Without James, there would be no book.

Similar thanks go to my agent, Rachel Mills, to the entire team at Profile, and to Charlotte Atyeo, whose editorial insight plucked me from the depths of despair, a month before the book was due in.

This is my second book, but the first I've produced as part of a community of writers, and I'm grateful to all of the fellow authors who have inspired, influenced, advised and coached me along the way, especially Kate Harris, Whitney Brown, Max Leonard, Jack Thurston, Kate Rawles, Chris Kassar, Fiona McGlynn, Jim Davidson, Christina Reynolds, Paul Pritchard, Ailsa Ross, Meghan Moya Finn, Eileen Keane, Kat Jungnickel, Jools Walker, Jenni Gwiazdowski, Claire Carter, Ursula Martin, Hannah Engelkamp, Michele Genest, Eva Holland, Nienke Beintema, Wayne Merry, Ishbel Holmes, Lauren Hough, Anna Kortschak, Laura Laker, Hannah Nicklin, Fearghal O'Nuallain, Alastair Humphreys, Hannah Reynolds, Heidi Swift and Rob Penn. Special thanks to Alison Criscitiello and Maria Coffey, whose writings on grief and bereavement helped me navigate my own.

Several chapters of this book came to life during the Banff Mountain and Wilderness Writing residency in 2018. Thank you to Tony Whittome, Marni Jackson, Harley Rustad and everyone at the Banff Centre, for giving me one of my most formative experiences as a writer, and helping to make *Where There's a Will* a far better book than it might have been.

Thank you to all of the riders, dot-watchers and guardian

angels who have helped me through my long nights on the bike, who forgave whatever extremes of misery, mania and rudeness I hurled at them, and were often, without necessarily knowing it, the reason I carried on. Many of their names I've forgotten, or never asked, but I am grateful to them all.

Particular thanks go to Robert Webb (aka Sir Wobbly), Marion Esfandiari, Kevin Cunniffe, Jo Burt, Sarah Outen, Kristof Allegaert, Shu Pillinger, Jayne Wadsworth, Paula Regener, Jenny Tough, Eleanor Jaskowska, Anabell Orenz, Mike Sheldrake, Rudy Rollenberg, Michał Plech, Matthijs Ligt, Patricia Hall, Philipp Schwedthelm, Zbyněk Šimčík, James Hayden, Rory Kemper, Anna Haslock, Steve Abraham, Jasmijn Muller, Chris Peacock, Bregan Faika, Cole Ruegg, Judith Postelmans, Kajsa Tylén, Sarah Hammond, Neil Phillips, Lee Craigie, Ferga Perry, Rickie Cotter, Jenny Graham, Zara Mair, Jo Thom, Naomi Freireich, David Jones, Mark Goodwill, Ian Fitz, Divya Tate, Franca Pauli, Barbara Frost, Jill Murray, Turloch O'Siochain, Jimmy, Brid and Morty O'Keeffe, Adrian O'Sullivan, Kirsten Hendricksen, the Trans-Provence boys, and of course Marija Kozin and her wonderful family.

And thanks also to Mike: it might have made sense to dedicate this book to you and put you on the front page, but a pedestal can be a lonely place, and I thought you'd prefer to be here at the back with the rest of us.

The journeys I undertook would have been impossible without the generous support of my sponsors, many of whom have played a far greater role in the story than merely supplying me with kit. Thank you to Apidura, Shand Cycles, Genesis Bikes, Hunt Bike Wheels, Swrve, Rapha, Endura, Findra, Alpkit, Schwalbe, Islabikes and Leigh Day Cycling, and particularly to Albert Steward, Steven Shand,

Russell Stout, Marta Gut, James Fairbank, Pamela Barclay and Tori Fahey. And the beautiful photography of James Robertson, Camille McMillan, Kristian Pletten, Jennifer Doohan and Matthias Wjst elevated my suffering, dignified my struggles, and illuminated my joys.

I was semi-itinerant while writing this book, and owe a huge debt of gratitude to all the people who welcomed me into their homes, sometimes just for the duration of a meal, and in some cases for days and even weeks at a time. Particular thanks to Fiona McGlynn and Robin Urquhart, for solitude, space and silence in their mountainside cabin, and to Juliana and Vito, for my impromptu writing retreat in Positano two weeks before the deadline. I was also comforted, cared for and kept going by Iain and Susie Ross, Chris Morris, Rebecca Geldard and Oz, the Gillows, the Pikes, the Bakke family, the Sauvé family, the Spackman family, the Copin Land family, Ulli and Kim Harding, Dick Fast and Maggie Darcy, Miche Genest and Hector Mac-Kenzie, Dee Jay and Kerry Cravatta, Cass Gilbert, Manos Christodoulakis, and of course my wonderful family. Thank you to my parents, for their emotional support during the writing process; thank you to Lucy and her family, for comforting and distracting me through the first shock of grief; thank you to Sam for company on the bike and off, and for keeping me going mechanically and spiritually during the Strathpuffer; thank you to Florence for companionship through the hardest of times, and for consistently setting me a good example; thank you to Harry for welcoming me in with charm, good grace and excellent cooking, at whatever antisocial hour I happened to pass through Leeds.

And it would take far more space than I have – or eloquence than I command – to describe how much I owe to the friends who got me through the last few years of challenge, growth, loss, grief and book-writing. I will attempt to make it up to them in deeds rather than words, but let it be known that I am forever grateful for the wisdom, support and love of Peter Fremlin, Danielle Welton, Hannah Darvill, Nhatt Nicholls, Andrew Ormerod, Kate Lines and Leo Tong, Isla Rowntree, Eleanor Moseman, Casper McMenamin (who unwittingly suggested this book's epigraph), Vicky Jacobs (who came back into my life after more than a decade, in a year when I'd lost so many others), and of course, Juliana Buhring, whose humour, affection, camaraderie and unwavering belief in me have kept me going through battles on the bike and off.

Picture Credits

The author and publisher would like to thank the following for permission to use their wonderful photographs:

Plates
James Robertson p. 1 (top), p. 1 (bottom), p. 2 (top), p. 2 (bottom), p. 6 (top), p. 7 (top) and p. 7 (bottom); Kristian Pletten p. 3 (top) and pp. 4–5; Max Leonard p. 8; Emily Chappell p. 3 (bottom).

Integrated photographs
James Robertson pp. 1, 20, 63, 78, 181, 195, 209, 226, 242; Kristian Pletten pp. 5, 89, 117, 132; Jennifer Doohan p. 49; Emily Chappell pp. 31, 100, 145, 161, 257.